Using insights about ancient and modern tragedy, this study offers challenging and provocative new readings of selected biblical narratives: the story of Israel's first king, Saul, rejected for his disobedience to God and driven to despair and madness by an evil spirit from the Lord; the story of Jephthah's sacrifice of his daughter in fulfillment of his vow to offer God a sacrifice in return for military victory; the stories of the members of Saul's house, each of whom comes to a tragic end; and the story of Israel's most famous king, David, whose tragedy lies in the burden of divine judgment that falls upon his house as a consequence of his sins. The book discusses how these narratives handle such perennial tragic issues as guilt, suffering, and evil.

TRAGEDY AND BIBLICAL NARRATIVE

TRAGEDY AND BIBLICAL NARRATIVE

NARRATIVE

Arrows of the Almighty

J. CHERYL EXUM

Associate Professor of Hebrew Bible, Boston College

CAMBRIDGE
UNIVERSITY PRESS

Published by the Press Syndicate of the University of Cambridge
The Pitt Building, Trumpington Street, Cambridge CB2 1RP
40 West 20th Street, New York, NY 1011-4211, USA
10 Stamford Road, Oakleigh, Victoria 3166, Australia

© Cambridge University Press 1992

First published 1992

Printed in Great Britain at the University Press, Cambridge

A catalogue record for this book is available from the British Library

Library of Congress cataloguing in publication data

Exum, J. Cheryl
Tragedy and biblical narrative: arrows of the Almighty / J. Cheryl Exum.
p.   cm.
Includes bibliographical references and index.
ISBN 0 521 41073 8
1. Tragic, The, in the Bible. 2. Narration in the Bible. 3. Bible. O.T. – History of Biblical
events. I. Title.
BS1199.T69E98   1992
221.6'6 – dc20   91-28325   CIP

ISBN 0 521 41073 8 hardback

For friends who saw me through tragedy, especially,
Alice
Bill
Jim
Pat
and
Richard

כפלגי מים בציון
כצל סלע כבד בארץ עיפה
Isa. 32:2

For the arrows of the Almighty are in me;
my spirit drinks their poison;
the terrors of God are arrayed against me.

                                         Job 6:4

Contents

Acknowledgments

This book has been many years in the writing. Though all my debts could never be fully recognized, it is a pleasure, finally, to acknowledge some of them. I began work on the topic of biblical tragedy, among other projects, in Jerusalem in 1981, supported by a grant from the National Endowment for the Humanities, administered by the American Schools of Oriental Research. A grant from the Penrose Fund of the American Philosophical Society helped support further research in Jerusalem in 1983–4. I am grateful to the American Schools of Oriental Research for appointing me as Honorary Post-Doctoral Fellow at the Albright Institute of Archaeological Research, and to the members of the Bible Department of the Hebrew University of Jerusalem for an appointment as a Visiting Research Associate in the Department and for the warm welcome I received there. A fellowship from the Alexander von Humboldt Foundation enabled me to spend the 1984–5 academic year conducting research in Germany; special thanks are due to my sponsors, Rudolph Smend of the University of Göttingen, and Rolf Rendtorff (now emeritus) of the University of Heidelberg, for making available the facilities of their universities and for their hospitality. Over the years, Boston College has been generous in granting released time and financial support; I am especially indebted to William B. Neenan, S.J., Academic Vice President and Dean of Faculties, and J. Robert Barth, S.J., Dean of the College of Arts and Sciences, for the personal interest and support they showed me.

Some sections of this book were presented as papers at meetings of the Society of Biblical Literature, the Catholic Biblical Association, the Bible Symposium at the Hebrew University, and the Kolloquium-Altes Testament, Göttingen. In addition, I wish to express my appreciation to Frans Jozef van Beeck, S.J., of Loyola University of Chicago, Edward L. Greenstein, of the Jewish Theological Seminary, New York, and Alan Cooper, of Hebrew Union College, Cincinnati, for invitations to present some of this material at their institutions. I profited considerably from the responses I received from the audiences who listened, challenged, and encouraged my developing ideas about biblical tragedy.

I have been particularly fortunate in having friends upon whom I could always depend for intellectual stimulation and sage counsel. Francis Landy, of the University of Alberta, and Edwin M. Good, of Stanford University, read portions of the manuscript and offered valuable suggestions. Alice Bach, of Stanford University, has been an indispensable conversation partner, whose advice, encouragement, and confidence in me saw me through when my vision flagged. David J. A. Clines, of the University of Sheffield, read the entire manuscript and gave generously of ideas and criticism. I am profoundly grateful for his careful attention to my text, and for his help during a difficult time. William Carl Ready was a gracious, if not always willing, listener and critic, and an unfailing source of support since the inception of this book; without him I could not have persevered. Heartfelt thanks go to Detlev Grohn for help in the preparation of the final manuscript, and for almost twenty years of friendship, and to James Michael Weiss, Patricia DeLeeuw, and Richard Jenson for sustaining me through the completion of this project.

Portions of Chapter 2 appeared in "Isaac, Samson, and Saul: Reflections on the Comic and Tragic Visions," co-authored with J. William Whedbee (*Semeia* 32 [1984]). An earlier version of Chapter 3 was published in *Signs and Wonders: Biblical Texts in Literary Focus* (Scholars Press, 1989). In Chapters 3 and 4, I have used material from my essay, "Murder They Wrote: Ideology and the Manipulation of Female Presence in Biblical Narrative," in *The Pleasure of Her Text: Feminist Readings of Biblical and Historical Texts*, ed. Alice Bach (Philadelphia: Trinity Press International, 1990). I thank Scholars Press and Trinity Press International for permission to use this material.

About translations and transliterations

Translations from the Hebrew are mine. In many cases, often unintentionally, they are close to the RSV. I have kept reference to Hebrew words at a minimum; transliterations from the Hebrew are not scientific. Throughout this book I use the proper name Yhwh to refer to the deity, since I believe the use of a personal name, even if unvocalized, helps underscore the status of the deity as a character in the biblical narrative. For the same reason I use "he" as a pronoun for the deity.

CHAPTER I

Biblical narrative and the tragic vision

Tragedy is alien to the Judaic sense of the world.
George Steiner, *The Death of Tragedy*

Of all ancient peoples, the Hebrews were most surely possessed of the tragic sense of life.
Richard B. Sewall, *The Vision of Tragedy*

This is a book about tragedy as we confront it in texts rather than as we abstract it in theory. It considers selected narratives from the books of Judges, Samuel, and Kings, arguing that in them we encounter a vision of reality that can properly be called tragic.[1] In appropriating notions of the tragic for the study of biblical texts, my aim is not to force the biblical material into Aristotelian categories, which are hardly applicable. Rather I am interested in exploring a particular dimension of biblical narrative, a dimension that reveals the dark side of existence, that knows anguish and despair, and that acknowledges the precarious lot of humanity in a world now and then bewildering and unaccommodating. Job experiences this dimension as the arrows of the Almighty, whose fierceness points beyond his physical suffering to the sudden, violent, and unprecipitated eruption of disaster into his life.

One encounters what I would define as the tragic vision in various biblical guises; for example, in the "jealousy of God" in the Primeval History of Genesis 2–11, or in the sufferings of the prophet Jeremiah, or in the book of Job – unless one choose to side with Job's three friends in maintaining that the suffering, the misery, the evil, and the inexplicable in the world are part of an inscrutable, larger plan for the good. Already within current biblical criticism, one finds the idea well established that Saul's fate is tragic, and one hears of the tragedy of Jephthah[2] and of David's tragic lot.[3] Something in the stories of these figures makes them recognizably "tragic," whatever meanings are assigned to that term. This book investigates that "something"

I

– what I call their tragic dimension – in an effort to render it more accessible and to explore its resistance to resolution as a source of its particular narrative power.

My use of the term "tragedy" is heuristic: it provides a way of looking at texts that brings to the foreground neglected and unsettling aspects, nagging questions that are threatening precisely because they have no answers. I offer neither a theory of tragedy nor an investigation of the genre as such. There exists a considerable body of criticism on the subject and no consensus. The idea that a work is tragic if it displays certain predetermined features, and not tragic if one or more of these features is missing, or even handled differently, cannot find support either in art or, for that matter, in the actual practice of criticism, where the description "tragic" has been claimed for works of widely different character. Since theories are based on existing tragedies, and then applied to other tragedies, they are neither absolute nor innocent; rather, the critic's choice of examples guides the theory.

Discussions of tragedy frequently begin with Aristotle but routinely and justifiably attack him for having dealt inadequately with the topic.[4] Neither tragedy in general nor even Greek tragedy in particular can be contained within Aristotle's conceptual framework, determined not just by his preference for *Oedipus Tyrannus* as a model but, more importantly, by his philosophical presuppositions. Michelle Gellrich, in a demonstration of tragedy's particular resistance to theory, shows how "the essential premises about dramatic consistency, intelligibility, and unity articulated in the *Poetics* and later absorbed into the mainstream of literary study...can be effectively secured only if obstinately unsystematic and destabilizing movements of language and action in tragedy are bypassed or somehow brought to heel."[5] In his attempt to treat tragedy systematically, Aristotle evades the problem of radical evil, the role of the gods, and tragic conflict – all important issues for critical discussions of tragedy and crucial issues for my investigation. And his insistence on rationality would deny the essence of tragedy, its representation of the irrational.

When one thinks of tragedy, what comes to mind as the supreme example is Greek tragedy as it flourished briefly in fifth-century Athens. Not that the experience of the tragic is unique to the Greeks, but by putting that experience into words, they gave us a rich and nuanced terminology to speak of it. Even Greek tragedy, however, is not of one fabric. Aeschylus, Sophocles, and Euripides wrote tragedies different not only in their dramatic structure, use of the chorus, characterization, and plot, but also in their very concepts of the tragic. Both Aeschylus and Sophocles, in their own ways, portray the gods in relation to some order beyond the apparent chaos, though one that can only be accepted, not understood. In Euripides the gods become incarnations of the irrational forces that determine our fates. They are more like us in their passions and pettiness – like his tragic heroes also, who are more often victims than the defiant protagonists whom Aeschylus and Sophocles present.[6] To Sophocles is attributed the claim that he portrayed people as they ought to be; Euripides, as they are.[7] As Euripidean characters, Electra and Orestes have lost the grandeur they had in Aeschylus. Aristotle considered plays with unhappy endings to be the most tragic. It is difficult to imagine a more tragic hero than Orestes, divinely compelled to kill his mother and relentlessly pursued by the Furies, yet the *Eumenides*, and with it the Oresteian trilogy, ends on a note of reconciliation with the prospect of harmony founded on justice. How unlike it is the violence of the *Medea* that Aristotle judged revolting, and how different again the *Bacchae*, where dionysiac frenzy triumphs. Though Aristotle called Euripides the most tragic of the poets, referring specifically to his unhappy endings, little Euripidean tragedy fits Aristotle's theory, and one modern critic can even claim that Euripides' works are not really tragic.[8]

Significant variety in the way the tragic vision is mediated can be seen in the corpus of another great tragedian. Regarding Shakespeare one scholar observes, "There is a greater resemblance among the Greek tragedies, those in the classic French or Spanish genre, or in the German Romantic tradition, or among the tragedies of Shakespeare's own contemporaries, than there is between *Macbeth* and *Timon of Athens, Troilus and Cressida, King Lear* or *Coriolanus*."[9] To appreciate the range of Shakespeare's view of the tragic, one need consider only the differences in temperament among his great tragic heroes – Lear, Hamlet, Macbeth, and Othello – and the vastly different tragic conceptions behind the plays that bear their names. As further illustrations of Shakespeare's tragic vision we might include his history plays, with their depiction of the rise and fall of princes and dynasties.[10]

That some purists would use the term "tragedy" only in a restricted sense, be it in reference to a dramatic form or in regard to a particular time or place, is no reason to abandon the word "tragic" for other works. The identification of tragedy with a dramatic form is far too limiting, as Northrop Frye observes:

Tragedy and comedy may have been originally names for two species of drama, but we also employ the terms to describe general characteristics of literary fictions, without regard to genre. It would be silly to insist that comedy can refer only to a certain type of stage play, and must never be employed in connection with Chaucer or Jane Austen. Chaucer himself would certainly have defined comedy, as his monk defines tragedy, much more broadly than that. If we are told that what we are about to read is tragic or comic, we expect a certain kind of structure and mood, but not necessarily a certain genre.[11]

Although there is no formula for deciding what constitutes the tragic, most people have a general idea of what tragedy is about. As George Steiner puts it so succinctly, "Tragedies end badly."[12] Though matters are never so simple, as I seek to indicate below, it is commonly acknowledged that tragedy portrays the hero's rise and fall, what Frye refers to as tragedy's binary form.[13] The notion of the hero's descent into misfortune is given its earliest expression in English literature by Chaucer in the Prologue to the *Monk's Tale*:

> Tragedie is to seyn a certeyn storie,
> As olde bokes maken us memorie,
> Of hym that stood in greet prosperitee,
> And is yfallen out of heigh degree
> In to myserie, and endeth wrecchedly.

Tragedy involves catastrophe, and the catastrophic events that bring the tragic tale to closure are irreparable and irreversible. But the tragic is more fully articulated in some works than others. As H. A. Mason points out, there are "degrees" of tragedy. "We are," he notes, "always ready to say, 'this is more or less tragic than that'..."[14] In this chapter I shall describe what I take to be central ingredients of tragedy and the tragic vision. The following chapters develop and expand this notion of the tragic as it applies to the biblical literature through analyses of particular texts. In what sense do they share the tragic vision? What features do they exhibit that elicit the response, "This is more or less tragic than that"?

I use, then, terms such as "tragedy" and "the tragic" in this book to refer not to a literary form but rather to a broader and more versatile concept, the "tragic vision,"[15] what Miguel de Unamuno calls a "sense of life." Susanne Langer writes about it as "the tragic rhythm," and Karl Jaspers speaks of "tragic atmosphere" and a "tragic mood." The tragic vision is a way of viewing reality, an attitude of negation, uncertainty, and doubt, a feeling of unease in an inhospitable world. It acknowledges, in Jaspers' words, "the ultimate disharmony of existence."[16] What distinguishes this vision from its opposite, the comic or classic vision, is that it lacks comedy's restorative and palliative capacity. Comedy gives voice to a fundamental trust in life; in spite of obstacles, human foibles, miscalculations, and mistakes, life goes on. But tragedy, in contrast, confronts us with what Richard Sewall has called "the terror of the irrational." The tragic hero is the victim of forces she or he cannot control and cannot comprehend, encountering on all sides unresolved questions, doubts, and ambiguities. Comedy may also embrace questions, doubts, and ambiguities, but, as Sewall points out, it removes their terror. The tragic vision isolates the hero over against an arbitrary and capricious world, a world in which – to get to the crux of the matter – the problem of evil is irreducible and un-resolvable into some larger, harmonious whole.

The representation, *mimesis*, of this vision in a particular literary work becomes an attempt to tame it by giving it aesthetic form. The tragic is inexpressible, unintelligible, and inexplicable; the rep-resentation of it – the showing of the absence of meaning – is an act that gives meaning, that brings the tragic within our perceptual grasp. Like primordial chaos in Genesis 1, the tragic is named and classified and thereby brought under control, though its threat to order remains:

If what is tragic can be *said* to be so then it has been fixed, it has become meaningful, and if that is so then one can no longer actually participate in it: the lack of knowledge has been canceled out. As something *named*, the tragic is the creation of the discourse, tragedy. To be in a position to show the tragic presupposes an analysis which, in providing the terms in which human activity is to be deemed possible, circumscribes the domain of the meaningful. If this were not so the tragic could not be shown.[17]

Because the tragic work *shows* it to us, we know the impossibility of knowing, the limits of meaning and order, which is something the protagonist in a tragedy does not know. The protagonist cannot name her or his situation as tragic because to do so would assign it

meaning.[18] Our knowledge spares us the protagonist's struggle –
perhaps it is a source of our feeling of satisfaction in reading or
watching a tragedy – but to what degree it eases our angst depends
on how profoundly we ponder the tragic situation. For while a
tragedy *represents* a vision of fundamental disorder and cosmic
unintelligibility, it resolves it only aesthetically, leaving it thematically unrelieved.[19] The tragic vision is thus contained in an
ordering discourse that it undermines from within by denying the
very possibility of meaningful discourse.[20]

Tragedy is made possible when human freedom comes into conflict
with the demands of the cosmic order. In its fully developed form it
requires, on the one hand, human possibilities and frailties
undiminished and pushed to their limits and, on the other, a cosmos
concerned with human actions. For this reason, the designation
"tragedy" has often been denied to modern works. Steiner, for
example, thinks that modern tragedy is not possible because we have
lost a sense of "the intolerable burden of God's presence." Earlier in
this century Joseph Wood Krutch published a major statement in the
controversy over the "death of tragedy," arguing that tragedy is no
longer possible because we no longer believe in the grandeur of the
human spirit or in the cosmic implications of human deeds. Ibsen's
Ghosts, he asserts, cannot reach the tragic plane of *Hamlet* because
"the materials out of which [Shakespeare] created his works – his
conception of human dignity, his sense of the importance of human
passions, his vision of the amplitude of human life – simply did not
and could not exist for Ibsen, as they did not and could not exist for
his contemporaries."[21] In spite of such passionate and forceful
arguments, the notion of tragedy has been profitably applied to a
range of modern works by a number of critics.[22] And, of course,
modern authors have continued to give expression to their own tragic
visions. One thinks especially of Eugene O'Neill, Tennessee Williams,
and Arthur Miller. Miller, in fact, has defended his tragic vision
against narrow academic definitions of tragedy based on Aristotelian
categories:

It matters not at all whether the hero falls from a great height or a small one,
whether he is highly conscious or only dimly aware of what is happening,
whether his pride brings the fall or an unseen pattern written behind the
clouds; if the intensity, the human passion to surpass his given bounds, the
fanatic insistence upon his self-conceived role – if these are not present there
can only be an outline of tragedy but no living thing. I believe, for myself,

that the lasting appeal of tragedy is due to our need to face the fact of death in order to strengthen ourselves for life, and that over and above this function of the tragic viewpoint there are and will be a great number of formal variations which no single definition will ever embrace.[23]

With the biblical literature, we remain in the world of bold assertions about the possibilities of freedom and the demands of transcendence. Yet even so, some critics would deny the presence of tragedy in the Bible on grounds of the biblical portrayal of God as just or, paradoxically, as merciful. Where there is justice there can be no tragedy, argues Steiner:

Often the balance of retribution or reward seems fearfully awry, or the proceedings of God appear unendurably slow. But over the sum of time, there can be no doubt that the ways of God to man are just. Not only are they just, they are rational. The Judaic spirit is vehement in its conviction that the order of the universe and of man's estate is accessible to reason. The ways of the Lord are neither wanton nor absurd.[24]

This may be true of some parts of the Bible but not, I believe, of others. And it could be said of some Greek tragedies. Aeschylus, for example, tries to reconcile the ideas of guilt and necessary suffering, especially in his appeal to divine justice at the end of the *Oresteia*. Interestingly, Steiner considers exceptional the Greek examples that might arguably fit his understanding of the Judaic vision (the *Eumenides, Oedipus at Colonus*), but he perceives the Bible as speaking univocally. For Baruch Kurzweil, who also denies the possibility of biblical tragedy, "a situation in Biblical narrative bereft of any hope of salvation, of God's mercies, is unthinkable."[25] At the heart of Kurzweil's argument is the conviction that, for the Bible, good and evil are clear-cut and absolute. There are no relative values, and since relativism is indispensable to tragedy, there can be no biblical tragedy:

...Biblical narrative by itself, if its essence remain unchanged and if it is not taken out of the sphere peculiarly suited to it – that is, the sacral sphere – lacks all the elements requisite to the tragic realm. The hero does not remain the captive of his self. Biblical narrative has no place for value relativism and no place for different truths equal in worth and importance. Biblical narrative defines what is good and what is evil in absolutely unambiguous terms, and that is something we do not find in tragedy.[26]

My disagreement with Kurzweil about relative values will become increasingly apparent in the following chapters. Good and evil are by

no means unambiguous in Saul's case, or in Jephthah's. And we shall
see how, in 2 Samuel 21, legitimate claims of the state come into
conflict with the elemental claim of the dead to burial. Even the book
of Job fails to resolve disturbing implications of the questions it raises.
Job has a truth: his integrity. It prompts his quest for justice as well
as his conviction that God treats him unjustly. God, too, has a truth:
justice is not the principle upon which the universe is founded.[27] The
relation between these truths is not entirely clear, since the book does
not indicate the place justice should have in the scheme of things, or
the principle upon which the universe is indeed founded.

Steiner and Kurzweil can extract from the Bible a unified and
coherent view of reality only by excluding alternative interpretations
of the biblical literature, by subsuming into their overall view texts
that are at odds with their claims – thus Steiner's qualification "over
the sum of time," and Kurzweil's insistence that the Bible should be
read as sacral art, not secular fiction. The same holds true for
Northrop Frye's impressive attempt to read the entire Bible (mainly
the Christian, but also the Jewish Bible) in terms of its central *mythos*
or plot.[28] Obviously such broad perspectives can be useful and
illuminating, but it is equally important to ask: what dissenting
voices are repressed or ignored in the interests of an overarching
view? what conflicting evidence is subsumed within the larger
schema? To claim, for example, as Steiner, Kurzweil, and Frye do,
that the book of Job is not tragic because Job in the end capitulates
and is rewarded with more possessions than he had before is to ignore
the terror of Job's experience: can a restored Job trust God again?
(Moreover, a strong case can be made that Job does *not* capitulate.[29])
Such explicitly "final" readings as Frye's and implicitly comprehensive readings as Steiner's and Kurzweil's can always be
challenged by close reading of particular texts.

My own study of the Hebrew Bible has led me to the conclusion
that the Bible contains a profoundly tragic dimension, and we deny
that dimension at the cost of our honesty about reality, and at the risk
of losing a precious affirmation of the indomitable human spirit. I
do not insist that the stories discussed in this book *must* be taken as
tragic in order to appreciate their insights, rather I maintain that
consideration of their tragic potential opens up a powerful and
inspiring, albeit disturbing, narrative dimension, a fullness of insight
into the human condition. It may be that there is a logical and
natural evolution toward the comic or classic vision in biblical

literature, but this is only by virtue of its open-endedness – the conditional nature of the future – and it does not lessen the tragic impact. Nor are there easy guarantees for a better future, only hopes. The entire Deuteronomistic History with its final dramatic gesture toward Jehoiachin, eating at the king's table in Babylonian exile, poignantly illustrates this point.

The tragic vision acknowledges those aspects of reality that we cannot incorporate into a comfortable, reassuring *Weltanschauung*. The Bible's particular resistance to closure, or to philosophical "neatness," has many sources. One is multiple authorship, reflecting diverse and sometimes contradictory viewpoints, spanning hundreds of years and held in marvelously redolent tension. Later redactors could give new meanings to their sources by giving them different contexts, but without necessarily silencing divergent voices. The Bible's eschewal of dualism further discourages systemization. If we seek the origin of evil, we find that it exists from the very beginning according to the creation stories. Darkness (*hosheq*) and the deep (*tehom*) are present when creation begins. Controlled and delimited by the deity in Genesis 1, they remain potentially threatening remnants of chaos. The forbidden tree of the garden of Eden offers knowledge of good *and evil*. God plants it; it is not imported into the garden. The prophets, too, recognize one source for both good and evil. "Does evil befall a city unless Yhwh has done it?" (Amos 3:6). "I make weal and create woe; I, Yhwh, do all these things" (Isaiah 45:7). And the "non-tragic" Job of the folktale can proclaim out of his piety, "Shall we receive good from God and shall we not receive evil?" (Job 2:10).

In the Bible, the association of good and evil within the divine provides fertile ground for tragic awareness to grow. An evil spirit from Yhwh torments Saul, driving him to despair and madness; and, as I argue below, Yhwh's spirit is implicated in Jephthah's fateful vow, in return for victory, to sacrifice the one who meets him. If there were no hint of divine involvement in these cases, if Saul's deterioration were entirely his own doing or if Jephthah's vow were a premeditated decision, the tragic power of these stories would be greatly diminished. By telling (and re-telling) stories rather than working out a philosophical system, the biblical authors bequeathed to us a multivalent, inexhaustible narrative world. To inherit the Bible is as if we had Sophocles without Plato, who, for his part, would have excluded tragedy from his ideal society.

At the core of tragedy lies the problem and mystery of evil. Paul Ricoeur captures the essence of the tragic in his discussion of the Aeschylean paradox of the wicked god and human guilt.[30] Fate *and* flaw present an essential combination in tragedy, though these terms can be misleading if understood too narrowly.[31] We describe tragic heroes as gripped by forces beyond their control. Ricoeur speaks cautiously of a "predestination to evil"; alternatively we may speak of hostile transcendence, arbitrary fate, an impending doom, a catastrophe waiting to happen. The tragic protagonist is caught up in a situation not entirely of her or his own making. At the same time she or he is also responsible, a guilty victim. Tragedy does not clearly distinguish guilt and innocence. Kierkegaard speaks of "authentic tragic guilt in its ambiguous guiltlessness."[32] The heroes of tragedy are innocent in the sense that their misfortune is far greater than anything their deeds have provoked, and guilty both as members of a guilty society and by virtue of living in a world where such injustices simply happen.[33] This is Ricoeur's "guiltiness of being" and Jaspers' "guilt of existence." As Ricoeur and Jaspers show, the tragic hero is *both* guilty of being *and* guilty of committing an act that need not occur and could also occur differently.[34] In the Bible, no one is innocent, except perhaps the Job of the folktale whose moral probity prompts divine boasting ("Have you considered my servant Job, how there is no one like him on earth, a blameless and upright man, who fears God and turns away from evil?"). Whereas the hero is guilty, the guilt need not stem from wrongful acts (Antigone insists she does right by doing wrong) nor necessarily be incurred willfully (as Oedipus' case demonstrates). Or the disaster that befalls the tragic protagonist may result from some sin or wrongdoing, a transgression deliberately pursued or innocently performed, a simple misjudgment, but in any case with the consequences out of proportion to the deed.

Nor is fate, though inexorable, simply mechanical. Bernard Knox shows the subtle but important distinction in *Oedipus Tyrannus* between fate predicted and fate predestined.[35] Tragic heroes do not consider themselves powerless when confronted with their fates. Oedipus leaves what he believes to be his home in order to avoid fulfilling the prophecy that he will kill his father and marry his mother. But because he does not *know* the identity of Laius and Jocasta the prophecy is fulfilled. His fate was not predestined, merely predicted; he could have killed himself or never married. Though he bears responsibility for what happens, because he acts in ignorance he is not to blame. In the biblical account, Saul knows God has rejected him and chosen another to be king over Israel, but this knowledge does not prevent him from struggling to retain his kingdom.

Tragedy deals with catastrophe, guilt, necessary suffering, and their essential but unfathomable connection. The suffering that tragedy brings cannot be explained simply in terms of human guilt. Something uncanny and contingent lies behind it. Jephthah vows to sacrifice the one who meets him upon his victorious return from battle, but why is that person his daughter and not someone else, someone less dear? On the other hand, calamity alone does not make a tragedy. Innocent suffering is usually not tragic, but only pathetic. What makes Job tragic is not his suffering, but his struggle to *know* its cause and his refusal to accept blame. When disaster befalls someone who deserves it, we call it justice, not tragedy. Tragedy requires that the disaster have some connection with the protagonist's guilt and some meaning in terms of the protagonist's life.[36]

At some point in tragedy, a catastrophe occurs. Disaster does not have to be the final word (as witnessed by the *Oresteia*, *Oedipus at Colonus*, and even the book of Job), but it usually breaks the hero, who dares to defy the universe. If they are not already exceptional people, rulers or leaders, tragic heroes are made exceptional by their experience, and so are commonly isolated from society. Greatness is within their grasp. Often a tragic hero responds to disaster – Oedipus to the plague, Saul to a crisis of leadership, Jephthah to a military emergency – and unleashes more disaster.[37]

A central feature of the tragic is the heroic struggle against fate. D. H. Lawrence located tragedy in this "supreme struggle," and his comments illuminate the difference between tragedy and disaster:

In tragedy the man is more than his part. Hamlet is more than Prince of Denmark, Macbeth is more than murderer of Duncan. The man is caught in the wheels of his part, his fate, he may be torn asunder. He may be killed, but the resistant, integral soul in him is not destroyed. He comes through, though he dies. He goes through with his fate, though death swallows him. And it is in this facing of fate, this going right through with it, that tragedy lies. Tragedy is not disaster. It is a disaster when a cartwheel goes over a frog, but it is not a tragedy. Tragedy is the working out of some immediate passional problem within the soul of man. If this passional problem and this working out be absent, then no disaster is a tragedy, not the hugest: not the death of ten million men. It is only a cartwheel going over a frog. There must be a supreme *struggle*.[38]

The Job of the folktale who acquiesces is not tragic, but the Job of the poem who argues tirelessly against his friends and what he perceives as God's injustice is profoundly so. Connected with this struggle is frequently the awareness that one is partly responsible and yet at the same time trapped by forces beyond one's control (the issue of guilt *and* innocence referred to above). Tragic heroes have the *hubris* – sometimes in authentic greatness, sometimes in delusion – to defy the universe, not in a stoic defiance but in an insistence on their moral integrity (justified or not). Because they refuse, they will be broken. "He may slay me; I am without hope. Yet I will defend my conduct to his face" (Job 13:15).[39] It is not that there is "no way out whatsoever," as Jaspers asserts,[40] but that there is no way out without denying oneself.[41] Saul refuses to acquiesce, he will hold on to the kingship whatever the cost, rejecting the easy way out. There is a "way out" and Saul's son Jonathan, by yielding his right to the throne to David, shows what it is, but at the cost of his identity, which, as we shall see, becomes submerged into David's. There is a way out for Jephthah, too; he could refuse to sacrifice his daughter. But to do so would mean denying himself, going back on his word, "I have opened my mouth to Yhwh, and I cannot take it back."

Whereas the struggle against fate plays an important role in tragedy, under certain circumstances and with certain qualifications, we may view helpless victims as tragic.[42] Status as tragic victim seems especially applicable to women, who in the biblical narrative rarely have real control over their lives, and for whom it is usually futile to struggle against their lot. In Chapter 3, I refer to Jephthah's daughter as tragic although her tragedy is of an entirely different order and magnitude from Jephthah's, where the tragic conflict is focused. And both Jephthah and his daughter ultimately fail to achieve true tragic stature. In Chapter 4, I discuss Michal's fate as tragic, though she, too, is a victim who can do no more than bitterly protest against her fate, a fate not of her own making. The tragic quality exhibited by the members of Saul's house, who share his grim destiny but not his heroic struggle, is the subject of Chapter 4.

In the Bible, Saul and Job are the pre-eminently tragic figures against whom to measure all others. The tragic dimension of the book of Job has long been recognized, and it is not my intention to take up the argument once again in this study.[43] The book of Job poses the problem of suffering, innocent or necessary, and the problem of moral order, examining them from various angles without resolving them.[44] The question of guilt, though the pressing issue for Job himself, is resolved for us from the start: we know that God considers Job innocent of any moral wrongdoing. In terms of the paradox of human guilt and hostile transcendence, Job is not guilty and God not wicked, only unknowable. But Job is guilty of *hubris* as he struggles, to the point of blasphemy, against what he perceives as God's injustice. And God is incited by the adversary to destroy Job without cause (2:3)[45] and remains absent during most of Job's suffering. The resolution, Job's restoration to prosperity (with a bonus) at the end of the book, is not such stuff as tragedies are made of. Neither is it sufficient in power or conviction to transform the book into a comedy,[46] chiefly because the dialogue brings cosmic terror, as well as human heroism, into such stark relief. In his defiance Job rivals God; comic heroes do not reach such heights. Frye observes of the *Oresteia* that Athena's appearance at the end of the *Eumenides* does not turn the trilogy into comedy but clarifies its tragic vision.[47] I would make the same claim about Job. God appears to Job in a whirlwind and overwhelms him with questions just as Job predicted he would (9:16–20),[48] holding before him the vision of a beautiful but morally unintelligible universe. The question is: can Job ever again feel secure in such a universe?

My investigation of biblical narrative in terms of "tragic vision" or "tragic themes" is likely to be judged a particularly modern preoccupation, a tragic worldview being well suited to our uncertain times. But after all, modern readings are what keep ancient literature alive for us, and without them, the Bible could well become a document purely of antiquarian interest or of concern only to the religious. I acknowledge my modern perspective, but I contend that the vision I call tragic is there – even if only implicitly – from ancient times, and my readings are an effort to demonstrate the enduring power of that vision. In this, I follow an approach which seeks to disclose the repressed and unconscious dimension of texts: "turn it and turn it again for everything is in it" (Avoth 5:22). My readings of the biblical texts proceed inductively, allowing the texts themselves to inform our understanding of the tragic. Thus my approach to the individual texts varies in accordance with their different tragic visions. I have sought to respect the ancient character of these narratives and to recognize their cultural assumptions, and I do not think I have wrenched them wholly or violently out of their ancient context in order to make them fit my notion of the tragic. Fortunately texts do not yield readily to our efforts to categorize them and assign them a particular place within a conceptual system. Thus my analysis also seeks to show how the stories of Jephthah, of Saul's family, and of David and his house resist interpretation along tragic lines and how they depart from my description above as well as from the classic representation of biblical tragedy in the story of Saul.

The narratives discussed in this book deal primarily with leaders – judges and kings and members of the royal household – perennial subjects of tragic treatment because their grandeur makes their lives and their "falls" so much more momentous. Chapter 2 deals with the story of Israel's first king, Saul, rejected by God and driven to despair and madness by the divine preference for his rival, David. Using Saul's tragedy as the backdrop, Chapters 3 through 5 consider how other biblical narratives fall short of realizing their full tragic potential, while nonetheless acknowledging and even embracing the palpable prospect of the tragic. Chapter 3 examines the scandalous story of Jephthah's unanticipated sacrifice of his daughter in fulfillment of his vow to offer God a sacrifice in return for victory. Chapter 4 analyzes the tragic lot of various members of Saul's family : Michal and Jonathan, Abner and Ishbosheth, and seven of Saul's descendants, whose ritual execution pollutes the land. Chapter 5 focuses on the working out of nemesis within the royal house of Israel's most famous king, David, exploring reasons why David does not attain true tragic status in spite of what appear to be the classic makings of tragedy in the account of his reign.

All these narratives belong to the complex literary composition known to scholars as the Deuteronomistic History, a comprehensive history of Israel from the exodus to the exile, encompassing the books of Deuteronomy to Kings. In singling out certain accounts from their larger literary context, I make no specific claims about sources used by the Deuteronomistic Historians or about literary independence. These are topics of great interest to some biblical scholars but they are not my concern in what is essentially a literary analysis. Thus I speak of the Saul story, the Samson story, the Jephthah story, and the David story. Because they deal with the fate of individuals, these accounts have the same kind of closure that any life story has : while every life intersects with others and forms part of a larger story, it also has its unique self-referential course from its beginning to its end. The accounts of Samson and Jephthah are autonomous units, inde- pendent episodes in the Deuteronomistic History that have clear boundaries. The Saul and David stories, on the other hand, appear interwoven in the same text, which tells their stories by means of interconnecting story-lines:

A story-line is structured like the complete story, but unlike the latter it is restricted to one set of individuals. Thus in *King Lear* one can distinguish the story-line involving Lear and his daughters from the one concerning Gloucester and his sons, although the two often intersect. Once a succession of events involving the same individuals establishes itself as the predominant story element of a text (and, unfortunately, there are no clear-cut criteria for predominance), it becomes the *main story-line*. A succession of events which involves another set of individuals is a *subsidiary story-line*.[49]

As complete in itself, Saul's story is a tragedy; in the ongoing narrative, the central figure is David, who establishes a dynasty still in existence when the Deuteronomistic History comes to an end.[50] We shall look at the text and its unfolding from Saul's perspective in Chapter 2 and from David's in Chapter 5.[51] In the case of minor characters, such as the members of Saul's house, investigating their "stories" requires reading from a different angle, focusing attention on their place in the larger narrative.

The excursuses that appear at the end of Chapters 2 and 3 move into different but related areas of interpretation. They are not afterthoughts but rather express my conviction that reading is never finished, that these texts remain ever open to new interpretive possibilities.[52]

The natural human need to make sense and order out of life and our desire for reassurance militate against the despair at the core of tragedy. As Sewall points out, the tragic vision "is not for those who cannot live with unsolved questions or unresolved doubts."[53] Others have also emphasized our reluctance and inability "to face a tragedy without turning it into something else."[54] The happy ending Nahum Tate gave to *King Lear*, where Cordelia is not killed and Edgar replaces the king of France as her suitor, was played on the English stage for a century and a half. The Bible, because its subject is the whole of human experience, cannot repress the chaotic side of reality and does not propose to, though its interpreters often seem anxious to make it do so. Human beings do suffer, and frequently unjustly though perhaps necessarily. The Bible's great virtue is that, like Abraham standing before God in Genesis 18, it calls God to account. Significantly, in this instance the scribes inform us that they changed an original text in which it was said that God stood before Abraham.

CHAPTER 2

Saul: the hostility of God

Whom god would destroy he first makes mad.

Euripides, fragment

A young Benjaminite, Saul son of Kish, becomes Israel's first king under adverse circumstances. The people's desire for a king "like the nations" displeases the prophet Samuel and arouses in Yhwh feelings of personal rejection. In spite of his initial reluctance to be king, Saul meets his first challenge admirably, delivering Jabesh-gilead from the threat of humiliating Ammonite oppression. But disobedience to the divine command, in ambiguous, if not extenuating, circumstances, soon costs him the throne. After his rejection by Yhwh, Saul views David's success and rising popularity with jealousy and growing apprehension. His attempts to kill his rival are thwarted by his own children, who, out of affection for David, help him escape. Saul's descent into madness and his alienation from those once closest to him, Samuel, David, and Jonathan, are painfully detailed as he carries his single-minded pursuit of David almost – but not quite – to the point of neglecting his duties as king. Abandoned by God, he must seek out preternatural and forbidden means of obtaining an oracle before facing the Philistines in a critical battle, only to receive from Samuel's ghost a scathing denunciation which dashes any hope he may have nourished. His career ends abruptly on the battlefield where, seeing no possibility of escape, he takes his own life.

The account of the rise and fall of King Saul found in 1 Samuel 8– 2 Samuel 1 offers the clearest example of biblical tragedy. It can best be described as "tempered tragedy."[1] For just as Denmark will be a better place under Fortinbras, and Scotland under Malcolm, Israel will find security and prosperity under Saul's successor, the king chosen after God's own heart. Nevertheless, all the essential tragic ingredients meet us in the story of Saul, chief among them, and

16

indispensable to the tragic vision, the Aeschylean paradox of human guilt and the wicked god.[2]

"Saul is the one great tragic hero of the Bible," says Northrop Frye,[3] an observation most biblical exegetes would take for granted. Few would quarrel with Gerhard von Rad's classic statement that "Israel never again gave birth to a poetic production which in certain of its features has such close affinity with the spirit of Greek tragedy."[4] In his 1965 study, *Irony in the Old Testament*, Edwin Good offers a compelling reading of the story of King Saul in terms of its tragic dimension. Good and others[5] have drawn attention to the theological problem addressed by this material: Yhwh opposes the people's demand for a king yet grants their request; he selects for them a king but one who fails to live up to his calling. Good analyzes the ambiguous nature of kingship and shows clearly how Saul's strengths are undermined by his weaknesses. He goes too far, however, in arguing the case for Saul's inability to meet kingship's challenges. For Good, Saul's major problem is his self-depreciation and concern for his status with the people; he is "little in his own eyes." The issue of Saul's qualifications for kingship is only part of the problem; Good neglects the essential feature of Saul's tragedy, the ambivalent role of the deity.

More recently, both Lee Humphreys[6] and David Gunn[7] have argued at length for the tragic character of the Saul story. Humphreys' interpretation is less congenial to the approach taken here, since it deals with successive stages of redaction in 1 Samuel. Humphreys posits an original tragic stratum that has been reworked by prophetic, and then royalist, circles who were "unable to accept the theological implications of the tragic vision."[8] His tragic stratum is a "hypothetical reconstruction."[9] By attributing to it the disturbing aspects of the present story, Humphreys arrives at a more comfortable final redaction, one that affirms what he considers a normative Israelite religious perspective. Such an approach, however, does not take the present shape of the story seriously. Regardless of how the ancient materials have been reworked and adapted (it is hard to imagine them so mechanically handled as Humphreys suggests), the tragic perspective is integral to the text as it now stands, and its threat to order and stability – as well as to a normative reading – cannot be dismissed.

Gunn's study, like the present one, is concerned with the final form of the story. His meticulous analysis of the issue of Saul's guilt in

1 Samuel 13 and 15 lies behind my remarks about these chapters. Unlike Good, Gunn recognizes the role God's dark side plays in Saul's tragedy and he exposes it forcefully. But because he unnecessarily seeks to distinguish between fate and flaw, he never treats human guilt and divine hostility as an essential combination, and in emphasizing Saul as a victim of God he sometimes loses sight of Saul as a victim of himself.

Rather than go over the same ground, repeating the valuable insights of these studies or arguing over details of interpretation, I propose to approach the story of Saul from a different angle, to investigate its tragic dimension by setting it over against the story of Samson, a narrative with enough points of contact with Saul's to merit Wellhausen's designation of Samson as a *Vorspiel* to Saul, but a narrative that moves in a different direction, away from the irreversible, somber ending of tragedy toward resolution and reconciliation. Both Samson and Saul are hailed as deliverers of Israel from the Philistines, both fail at the task, and both die seemingly ignominious deaths at the hands of their oppressors in the process. Yet Saul reaches tragic depths not experienced by Samson, however grim his disfigurement and death in Philistine captivity may be. Comparison of the two accounts, with their different handling of similar elements, reveals two contrasting visions of reality, the tragic and the comic. To offset the tendency to confuse the designation "comic vision" with something funny, I shall use it interchangeably with "the classic vision," Murray Krieger's term for the affirmative alternative to the tragic vision. Whereas the comic or classic vision can be funny, it is not limited to the humorous and laughable. The classic is not naive but rather an inclusive vision, as Krieger shows, able to acknowledge a tragic vision and yet refuse it. It accepts, without illusion and without despair, the imperfections of the human condition.[10]

Although fundamentally opposed, the classic and tragic visions are not mutually exclusive. They may appear in various combinations, great tragedies often offering a glimpse of the assuring universe of comedy and great comedies acknowledging a tragic potential only to deny it in the end – thus the difficulty of differentiating sharply between comedy and tragedy, except in their extreme forms (for example, most Greek tragedy). As Susanne Langer points out, "The matrix of the work is always either tragic or comic; but within its frame the two often interplay."[11] Interplay lends vitality to these visions. Tragedy without comedy can easily slip into melodrama, while comedy without a sense of tragic possibility becomes farce.

Stock elements of comedy abound in the story of Samson in Judges 13–16: wit and humor, bawdy riddles and amorous escapades, a rapid pace, an episodic structure, and a hero of incredible vitality. The Philistines are blocking characters who inhibit movement toward a harmonious society; they are caricatured, as is Samson himself, and clear distinctions are made between hero and villains. Unmistakably tragic elements appear as well – the hero's betrayal, blinding, and death providing the most obvious examples. When Milton sought to make a tragedy of the Samson story he produced a powerful drama, but even here the inherent comic plot-line which he took over from the biblical tradition defeats the realization of the tragic vision. Neither in *Samson Agonistes* nor in the biblical account does the hero's death carry the final or the central message. It is entirely in keeping with the spirit of the biblical story, as I shall argue below, that Milton's Manoah offers us the crucial insight, "No time for lamentation now, / Nor much more cause; Samson hath quit himself /Like Samson..." and the chorus assures us, "All is best, though we oft doubt..."

Samson has been variously characterized as comic, as tragic, or as tragicomic.[12] Although tragic elements are present, the matrix of the Samson story is best described as comic, which does not necessarily mean that we like the way the story ends. In spite of Samson's suffering and death, the story, with its emphasis on restoration and resolution, exemplifies the classic vision, a vision that can tolerate distress and defeat because life, Israel's life, goes on. Thus, while Saul's is a tempered tragedy, Samson's might be considered a grim comedy.[13] Unlike Saul's, Samson's story does not threaten our assumptions about the nature of things. There is a fundamental rightness in the way events are resolved, a sense that a proper and fitting outcome has been achieved.

Whereas Samson combines comic and tragic features in unique ways, there is little, if any, comic relief in the Saul story.[14] A few incidents relieve the foreboding atmosphere of 1 Samuel 8, which predisposes us to expect the worst from the institution of a monarchy; for example, the narrative of the unsuspecting lad who seeks lost asses and finds a kingdom (1 Samuel 9–10), and the vignette of the future king hiding among the baggage when he is chosen by lot (11:20–4). But such potentially moderating incidents occur only at the beginning of the narrative; the only real alternative to the tragic perspective in 1 Samuel 8–2 Samuel 1 is provided by the account of David's rise to power. If we shift our perspective from Saul's to David's, we find in the narrative another, sanguine, mood alongside the somber mood of Saul's tragedy. Shortly after he is introduced, this ruddy, handsome shepherd boy with a sling slays the Philistine champion, "a man of war from his youth," and from this point on, David and Saul become foils for each other. David's rise matches Saul's decline, with David's good fortune underscoring Saul's failure.

In comparing Samson and Saul, let us first consider the course of their fortunes as plotted in Judges 13–16 and 1 Samuel 8–2 Samuel 1. Both Samson and Saul die fighting Yhwh's battles against the Philistines. Preceding the death account in each story comes the point where the hero experiences his moment of greatest desolation. These two elements in each story, the low point in the fortunes of the hero and the account of his death, provide the points of greatest similarity between the tales and thus serve well to demonstrate how the classic and tragic visions clearly diverge, one moving toward reconciliation and affirmation, the other toward isolation and lamentation.

The Samson saga exhibits what Northrop Frye describes as the ternary form of comedy. The first phase, an original state of harmony, lies in the background, before the events of the story get underway.[15] As the story opens, conflict between Israelites and Philistines is evident, with Samson contributing his fair share to the animosity, ever savoring the opportunity to nettle the Philistines.[16] One side, then the other, gets the upper hand in a series of skirmishes, reprisals, and counter-reprisals, until the low point in Samson's fortunes is reached when Samson is shaved and Yhwh leaves him. Yhwh's departure is all the more devastating because Samson, at first, does not realize it. On three earlier occasions, when Delilah had tried to subdue him, Samson tricked her and remained invincible. But her fourth attempt brings about his undoing, just as she knew it would (16:18). In what we might consider a moment of *hubris*, Samson sets out "as at other times" to best the Philistines, only to confirm his prediction, "If I be shaved, my strength will leave me, and I will become weak like other men," and to discover the bitter reality that "Yhwh had left him." Betrayed by Delilah, bereft of his hair, his strength, and the presence of his god (and these three things are inseparably connected in the narrative), Samson is blinded and imprisoned. He is brought out for "sport," to amuse the crowd at a sacrifice to Dagon, where vast numbers of Philistines gather to celebrate victory over their enemy. In this, his moment of deepest humiliation, Samson calls on Yhwh with a petition for vindication and death:[17]

Samson called upon Yhwh, "O Lord Yhwh, remember me please and strengthen me please only this time, O God, that I may be vindicated against the Philistines for one of my two eyes." Samson grasped the two middle pillars upon which the house rested, and leaned upon them, one with his right hand and one with his left, and Samson said, "Let me die with the Philistines." (Judg. 16:28–30)

Samson's prayer, with its conventional invocation and plea to be remembered, expresses his sense of abandonment by God,[18] as he makes urgent supplication for divine favor this last time. His prayer reestablishes his relationship to Yhwh and thus gives the plot its upward surge. This restoration of relationship is decisive for the classic vision in Judges 13–16. Yhwh's departure from Samson, which occurred when he was shaved, is not final; rather, Yhwh is a responsive deity who can be swayed by prayer. Samson's petition for strength "only this time" is granted, as is his grim request to die with the Philistines. Strictly speaking, his death is not a suicide, for death is in Yhwh's hand, not Samson's. The distinction is an important one: Yhwh's power – not Samson's own or some mysterious force that resides in his hair – enables Samson to kill Philistines and die in the process. Samson's death is the logical conclusion of the narrative; it releases him from a world of darkness (an aspect heightened by Milton) and avenges the ignominy he has suffered at the hands of the Philistines (the aspect emphasized in the biblical account).[19] At his death, Samson fulfills the destiny Yhwh had appointed for him, to "be the first to deliver Israel from the Philistines" (13:5). Moreover, his final triumph over the Philistines surpasses his earlier exploits, winning him even greater glory: "The dead that he killed at his death were more than those he had killed in his life" (16:30). His burial by his brothers in the tomb of Manoah, his father, symbolizes his ultimate integration into the society he represents, but on whose periphery he has functioned so obstinately and individualistically.

In contrast to the movement toward reincorporation and re-integration in Judges 13–16, the story of Saul in 1 Samuel 9–31 follows the typical movement of tragedy, what Frye terms its binary form, from success (the hero's rise) to catastrophe (the hero's fall).

The story develops against the negative backdrop of Samuel's and Yhwh's misgivings about kingship in 1 Samuel 8,[20] and its downward movement is impelled by the rejection stories of 1 Samuel 13 and 15. Samuel, Yhwh, and Saul are all drawn into the conflict over kingship. Saul's anointing as *nagid* (king-elect) in 1 Samuel 9–10 and his impressive victory over the Ammonites in 1 Samuel 11 (the people wanted a king to lead them against their enemies, 8:20) are surrounded by negative evaluations of kingship. Samuel and Yhwh accuse the people of rejecting Yhwh in favor of a human king in 1 Samuel 8; 10:17–19; and 12, and divine authority is violently asserted when Yhwh, in answer to Samuel's request, sends a thunderstorm during the dry season (12:16–19). The first rejection scene follows closely upon Samuel's threat to the people, "If you still do wickedly, both you and your king shall be swept away" (12:25). After his rejection, Saul achieves another military victory (1 Samuel 14), but unlike the victory over Ammon, this one is ambiguous and problematic. A battle also provides the context for the second, climactic rejection, after which the successor is introduced (1 Samuel 16). Another battle scene follows, but this time Saul, "dismayed and greatly afraid" (17:11), does not fight; David meets Goliath in single combat. In the wake of David's success, Israel defeats the Philistines.

From this point on, Saul encounters various setbacks, from anxiety over his loss of prestige in the eyes of the people (18:7) to his inability to apprehend David, and his fortune, not to mention his sanity, deteriorates until the narrative reaches its lowest point with the vision of Samuel conjured up by the medium at En-dor. For sheer starkness and terror, and in its gripping evocation of isolation and hopelessness, this scene stands out in biblical narrative. Saul's anguished state of mind is plentifully signaled by the text: he is afraid (1 Sam. 28:5), his heart trembles greatly (v. 5), he is in great distress (v. 15), filled with fear (v. 20), there is no strength in him (v. 20), he is terrified (v. 21). After this journey into the abyss of divine abandonment, Saul's death can only be seen as anticlimactic.

The scene is set at night. Night not only covers the movements of the king, hiding him from Philistine observation, but symbolizes as well the realm of darkness and uncertainty he is about to enter. Night is traditionally the time of spirits and necromancers' rites, and it provides an archetypal symbol for the ultimate darkness, death. It is no accident that, just as Saul left his first meeting with Samuel in 1 Samuel 9 at the break of day (that is, the dawn of his career), he both arrives at and departs from his last encounter with Samuel while it is still night.

The isolation Saul experiences manifests itself even before this final rejection by Samuel. Try as he may – and there have been no indications that Saul was not a faithful Yahwist – Saul cannot get Yhwh to answer him: "And when Saul inquired of Yhwh, Yhwh did not answer him either by dreams, or by Urim, or by prophets" (28:6); indeed, Yhwh never addresses Saul directly in the narrative, but speaks to him only through Samuel, or, as in 1 Samuel 14, through the sacred lots. Why does Saul seek out the prophet Samuel, who has already rejected him? When Gunn answers that Saul can stand no more ambiguity, he identifies the root of the dilemma of the tragic hero.[21] Not content to let his tragic destiny unfold, the tragic hero stalks it. Like Oedipus, who relentlessly pushes for the full truth to be disclosed while the answers steadily close in upon him, Saul *must know*.

A feeling of uncertainty and apprehension permeates the chapter; what occurs is not only secretive but forbidden as well. Ironically it was Saul himself, apparently in the service of Yhwh, who put the mediums and wizards out of the land (28:3). Now Yhwh's silence and the failure of ordinary means of inquiry drive Saul to consultation with the dead. Though reluctant, the medium, whose life stands threatened by Saul's edict against necromancy, becomes the sole source of the knowledge he seeks. Neither Saul nor Samuel is identified at first; Saul goes in disguise and instructs the woman, "Bring up for me whomever I say to you" (v. 8). The seance reveals Saul's and Samuel's presence simultaneously: at the moment she sees *Samuel* the woman recognizes *Saul*. Saul, for his part, recognizes Samuel on the basis of the woman's description, "an old man...wrapped in a robe."[22] It has taken twelve verses to establish the mood and set the scene, during which time suspense has been mounting as we await the fateful confrontation.

With characteristic brusqueness, Samuel asks Saul's reason for disturbing him. Saul's reply that "the Philistines are waging war against me" recalls the situation of 1 Samuel 13, when Saul first erred by offering the sacrifice in Samuel's absence. And when he implores, "I have called you *to reveal to me what I should do*," we remember that he did not wait for Samuel to tell him what to do then: "Seven days you shall wait until I come to you and I will *reveal to you what you shall do*," Samuel had said (10:8). Samuel's reply, "Why do you ask me?"

(*welammah tish'aleni*), puns ironically on Saul's name, and his answer reiterates in painful detail what Saul knows already: because Saul disobeyed Yhwh in not carrying out the ban against the Amalekites (1 Samuel 15), Yhwh has rejected him and given the kingdom to David. Moreover, Israel will be defeated and Saul and his sons will die in the coming battle. Overcome by weakness and fear, Saul collapses (v. 20), prefiguring as it were his fall on the field of battle.

Though the meal which follows provides one of several points of contact between Saul's last meeting with Samuel and his first (in this case the meal that takes place in 1 Samuel 9),[23] it seems at first glance somewhat incongruous in this terrible rejection scene. A remark by George Steiner with reference to Racine's *Bérénice* not only provides, in my opinion, the clue to the meal's function, but also sheds helpful light on the nature of the tragic vision in 1 Samuel 28 – a vision as terrifying and uncompromising as any in the tragic corpus, yet ever so slightly tempered:

Can Bérénice remain standing under the hammering of sorrow on Racine's naked stage or will she have to call for a chair, thus bringing on to that stage the whole contingency and compromise of the mundane order of the world? I admit that, today, this question and the executive conventions from which it springs, seem to me to crystallize the truth of absolute tragedy with an integrity, with an economy of means, with a transcendence of theatrical "business" and verbal orchestration beyond that which we find on Shakespeare's loud and prodigal scene. It needs no cosmic storms or peregrine woods to reach the heart of desolation. The absence of a chair will do.[24]

Henri Bergson, in a classic essay on "Laughter," makes a similarly applicable point:

No sooner does anxiety about the body manifest itself than the intrusion of a comic element is to be feared. On this account, the hero in a tragedy does not eat or drink or warm himself. He does not even sit down any more than can be helped.[25]

In a scene built around dialogue, Saul's words are dramatic in their brevity, "I will not eat." The meal which Saul finally allows to be prepared and which he eats with his servants ameliorates the despair and pathos of the scene. Saul would have it otherwise, but he gives in, as he has before, to human urging. Pure tragedy would have left him without any recourse. Samson prays for and receives strength (*koah*, Judg. 16:30) from Yhwh; but as for Saul, he has no strength in him (*koah*, v. 20). Relief comes as he receives nourishment from the medium whose kindness contrasts dramatically with Samuel's severity.[26] This delicate tempering of the tragic vein enables Saul to eat, rise, and go on his way – though he goes now with the sure knowledge of the fate that awaits him: "tomorrow you and your sons shall be with me..." (28:19).

In the account of Saul's death in 1 Samuel 31, the narrative yields fully to the tragic vision. Wounded and fearing abuse by the Philistines, Saul tells his armor-bearer to thrust him through. But the young man is afraid. As in the ill-fated decision to make the offering himself in 1 Samuel 13, it appears that Saul again has no option but to take matters into his own hand. Unlike Samson, whose prayer re-establishes his relationship with Yhwh, Saul cannot call on God to let him die, because already in 1 Samuel 28 God has effectively and decisively ended communication. Thus, whereas Samson's death is in the hands of Yhwh, Saul's comes by his own hand. In contrast to Samson's death, which belongs to a larger, classic resolution, Saul's death stands in tragic isolation. Whether grounded in a "failure of nerve"[27] or symbolic of a "final moment of grandeur [when] he seizes control of events,"[28] Saul's suicide functions as his last desperate attempt to wrest from his destiny its final meaning. As an act of his own will, it can be compared to Oedipus' self-blinding, even though in both cases the circumstances are from God:

> It was Apollo, friends, Apollo,
> that brought this bitter bitterness, my sorrows to completion.
> But the hand that struck me
> was none but my own.[29]

Tragic events mount in 1 Samuel 31. First, Israel is routed and many are slain (v. 1); then Saul's sons meet their deaths (v. 2); next comes Saul's suicide and that of his armor-bearer (vv. 3–6), after which the Israelites abandon their cities to the Philistines (v. 7). The next day brings further dishonor: the Philistines mutilate and desecrate Saul's corpse (vv. 8–10). They send messengers throughout their territory to carry the good news, and, as a token of their victory, they exhibit Saul's armor in the temple of Ashtaroth and his body on the wall of Beth-shan. The scene recalls the Philistines' celebration of Samson's defeat and their merrymaking in Dagon's temple over his disgrace ("Our god has given [Samson] our enemy into our hand," Judg. 16:23, 24). But no *deus ex machina* steps in to aid Saul and bring about a resolution, as in the Samson story. The cruelest part of Saul's fate lies in his death in isolation from Yhwh. Typically of the tragic vision, there is no reconciliation, no restoration. Nor will there be a future for the house of Saul.

Catastrophe does not strike the tragic protagonist alone. Like the curses that work themselves out in the house of Atreus and the house of Cadmus, Saul's misfortune extends beyond himself to his family. Three sons, Jonathan, Abinadab, and Malchishua, are also killed in the battle on Mount Gilboa, and their bodies exhibited with their father's at Beth-shan. We shall examine below in Chapter 4 the tragic circumstances that befall the remaining members of Saul's house: his son Ishbosheth, slain in his bed; his cousin Abner, ruthlessly assassinated; sons and grandsons executed to expiate Saul's crimes against the Gibeonites. Only Jonathan's son Mephibosheth escapes the Gibeonites' vengeance, but Mephibosheth has his own troubles. Not only is he lame, but David shows him questionable loyalty and his loyalty to David is questioned.[30] Finally there is Saul's daughter Michal, who is taken from David, whom she loves, and given to Palti, only later to be taken from Palti and returned to David. Michal and David quarrel over his behavior before the ark of Yhwh and the outcome for Michal has an air of tragic finality about it. She dies childless, bringing to an end another branch of the house of Saul.

The accounts of Samson and Saul handle repetition, a distinctive feature of biblical narrative, differently. Frye, in his *Anatomy of Criticism*, observes that repetition overdone or not going anywhere is comic.[31] Samson, as we are all aware, keeps doing the same thing, and in this, he is quite laughable. True, he encounters obstacles and suffers temporary setbacks, but we see over and over again that Samson bounces back, and we come to expect it. Samson exemplifies Ben Jonson's theory of the "humor" and Bergson's concept of mechanical behavior as a central element of comedy. He has a fatal weakness for women, and this leads him into repeated scrapes with the Philistines (Judg. 14:1–15:17; 16:1–3; 16:4–22). Twice he falls for the same ruse and reveals his secret to a woman, and the repetitive factor in these episodes accentuates his incorrigibility. The Philistines threaten one woman and bribe the other to "entice" (14:15; 16:5) Samson to "tell" them his secret (*ngd*, "to tell," figures prominently throughout both accounts). Through the Timnite they seek to learn the answer to his riddle, and through Delilah, to discover the source of his strength. Both women manipulate Samson by appealing to his affection. "You only hate me, you do not love me," protests the

Timnite (14:16), while Delilah badgers him with the words, "How can you say 'I love you' when your heart is not with me?" (16:15). After enduring the Timnite's urging for seven days (14:17), and Delilah's every day (16:16), Samson gives in. In both cases "he told her" (14:17; 16:17) "because she harassed him" (14:17; 16:16). The betrayal of his secret leads both times, first indirectly and then directly, to the handing over of Samson to the Philistines. In Judg. 15:13 the Philistines bind Samson with two new ropes and bring him up from the rock of Etam. In Judg. 16:21 they bring him down to Gaza and bind him with bronze fetters. The climax of both accounts occurs when Samson calls on Yhwh (*wayyiqra'* [*shimshon*] *'el yhwh*, 15:18; 16:28). Divine intervention dramatically reverses Samson's desperate situation. In the first instance, Yhwh provides water so that Samson, who has just slaughtered a thousand Philistines and is now overcome by thirst, can live. In the second, Yhwh grants Samson's petition for strength to pull down the Philistine temple and for death. The extensive repetition both amuses and instructs, for these two episodes in the story make the same point: ultimately the strong man cannot save himself; Samson depends on Yhwh to preserve his life and to grant his plea for death.[32]

The repetitive phenomenon in Judges 13–16 differs noticeably from the twofold account of Saul's disobedience and rejection and other doublets in the narrative, such as the two reports of Saul's casting his spear at David, and the two versions of Saul's pursuit of David that results in David's sparing Saul's life – all of which have a cumulative effect. When, for example, Samuel rejects Saul for disobedience the first time (1 Samuel 13), a number of details remain hazy.[33] It is not altogether evident wherein Saul's disobedience lies: he did wait the seven days required by Samuel, and only then made the offering because his army was scattering and because he feared the Philistines would attack before he had entreated Yhwh's favor. Faced with the dilemma of choosing between competing and mutually exclusive courses of action, each with its own validity, Saul offers a sacrifice rather than wait any longer for Samuel. The choice is his, but necessity forces his hand.

Samuel's failure to keep the appointment on time, followed by his arrival just as Saul finished offering the sacrifice, suggests something beyond mere chance.[34] Moreover, his accusation, "You have not kept the commandment of Yhwh," sheds no light on precisely what Saul had done wrong, especially since the narrative records no instructions from Yhwh but only from Samuel (10:8).[35] In fact, Samuel had earlier given Saul confusing instructions. After anointing Saul, Samuel tells him, "do (*'aseh*) what your hand finds to do for God is with you," but then admonishes him to wait seven days "until I come to you and make known to you what you should do (*ta'aseh*)." Now he demands an accounting, "What have you done (*'asita*)?" Even the outcome of the prophet's confrontation with the new king lacks an apparent resolution, for it leaves us in the dark about Saul's response. Having delivered his diatribe, Samuel simply goes off to Gibeah, leaving Saul to prepare for battle, and the narrative makes no further reference to Saul's error in offering the sacrifice.[36]

By the second rejection scene, however, there is no mistaking that Yhwh has had second thoughts about the fledgling monarch. 1 Samuel 15 reinforces and spells out what 1 Samuel 13 presented tentatively, and it confirms what we may have suspected about Saul there. Yhwh clearly gives the command to annihilate the Amalekites and Saul equally clearly does not carry it out, whatever the reason. Here we see more deeply into Saul's character, and his motives emerge as bafflingly complex. Saul may well be acting in good faith; that is, he may view a sacrifice of the spoils to Yhwh in Gilgal as compatible with Yhwh's demand of total destruction (*ḥerem*) of the Amalekites. His presence at Gilgal with the booty argues for his sincerity, and, as Gunn points out, it makes sense to save only the best for sacrifice, while destroying on the spot what was despised and worthless.[37] Saul insists so strongly on his obedience to Yhwh's command (vv. 13, 20–1) that his understanding of sacrifice as fulfilling (perhaps going beyond?) the demands of destruction takes on cogency. He has interpreted this command already: though Yhwh says nothing about sparing the Kenites, Saul warns them to leave the area before he attacks (v. 6). But whereas Saul's earlier defense against the charge of disobedience seemed reasonable, here his justification of his behavior is somewhat feeble, as he shifts his pronouns as well as the blame:

" *They* have brought them from the Amalekites; for *the people* spared the best of the sheep and the oxen, to sacrifice to Yhwh your God; and the rest *we* have utterly destroyed." (1 Sam. 15:15)

"*I* obeyed the voice of Yhwh and *I* went on the course on which Yhwh sent me. *I* brought Agag king of Amalek and the Amalekites *I* utterly destroyed. *The people* took from the spoil, sheep and oxen, the best of the things devoted to destruction, to sacrifice to Yhwh your God at Gilgal." (1 Sam. 15:20–1)

When Samuel snaps back, "to obey is better than sacrifice," Saul confesses to "obeying the voice" of the people rather than "obeying the voice" of Yhwh. "I have sinned," he says (*hata'ti*, vv. 24, 30; "my sin," v. 25). In the literal sense of the word *hata'* he has "missed the mark." He has transgressed Yhwh's command – and Samuel's words[38] – though, as in the earlier rejection scene, his intentions may be virtuous. He "obeys" or "listens to the voice" of the people because he "honored" or "respected" them (*ki yare'ti 'et ha'am*, 15:24). This is hardly the behavior of the kind of despot Samuel warned the people about in 8:11–18.[39] Certainly a great sacrifice of the spoils of battle to Yhwh would be a way of honoring Yhwh. Saul's devotion to Yhwh is underscored in word – he confesses his sin and asks forgiveness "in order that I may worship Yhwh" (15:25, 30) – and deed: "Saul worshipped Yhwh" (15:31). But whether his intentions are judged good or bad, they are irrelevant.[40] The scene concludes on a tragically dramatic note: "Samuel did not see Saul again until the day of his death but Samuel grieved over Saul. And Yhwh repented that he had made Saul king over Israel" (15:35).[41]

Saul fails repeatedly where Yhwh is concerned. Try as he may to do the right thing, he invariably does the wrong thing. In the first rejection scene, Saul seeks to gain divine favor before battle, but instead loses it for all time: "Yhwh would have established your kingdom over Israel for ever, but now your kingdom shall not endure" (13:13–14). In the second, Saul returns to Gilgal, the scene of his first rejection, to sacrifice once again – this time the spoils of battle. Is he too pious, or simply insecure? Is his problem that he tries too hard, misguidedly seeking to go beyond what is required of him? Between the two rejection scenes we find further evidence of Saul's efforts to do the correct thing being frustrated at every turn (with a portentous shadow cast over the events by Samuel's absence). Saul's consultation with the priest Ahijah and the ark of God is interrupted by the battle; his oath laid on the people against eating before evening is unknowingly violated by his son Jonathan; his ravenous army falls on the spoil without slaughtering it properly, and he must build an altar to prevent them from sinning further. To add to his problems, God does not answer his inquiry about pursuing the Philistines because Jonathan violated the oath. Finally, an overly zealous Saul is prepared to sacrifice his son and heir in order to remove the guilt incurred by Jonathan's ritual infraction.[42]

Samson repeats his folly and Saul repeats his errors. The repetition has different force and is evaluated differently in the comic and tragic worlds. Samson is not judged negatively by Yhwh. Though certainly not the most perceptive of heroes, he is never castigated by Yhwh for lacking discretion, and commentators who condemn Samson for betraying his Nazirite vow engage in a moral evaluation that the narrative itself does not make.[43] In contrast, Saul is judged negatively by both Yhwh and Samuel; and each repeated weakness, each instance of vacillation, each violent and unstable action adds to the case against him.

A comparison of the treatment of the two heroes shows how little Samson is held accountable by Yhwh. Judges 13–16 does not make an issue of obedience. At best, it is implied in 13:5 and 16:17, where we are told that Samson will be a Nazirite and no razor should touch his head. But demands for obedience, warnings against disobedience, and homilies about the results of disobedience are strikingly absent in the story. Neither Yhwh, nor the narrator, nor any of the characters (except Philistines) censures Samson for any of his actions, though his parents demur at his choice of a spouse (14:3). This lack of specific moral judgment finds its most natural home in comedy. The comic hero is neither good nor bad, as Langer points out, "but is genuinely amoral – now triumphant, now worsted and rueful, but in his ruefulness and dismay he is funny, because his energy is really unimpaired and each failure prepares the situation for a new fantastic move."[44] Tragedy, on the other hand, plunges its protagonist into moral conflict. Obedience plays a central role in the tragedy of Saul. Samuel stresses its importance for both king and people: "If you fear Yhwh and serve him and obey his voice and do not rebel against the commandment of Yhwh, and if both you and the king who reigns over you will follow Yhwh your God, it will be well; but if you do not obey the voice of Yhwh, but rebel against the commandment of Yhwh, then the hand of Yhwh will be against you and your king" (12:14–15, following LXX). This admonition sets the stage for Saul's failure and consequent rejection when he obeys the people (15:24) rather than Yhwh (15:1, 19, 20, 22). And Samuel does not miss a posthumous opportunity to remind Saul that disobedience lost him the kingdom (28:18).[45]

On various occasions people around him draw attention to Saul's weaknesses and shortcomings. Samuel calls him a fool (13:13) and rebukes him for his feelings of inferiority (15:17), his own son observes that he has "troubled the land" (14:29), and David twice forces him to admit his failings ("You are more righteous than I," 24:17; "I have sinned…I have acted foolishly and erred exceedingly," 26:21). In his final encounter with David, preceding his agonizing audience with Samuel's ghost, Saul symbolically relives his rejection. His confession to David in 26:21 recalls both the first rejection scene, where Samuel accused him of acting foolishly (13:13), and the second, where Samuel forced him to admit his sin (15:24–30). Such negative assessments expose Saul's vulnerability while assuming his accountability.

Looking again at the death scenes in Judges 16 and 1 Samuel 31 in terms of the different literary techniques they employ, we find support for critical claims about the artifice of the comic expression and the high seriousness of the tragic style.[46] The techniques of irony and reversal as used in Judges 16:23–31 are not appropriate to the seriousness of tragedy. The entire scene depends for its surprise and its grimly satisfying sense of closure on the technique of ironic reversal, and its unfolding is splendidly manipulated by the skillful employment of paronomasia. The Philistines assemble to praise their god for victory over their Israelite enemy, but in the end Yhwh (through Samson), not Dagon, is the victor. The Philistines rejoice at the captivity of one who has greatly multiplied (*hrbh*, v. 24) their slain, and ironically, these very merrymakers become the slain who outnumber (*rbym*, v. 30) those he killed in his life. When Samson is brought out for the Philistines' amusement, he leans on the pillars of the temple initially for support ("Let me feel the pillars on which the house rests, that I may lean against them," v. 26) but later for destruction ("Samson grasped the two middle pillars upon which the house rested, and he leaned his weight upon them," v. 29). At first, the sightless Samson depends on a mere lad for support (*hn'r hmḥzyq bydw*) but his petition to Yhwh to strengthen him (*wḥzqny*) results in a dramatic change of circumstances. The crowning pun, and the one which carries the scene, revolves around Samson's prayer: the people call (*qr'*) Samson to make sport, but while they watch, Samson calls (*qr'*) on Yhwh! This ironic twist reverses the downward movement of the narrative and turns Dagon's festival into Yhwh's victory.

The situation is different in 1 Samuel 31. The tragic vision at this point could not tolerate a delight in word-play. The account is terse and straightforward, with an almost uncharacteristic lack of repetition. Of the few repeated terms, the recurrent phrase "Saul and his (three) sons" reminds us of the end of the Saulide dynasty prophesied by Samuel, and the reappearance of such words as "fall" (*npl*), "dead" (*mwt*), "slain" (*ḥll*), and "fled" (*nws*) reinforces the somber tone.

Restoration in Judges 16 comes from God. In spite of the brute fact of Samson's death among the enemy, the story ends on a note of triumph: through Samson, Yhwh achieves a glorious victory over Israel's oppressors. There is no restoration in 1 Samuel 31, but there is relief. Just as in 1 Samuel 28 relief had come in the form of human kindness on the part of the woman of En-dor, so now it comes from the men of Jabesh-gilead. Again, it is a kindness *of the night*. In one of many instances of *inclusio* in the Saul narrative, the men of Jabesh act on Saul's behalf as he had on theirs, at the beginning of his kingly career (1 Samuel 11). Whereas he delivered them in the morning from the threatened shame of mutilation, they, under cover of night, retrieve his mutilated corpse, sparing it further humiliation. Saul's burial does not have the integrating symbolism of Samson's. The fact of divine rejection overshadows this act of acceptance into human society, though it does not negate it. Moreover, the treatment of Saul's body raises uneasy questions.[47] Mutilation and desecration of the body occur; in a practice uncommon in Israel, the body is burned; and only then are the bones buried in Jabesh, a location remote from Saul's home in Benjamin. The tragedy of King Saul ends with fasting (1 Samuel 31:13) and lamentation (2 Samuel 1:17).[48] David's lament, "How are the mighty fallen," like the chorus' "Behold, this was Oedipus, greatest of men," serves as a commentary, not just on the fate of Saul, but on the tragedy of the human condition in general.

The comparison of the deaths of the heroes can be extended by looking at companion scenes in each narrative. The account of Saul's suicide in 1 Samuel 31 has its counterpart in the Amalekite's report to David in 2 Samuel 1. In some respects the Amalekite's story agrees with the information given in 1 Samuel 31, as, for example, when he relates that the Israelites fled before the Philistines and many fell in battle, including Saul and Jonathan. It differs, however, in some important details. The Amalekite passes over in silence the death of Saul's other sons and, more significantly, he neglects to mention Saul's armor-bearer. The Philistine archers close in upon Saul in the earlier account, but the Amalekite speaks of chariots and riders. Whereas 1 Samuel 31:4 reports that Saul fell on his sword, the Amalekite describes him as leaning on his spear. Saul's preference to die by his own hand rather than become an object of ridicule for the Philistines becomes the somewhat less noble desire for death as a quick end to the agony (dizziness? cramp?) that has overcome him.

Quite possibly the Amalekite is lying in hopes of gaining a reward from David, who stands to profit considerably from Saul's death. The very fact that an Amalekite claims to have killed Saul has ironic overtones, for, presumably, had Saul carried out the *ḥerem* against Amalek (1 Samuel 15), this man would not be alive to tell his tale. But even if unreliable, the Amalekite's story complicates Saul's death. Occurring immediately after the suicide account, it undercuts its central tragic impression, making Saul's death seem more pitiful than heroic. Whereas we are privy to two versions of Saul's death, presumably David and his retinue know only this one. David uses the opportunity to honor Saul with a lament, but, as we shall see below, the ironies of the lament raise doubts about David's sincerity.

In the Samson story, there is a scene that corresponds to the death scene in Judg. 16:28–30, a near-death scene in Judg. 15:18–19.[49] Unlike the two versions of Saul's death, these two scenes in the Samson saga are not duplicate accounts of the same event but rather variations on the same theme. Judges 15:18–19 and 16:28–30 occur, as we have seen, at the climax of two similar sequences of events. Only on these occasions does Samson call directly on Yhwh. In Judges 15 his entreaty follows a great slaughter of Philistines; in Judges 16 it precedes the slaughter. Both accounts take the opportunity to pun on the word "call": in 15:19 Samson's call provides the etymology for En-haqqore', "the spring of the caller." In 16:25 and 28, Samson's calling on Yhwh is set ironically over against the Philistines' call for Samson to provide amusement for them. The possibility of death and the hero's call on Yhwh are intimately connected. In 15:18 Samson attracts the divine concern with the words, "I shall die of thirst"; 16:30 is more direct, "let me die with the Philistines." In response to Samson's call, Yhwh intervenes, sustaining life:

he drank, his spirit returned, and he lived (15:19),

and granting death:

the dead he killed at his death were more than those he killed in his life (16:30).[50]

We have seen how Judges 16 concludes with Samson's relationship to Yhwh restored and with his vindication against the Philistines, thus bringing a satisfying result out of tragic circumstances. The corresponding scene in Judg. 15:14–19 offers a thoroughly comic episode with a delightful resolution. Having killed a thousand Philistines with the jawbone of an ass, the strong man encounters a simple threat from which he cannot deliver himself – thirst. Part of the pleasure of the scene derives from seeing Samson's boastfulness undercut by his dependence on Yhwh. Though empowered by Yhwh's spirit, Samson is the real center of attention in 15:15–17. *He* finds the jawbone, *he* seizes it, and *he* slays with it a thousand men. His boast, "With the jawbone of an ass *I* have slain a thousand men," emphasizes his accomplishment. Thirst humbles him somewhat, but even when attributing victory to Yhwh, he manages to credit himself: "You have given this great deliverance by the hand of your servant."[51] Yhwh dramatically intervenes to save Samson from thirst, and Samson's slaughter of Philistines pales by comparison with Yhwh's feat of bringing forth water from the crater. Both in this scene and in the death scene of Judges 16, we are shown that life and death are in Yhwh's hands, and there is a certain security in that knowledge.

Northrop Frye observes that tragedy demonstrates the inexorable workings of law, whereas comedy reveals the arbitrary activity of grace. Thus we speak of inevitable tragedy but not of inevitable comedy.[52] Both Samson and Saul break rules. Samson violates not merely the injunctions placed upon a Nazirite against drinking, contact with the dead, and cutting the hair;[53] in his amorality he transgresses all sorts of societal norms. Nonetheless, in Samson's hour of need, God intervenes. A *deus ex machina* frequently operates in comedy to resolve events in miraculous and unexpected ways. Samson's prayer is granted, not because Samson merits God's help, but simply because God is willing to respond on Samson's behalf.[54] In contrast, the demands of law operate unmercifully in the Saul story. Saul disobeys, and disobedience requires punishment. God shows Saul no compassion, and because God is unrelenting (God "is not a man that he should repent," says Samuel [15:29]), Saul's demise is unavoidable.

The comic or classic vision can embrace pain and death in the larger context of restoration. For Samson, this is possible because he is an instrument of the divine plan, a plan that does not appear inscrutable. In contrast, the tragic vision shows the uncompromising terror of suffering and death that Saul must face alone. Here we find a crucial difference between the tales: divine intention and motivation are ambiguous in Saul's case but not in Samson's. Though we are introduced to Samson with high expectations that remain unrealized – the birth account of Judges 13, with its theophany and promise of a deliverer[55] – we are nevertheless repeatedly reminded that Yhwh controls Samson's folly and ludicrous escapades, "for [Yhwh] was seeking an occasion against the Philistines," 14:4. This fact allows perhaps for perplexity on the part of the reader, but not ambiguity. We, like Samson's parents, may find it odd that Samson desires a Philistine wife, but the text assures us that "it was from Yhwh," 14:4. Not just sexual desire but also the spirit of Yhwh drives Samson to confront the Philistines (14:19; 15:14). Significantly, Yhwh does not promise that Samson will ultimately deliver Israel from the Philistines, only that he will be the first to do so, 13:5. The opposite holds true for Saul, of whom Yhwh says, "he will deliver my people from the hand of the Philistines" (9:16). Do we have here a hint of divine unreliability? Samson unwittingly fulfills Yhwh's plan for him; Saul's tragedy derives poignancy from the fact that Yhwh's prophecy about him does not come to pass.[56] Saul's early successes against the Ammonites and the Philistines are cancelled out by his final failure to deliver Israel.

In the account of Saul's vicissitudes, the portrayal of the deity is uncomfortably ambiguous. Any way we look at it, Yhwh has an ambivalent attitude toward kingship. Gunn has argued, with good evidence, that the deity's angry feelings of rejection as king by the people give rise to a predisposition to reject Saul. Rejection (*m's*) appears at strategic points in the narrative. Samuel's biting denunciation in 15:23, "Because you have rejected the word of Yhwh, he has rejected you from being king," echoes Yhwh's bitter complaint of 8:7, "They have not rejected you, but they have rejected me from being king over them." Yhwh selects Saul as Israel's first king, but at the same time views him as an unwelcome usurper of divine leadership. Thus the first king must pay dearly for the people's sin, their "evil" according to 12:17 and 19, of requesting a human monarch. To use Gunn's phrase, Saul becomes kingship's scapegoat. Whether one accepts Gunn's conclusion or sides with commentators who defend Yhwh as justified in rejecting Saul, such widely differing interpretations bear witness to a complex picture of deity in the narrative.

But it is not just Yhwh whose portrayal is ambiguous. Saul himself appears as a particularly complicated personality. He emerges as a strong leader when he responds to the desperate plight of Jabesh-gilead, yet wavers in precarious situations (1 Samuel 13 and 15). Appearing not to want the kingship at the beginning of his career, at the end he struggles to hold on to it at all costs. Though capable of magnanimity (11:13) and inspiring loyalty among his followers, he sometimes displays sinister, inflexible qualities one hardly anticipates – for example, his willingness to carry out his rash oath and have his son killed in 1 Samuel 14, his evil designs against David, and his supererogatory slaughter of the priests of Nob. If, in fact, Saul acted in good faith in 1 Samuel 13 and 15, then even Saul's best intentions bring about the worst of consequences. Is his problem that he is, as Good puts it, "a man not fitted for a job that should not have been opened"?[57]

The tragic vision, until relatively modern times, has typically cast as its hero a royal figure such as we find in Saul. The privileged position of kings, which enables them to break laws ordinary people must respect, renders them well suited to tragic treatment. In Israelite as in Greek thought, the king in his roles as mediator and representative of the kingdom stands in a special position between the sacred and the profane[58] and, as the Deuteronomistic Historian is fond of pointing out, the people's welfare depends upon the king's proper performance of the royal functions symbolized by obedience. The tragic events involve the whole society, while at the same time isolating the king who represents it. In response to a crisis of leadership a king is asked for (*sha'al*, 8:10; 12:13, 17, 19). Saul (*sha'ul*) appears in answer to the demand, but instead of resolving the crisis he exacerbates it.[59] We observe him at the height and depth of his worldly fortunes. Though Saul stands "head and shoulders above the people" (10:23), all too soon we discover that he is little in his own eyes, and we follow his decline to his final rejection when his imposing stature lies "full length upon the ground, filled with fear" (28:20). Saul is thrust into a position of leadership he did not seek, only to have it torn away from him and promised to another who is better than he. Though he remains head and shoulders above the people who, like us, are less significant in the shaping of history, he is not so far above us that we fail to recognize in his *hamartia* our own potential to make similarly destructive, though no doubt less far-reaching, errors of judgment.

And what of Samson? We are told he "judged Israel," but commentators have long observed that he does not behave like a judge. Samson, rather, is the typical rogue, a Hebrew Rob Roy, a Till Eulenspiegel in biblical dress. His wit and prowess provide the occasion to ridicule the Philistines and have a good laugh at their expense. He constantly gets the better of them, and the narrative shows a hearty, lusty approval of his unconventional conduct. Comedy can serve as a release from antisocial instincts and as a form of aggression.[60] Samson is a comic hero not only in his ability to bounce back but also in his capacity to inflict pain on his enemies. The frequently cruel laughter at the Philistines gives vent to Israelite hostility – so much so that one commentator has aptly described these anecdotes as "resistance stories" through which the underdog Israelites poke fun at the militarily superior Philistines.[61] The story allows no place for remorse over the Philistine casualties of Samson's pranks and angry outbursts. The lively spirit which animates these escapades does not permit us to pause over any of them long enough to ponder the potential tragic dimension before plunging us into another laughable adventure.[62] Only in Judges 16, with Samson's betrayal, blinding, and death, does a tragic perspective threaten seriously to intrude. But here also the classic vision prevails. Immediately after the betrayal and blinding, we catch a glint of hope and a hint of victory which is to come: Samson's hair begins to grow (v. 22). The clue to its direction planted, the comic movement proceeds, as we have observed, reversing the fortunes of our hero and his captors, and finally bringing about a victory for Yhwh and Israel.

A typical comic hero, Samson displays a remarkable absence of character development, a factor Milton was forced to alter considerably if his hero was to attain tragic proportions. We all know that the biblical Samson does not learn from past mistakes. This simple, if not simplistic, characterization is not merely a function of the short span of the story – only four chapters as opposed to the much longer narrative about Saul. One gets the impression that even if there were more Samson stories, they would be essentially the same. Characteristics of the picaresque are evident not only in the episodic structure of the narrative but also in the hero who moves from one adventure to the next with little or no character development. In the end, of course, Samson is released from his "humor." Whether or not he learned anything about himself or his mission in the process, the narrative does not say. We may take our clue from other comic heroes that the freedom from an obsessive trait does not necessarily bring with it a deeper self-understanding.[63]

Samson lives on the margins of two cultures, Israelite and Philistine. His isolation is symbolized preeminently by his status as a lifelong Nazirite, a word meaning "separate, dedicated." He is a "personification of intoxication who cannot drink wine,"[64] an Israelite who prefers Philistines. He fights alone, motivated by personal grievances, and his incredible strength renders him different, not "like other men" (16:7, 11, [13], 17). He has no close family or tribal ties (except his parents, who soon disappear from the scene), and he dies without offspring.

Barbara Babcock-Abrahams observes that marginality may be distinguished into its comic and tragic modalities, represented by the trickster and the scapegoat.[65] In many respects Samson exhibits the contradictions associated with the well-known trickster figure, a marginal character with abnormal strength and an enormous libido, witty, uncontrollable, destructive, and beneficial, finally destroying himself:

[Trickster] is positively identified with creative powers [in Samson's case as an instrument of Yhwh]...and yet he constantly behaves in the most antisocial manner we can imagine. Although we laugh at him for his troubles and his foolishness and are embarrassed by his promiscuity, his creative cleverness amazes us and keeps alive the possibility of transcending the social restrictions we regularly encounter.[66]

Samson's adventures, like the adventures of numerous trickster figures, are episodic and picaresque. Society's structures do not apply to him; he regularly violates social, kinship, sexual, and natural boundaries. Cultural hero and buffoon, he dupes others and is duped himself.[67] Whereas he profits his people by breaking rules, he hurts not just his enemies but also those close to him, his Philistine wife and father-in-law, whom the Philistines burn because Samson destroyed their crops, and the Judahites, whom the Philistines attack in order to capture Samson through them.

The tragic hero's marginality is well established. Saul is a *pharmakos*, the scapegoat for the people's sin of requesting a human king. That Israel's first king – desired by the people and selected by God – should be kingship's scapegoat finds support in the sacrificial theory of René Girard. According to Girard, the king's position precisely at the center of his society serves to isolate him, and thus render him an ideal sacrificial victim. The king must, by committing the requisite transgressions, show himself "worthy" of punishment in order to take upon himself society's sins and transform them into something beneficial.[68] Saul's sins are well documented. The Davidic monarchy, blessed by Yhwh, will be among the benefits, though David, as we shall see, will in turn become a victim of violence, and the cycle will repeat itself in a series of false starts until the monarchy comes to an end.

In pursuing their nemesis, tragic heroes usually take a course that isolates them from others. Saul loses God's and Samuel's support. Samuel, on whom he once relied, has nothing more to do with Saul after his rejection (19:24, where Samuel sees Saul again at Naioth, contradicts 15:35, but Saul is not himself, and clearly the rift remains). Initially Saul seeks out David, but when he recognizes him as a potential rival for the throne, Saul drives David away. To Saul the *pharmakos*, David serves as *pharmakon*, both cure and poison. Whereas David's lyre playing relieves the troubled king, his military success and popularity evoke jealousy and fear. On the two occasions that Saul "falls" into David's hands, David spares his life, but with a theatricality that underscores Saul's impotence, reduces him to groveling, and robs him of dignity (1 Samuel 24, 26). Saul hates David so intensely that he alienates his own children, who love David. Though Saul has loyal subjects who inform him regularly of David's whereabouts,[69] his paranoia feeds his isolation. He accuses his followers of conspiracy, blames his son Jonathan for inciting David to rebellion, and irrationally levels these same charges against the priests of Nob (1 Samuel 22). At his most violent Saul is most isolated. When he commands his soldiers to slaughter the priests of Nob, only Doeg the Edomite carries out the order, putting the entire city to the sword, "men and women, children and infants, oxen, asses, and sheep." What he failed to do to Amalek, Saul does to Nob, destroying the city of priests in a displaced attack on God.

Whereas Samson's insouciant, comic character does not develop, Saul's tragic one becomes a veritable battleground for opposing emotions and traits. Unquestionably Saul is a troubled man. Not only does he display uncommon rigidity with regard to Jonathan's ritual infraction (1 Samuel 14), he also transfers to Jonathan the frustration and fury he feels toward David, throwing his spear at Jonathan as he had earlier at David (20:30–3). His repeated attempts on David's life show how desperately insecure and unscrupulous he has become. When Saul combs the countryside for David, we know he cannot catch him because Yhwh is with David. Saul, however, is so painfully deluded that on one occasion he presumes that "God has given him into my hand" (23:7). Saul's obsession with David and his random paranoia regarding the loyalty of family and servants, culminating in his massacre of the priests of Nob, are clear signs that something is amiss. The tragic hero is haunted by demonic forces from both within and without. We witness as Saul, driven by petty fears and jealousies, becomes a disintegrated personality, but most disturbing is the realization that the evil spirit which torments him and makes his plight even more desperate is the agent of none other than Yhwh. In this acknowledgment of the root of Saul's distress, we discover why Saul alone of biblical heroes attains a truly tragic stature, and we reach the core of the tragic vision: the problem of evil.

In no other biblical story is the problem of evil so pressing and so uncompromising as in the story of Saul. Saul's downfall is of his own making; and in more than one instance he has incurred the divine wrath. But whereas Saul is guilty, he is not really wicked. The tragic vision gives rise to the uneasy awareness that the hero's punishment exceeds any guilt. The question is not why Saul is rejected. That we know, regardless of whether or not we consider the rejection justified by Saul's actions. The question is why there is no forgiveness.[70]

Saul encounters God's dark side in a way that Samson never experiences it. Even though Samson endures divine abandonment, God responds to Samson's prayer in his hour of need. Saul, however, knows the demonic side of God not only through divine absence, but also, paradoxically, through Yhwh's persecuting presence in the form of an evil spirit. Yhwh and Yhwh's spirit take possession of Saul immediately after his anointing. God gives him another heart (1 Sam. 10:9), the spirit of God makes him prophesy (10:10), and when he hears of the plight of Jabesh-gilead, the spirit inspires him to come to their aid (1 Sam. 11:6–7).[71] Saul's possession in these instances resembles Samson's when the spirit rushes on him (Judg. 14:6, 19; 15:14), and may also be compared to the cases of Othniel, Gideon, and Jephthah in the book of Judges. Divine possession leads to bizarre deeds. But we do not recognize it as especially problematic until after Saul's rejection, when we are told pointedly, "the spirit of Yhwh departed from Saul and an evil spirit from Yhwh tormented him" (1 Sam. 16:14). Under the evil spirit's influence, Saul tries to kill David with his spear on two different occasions (18:10–11; 19:9–10).[72] The second time, the evil spirit undermines the reconciliation Jonathan has just brought about between his father and his friend. Not only Saul but also the messengers he sends after David are driven to prophecy by God's spirit (19:20–4). This second prophetic seizure leaves Saul in a frenzy all that day and all that night, naked and completely vulnerable, before Samuel. Later he will lie vulnerable before David, when Yhwh sends a deep sleep on him and his entire army, allowing David and Abishai to enter his camp undetected (1 Samuel 26).

In Greek tragedy, the hero faces an indifferent, arbitrary world alone. Saul, in contrast, knows the agony of rejection by the God whose aid he repeatedly seeks – and more, he feels directly the terror of divine enmity. In a turn of phrase as telling as it is disquieting, Samuel exposes the problem, "God has become your enemy."[73] Hostile transcendence is a vital force in tragedy. Paul Ricoeur, in a discerning discussion of it, observes:

The tragic properly so called does not appear until the theme of predestination to evil – to call it by its name – comes up against the theme of heroic greatness; fate must first feel the resistance of freedom, rebound (so to speak) from the hardness of the hero, and finally crush him, before the pre-eminently tragic emotion – φόβος – can be born.[74]

It is hardly necessary to point out that when we speak of predestination to evil in the biblical story of Saul, we are not speaking of predestination in any simple sense, but rather as something undefinable and irreducible, and therefore all the more terrifying. Saul is caught between his own turbulent personality and the antagonism of God toward human kingship. He displays heroic greatness in his refusal to acquiesce in the fate prophesied by Samuel, taking extraordinary steps to hold on to his kingdom. A lesser man, a man without *hubris*, might merely accept his destiny. Saul, however, wrestles against it. Again, to borrow an insight from Ricoeur that fits Saul's story admirably:

Without the dialectics of fate and freedom there would be no tragedy. Tragedy requires, on the one hand, transcendence and, more precisely, hostile transcendence ... and, on the other hand, the upsurge of a freedom that *delays* the fulfillment of fate, causes it to hesitate and to appear contingent at the height of the crisis, in order finally to make it break out in a "dénouement," where its fatal character is ultimately revealed.[75]

Yhwh rejects Saul on two occasions early on in the narrative, and while tormenting Saul with an evil spirit, proceeds to further the fortunes of his rival. Since a large part of the narrative develops the plot of David's rise, we see Yhwh act simultaneously to subvert Saul and to strengthen David. Saul manages to delay his downfall but not to avoid it. He rules some years after his rejection; there are signs that he still commands loyalty even though he himself doubts it; for a time he keeps the Philistines at bay; and he even shows on occasion a conciliatory attitude toward David (19:6–7; 24:16–22 [Heb. 17–23]; 26:21–5). Moreoever, to the end, he seeks Yhwh's counsel (1 Samuel 28). But, as we have seen, he meets ultimately with divine silence and a crushing reiteration of rejection from the ghost of Samuel.

EXCURSUS: HOSTILE TRANSCENDENCE IN THE SAMSON STORY

Can the Samson story be read as a tragedy? Throughout this chapter, I have argued it cannot. But there are commentators who consider Samson's failure to learn from his mistakes to be his tragic flaw; or who find him guilty of violating his Nazirite vow; or who point to his isolation, his marginality to both Israelite and Philistine culture, as lending a tragic quality to his life.[76] Any attempt to make Samson into a tragic hero, however, encounters serious difficulties with Samson's character. Francis Landy argues that for tragedy to have moral power, the hero must be held responsible for his or her flaw.[77] Though one can always find exceptions to generalizations about tragedy (for example, Job and Orestes, in this case), Landy's point clarifies an important difference between Saul and Samson. Clearly Saul is held responsible for his shortcomings, but not Samson. Samson simply does not have the makings of a tragic hero. In particular he lacks the ability tragic heroes have to win our respect, even if we oppose their choices. Saul has a lofty purpose. He is chosen by Yhwh to "save my people from the hand of the Philistines" (1 Sam. 9:16). Though little in his own eyes, he is head of the tribes of Israel (1 Sam. 15:17) with all the responsibilities that office entails. His purpose is thwarted by challenges unsuccessfully met. In contrast, Samson occupies himself with personal vendettas and only unwittingly serves God's purpose. As Humphreys observes, Samson's choices "rather too narrowly serve his self-interests."[78] Not even at his death does Samson show any deeper understanding of his role or of God's purposes. In his dying prayer, Samson asks not that he might bring glory to God or to Israel, but for personal vindication "for one of my two eyes" (16:28).

The tragic hero's struggle against fate plays no role in the Samson story. Indeed, Samson shows no awareness of fatedness. Samson and Saul illustrate an effective distinction Stephen Booth draws between comedy and tragedy. Comedy, he suggests, operates from, and demonstrates, the proposition that there is a way things are and fools forget what it is. Tragedy also operates from, and demonstrates, the proposition that there is a way things are, but in its case fools assume it is knowable and known.[79] Saul, though fated, maintains the illusion of freedom; he does not behave as if he were powerless in the face of his destiny prophesied by Samuel. In a sense he refuses to know what he knows. Samson, in contrast, displays no knowledge or understanding of his place in Yhwh's plan. This is not surprising since no dialogue ever takes place between Yhwh and Samson.

Though the Samson story is not tragic, we can pursue a reading according to which it ceases to be comic. Samson, as we have seen, is the instrument of a divine plan. If God's behind-the-scenes activity through Samson inspires our confidence, the classic vision prevails. If, however, we choose to foreground hostile transcendence by focusing on Samson as a *victim* of forces beyond his control, our interpretation no longer finds accommodation in the classic vision. In such a reading the divine plan becomes problematic because it remains hidden from the participants. Secrecy figures prominently in the story, from Samson's secrets (the answer to his riddle; the source of his strength) to Yhwh's hidden activity in Samson.[80] Everything that happens to Samson seems determined by God without his knowledge or consent, leaving Samson with little, if any, control over his own life. He is passive with regard to the most important events that concern him, making and breaking the Nazirite vow. Nazirite injunctions are placed upon him before his birth, and his hair is cut while he sleeps.

Only in death does Samson fulfill his destiny, to begin to deliver Israel from the Philistines. One might argue that Samson's role as Yhwh's instrument against the Philistines, because it was unwitting and because he was not offered a choice, is no compensation for his personal loss, his blindness, humiliation, and death. Perhaps most disturbing is the fact that Samson is dispensable in God's plan. What purpose has his life served? He accomplishes no lasting deliverance. He has no followers or supporters, but remains an outsider, living between two cultures and dying without offspring. He is betrayed by his wife and by Delilah, whom he loved, as well as by the Judahites, who hand him over to the Philistines (15 : 11–13). Yhwh, too, hands Samson over to the Philistines, who blind and enslave him, and make him an object of amusement. Is he then also betrayed by Yhwh?

If pursued, such a reading, bleak as it is – and it could easily be reinforced by a subversive reading of the entire book of Judges[81] – still would not be tragic. Where there is no struggle, no awareness of fatedness, there can be no tragedy, though there can be despair. Perhaps this could be characterized as the ironic vision, "the non-heroic residue of tragedy."[82]

CHAPTER 3

Jephthah: the absence of God

> From the gods who sit in grandeur grace comes somehow
> violent.
>
> Aeschylus, Agamemnon

Accounts of human sacrifice are rare in the Bible. The practice figures prominently in only two biblical narratives, the tragic tale of Jephthah and his daughter (Judges 11–12) and the story of the execution of Saul's sons and Rizpah's vigil (2 Samuel 21), which we shall examine in Chapter 4. Whereas human sacrifice appears to have been practiced at various times throughout the ancient Near East, its place in the Bible is ambiguous.[1] In Genesis 22, for example, God commands Abraham to sacrifice his only son Isaac but, at the last possible moment, intervenes to save the child. Exodus 22:29–30 calls for every first-born son to be given to the deity, though Exod. 13:13 allows for their redemption. As a rule, the Bible condemns human sacrifice (Lev. 18:21; 20:1–5; Deut. 12:31; 18:10), and in the actual biblical examples of it, which are few, it is viewed with horror (e.g., 2 Kings 3:27; 16:3; 17:17; 21:6).[2] The Jephthah story stands apart as something of an anomaly: Jephthah vows a sacrifice to God in return for military victory, and the sacrificial victim turns out to be his daughter, his only child. The sacrifice is made to Israel's God, not to some pagan deity, and, surprisingly, no condemnation of the deed appears in the narrative.

When we turn from Saul's tragedy to Jephthah's, we thus find ourselves in a different atmosphere. Jephthah's human sacrifice appalls us more than any act Saul has committed, even the wanton slaughter of the priests of Nob, for Jephthah is unwittingly responsible for a situation that calls for him to take the life of his own child. A vow made in ambiguous circumstances and in ignorance of its outcome forces his hand. But unlike the case of Saul, there is no apparent reason for the disaster that befalls Jephthah, nothing of the divine displeasure which drives Saul to despair and madness. Nor does Jephthah suffer perceptibly as a result of his deed. Strangely, we are not told how the act affects him; nor, for that matter, do we learn of God's reaction. Jephthah's life does not end in disgrace; there is no outright rejection, no clear sense of alienation from God – central elements for Saul's tragedy.

Wherein, then, does the tragedy of Jephthah lie? Not in Jephthah's relationship to the deity *per se* nor in the character of Jephthah or his daughter, neither being sufficiently developed in terms of the struggle against fate that distinguishes the tragic hero – but in events themselves, in a certain ambiguity that surrounds all that transpires, and finally, in the divine silence, the refusal of the deity to take a position *vis-à-vis* these events. Jephthah's sacrifice of his daughter to Yhwh is the preeminently tragic moment; it brings into relief an ambivalent quality surrounding everything else about him.

The story of Jephthah opens, like that of Saul, at a point of crisis: Gilead, the home from which Jephthah has been expelled, comes under attack by the Ammonites. Judges 10:6–18 forms the backdrop of the story, and portrays the Ammonite threat as affecting not only Gilead but also the tribes of Judah, Benjamin, and Ephraim. The book of Judges offers a pessimistic testimony to the deterioration of order and stability in Israel before the monarchy. A pattern is established early in the book (2:11–23) into which are set the stories of leaders such as Othniel, Ehud, Deborah, Gideon, Jephthah, and Samson. Its essential features are: the people of Israel do what is evil in the eyes of Yhwh (understood as worship of other gods); they provoke Yhwh to anger so that Yhwh gives them over to plunderers (the statement about provocation is sometimes missing); as a result of their groaning, Yhwh is moved to pity and raises up judges who deliver them. Israel is doomed at the outset to repeat this pattern:

Whenever Yhwh raised up judges for them, Yhwh was with the judge, and saved them from the hand of their enemies all the days of the judge ... but whenever the judge died, they turned back and behaved worse than their ancestors ... (Judg. 2:18–19)

Disorder is thus a fact of life, interrupted routinely by periods of respite. Even the judges who deliver Israel in times of need reveal unexpected shortcomings and serious faults. Before Jephthah, we have the example of Gideon, who builds an ephod that becomes a snare to the people; and after him, we encounter Samson, who not only fails to live up to his Nazirite calling, but worse, fails to achieve Israel's deliverance from the Philistines.

As the prelude to Jephthah's rise to power, Israel's rebellion is nothing new, "And the Israelites continued to do evil in the eyes of Yhwh" (10:6). Punishment follows ineluctably upon sin. Yhwh sells them into the hand of their enemies (v. 7) and they cry out in their distress. So far we have the usual pattern of sin and punishment. Verses 11–14, however, introduce a new element, the divine refusal to intervene, "therefore I will not continue to deliver you." The people implore divine assistance at any price, "We have sinned; do to us whatever is good in your eyes, only deliver us this day," and demonstrate their resolve by putting away their foreign gods and serving Yhwh. Interestingly, this is the only place in Judges where the people actually repent, rather than merely appeal to God for relief from oppression. And yet Yhwh, though plainly affected by Israel's behavior, does not react by providing a deliverer, as he had earlier with Othniel (Judg. 3:7–11), Ehud (Judg. 3:12–30), Deborah (Judges 4–5), and Gideon (Judges 6–8). In fact, the deity's response is far from clear. Whereas Judg. 10:16 is frequently understood to mean that Yhwh is moved to intervention by Israel's suffering, the verse states only that Yhwh "became impatient with Israel's misery." How God acts as a result of this exasperation is not specified.[3]

A crisis and a question set the stage for the appearance of Jephthah: "Who is the man who will be the first to fight the Ammonites? He will be chief over all the inhabitants of Gilead" (10:18). Jephthah is selected by the elders of Gilead (11:4–5), who turn to him only in distress (11:5–8), just as the Israelites have repeatedly turned to Yhwh only in distress. If Saul is "kingship's scapegoat,"[4] Jephthah is the judge Israel deserves. "Do to us what is good in your eyes, only deliver us this day" (10:15). Yhwh grants them the deliverer they have chosen, a man who will win a great victory for them over the Ammonites, but at high personal cost, and who, though capable of providing effective leadership against an external threat, will prove unable to forestall internecine warfare.

The introduction to Jephthah in Judg. 11:1 alerts us from the beginning to an ambivalent quality about him. From the Gileadites' point of view, Jephthah combines the desirable with the unacceptable: "Jephthah the Gileadite was a mighty warrior and he was the son of a harlot."[5] The conjunction *waw* joins the two sides of this statement, giving them equal weight. This duality characterizes

Jephthah's life: he will achieve desirable goals, victory for Gilead against Ammon, victory against Ephraim, but in both cases by what will strike us as unacceptable means. Even his name hints of his ill-fortune: *yiphtah*, "he opens," perhaps a hypocoristic form of *yiphtah-el*, "God opens [the womb]," but, knowing what is in store for him, we cannot help connecting it to the fatal moment when he opens his mouth and out comes the vow that seals his tragic fate. The verbal root in his name is *pathah* whereas the verb used of the vow in 11:35 and 36 is *patsah*, but the association is not farfetched. Both *pathah peh* and *patsah peh* mean "to open the mouth," and in Num. 16:30 and 32 and Ezek. 2:8 and 3:2 the verbs are used interchangeably. *Yiphtah*, "he (God) opens the womb"; *yiphtah*, "he (Jephthah) opens his mouth." And may we not speculate on the possible implications of another way of reading the name: "he (God) opens his (Jephthah's) mouth," for is not Jephthah under the influence of the spirit of Yhwh when he makes his ill-fated vow?

Jephthah's unacceptable origins mark him as an outcast. His brothers drive him away from the paternal household, and he flees to the land of Tov, perhaps for him a "good" (*tov*) land, from where he goes raiding with *'anashim reqim*. The fact that he commands a following demonstrates his leadership abilities, but the nature of this company, worthless fellows, literally "empty men," shows Jephthah's unacceptable side.

If Jephthah's origins are questionable, so is his rise to power. Twice the text states that the Ammonites attacked Israel (11:4 and 5). Only a crisis makes Jephthah's desirability as a mighty warrior outweigh his unacceptability as an outsider. Like Saul, who was first demanded by the people and then chosen by Yhwh, Jephthah is first sought out by the elders, and only later affected by the spirit of Yhwh. Yhwh's attitude here is not so evident as in 1 Samuel 8, but may be hinted at in the absence of divine involvement in the elders' choice. Jephthah's retort in 11:7, "Why have you come to me now that you are in distress (*tsar*)?," echoes Yhwh's response to the wayward people in 10:14, "Go and cry to the gods you have chosen; let them deliver you in your time of distress (*tsarathekem*)." Both mock those who, having rejected them in the past, seek them out only as a last resort. Like the people in 10:15–16, the elders persist. But assistance granted under such conditions will have ambiguous repercussions.

Jephthah's rise to leadership occurs immediately, before his confrontation with the Ammonites. The people appoint him chief (*ro'sh*) and leader (*qatsin*), even though he had made becoming leader conditional upon victory. In his newly attained position of authority, the former outcast speaks, through messengers, as the singular representative of his people, "What is between *me* and you that you have come against *me* to fight against *my* land?" (11:12). Jephthah tries to resolve the differences between Israel and Ammon through diplomacy, but his attempt fails and fighting ensues. Israel achieves a great victory over the Ammonites; the threat posed at the beginning of the story is resolved; the spirit of Yhwh with Jephthah appears to signal the divine sanction of the people's choice of a leader; and the elders' confidence that Jephthah could deliver them is justified. We seem to have here all the ingredients for an ideal conclusion – but not quite. Success has a price. Jephthah's victory, won against the backdrop of his failed negotiations, is Pyrrhic. The pinnacle of his career, his moment of greatest glory, contains the seeds of his tragedy, for Jephthah has vowed a sacrifice to Yhwh, and victory demands its scandalous performance.

What provokes Jephthah's vow, which pops out of his mouth (*patsiti pi*), bringing in its wake disastrous consequences? It seems almost superfluous, excessive, since the obvious reason for making a vow, to ensure success, would appear unnecessary if the spirit of Yhwh is with Jephthah. Our speculations about what lies behind Jephthah's vow are efforts to resolve its un-reason, its sinister and seemingly unnecessary quality, its ultimately tragic dimension. Because the situation lacks the urgency that calls for a vow, Phyllis Trible views Jephthah's vow as an act of unfaithfulness, an attempt to manipulate Yhwh, who has already freely bestowed upon Jephthah the gift of the spirit.[6] But one could more plausibly argue that Jephthah makes his vow under the influence of Yhwh's spirit. The text reads: "The spirit of Yhwh was upon Jephthah, and he passed through Gilead and Manasseh, and passed through Mizpah of Gilead, and from Mizpah of Gilead he passed on to the Ammonites. And Jephthah vowed a vow to Yhwh..." (11:29). Is the spirit of Yhwh the driving force behind all of these activities or only some of them – and if only some, which ones? On the basis of its role in inciting other heroes to mighty, and sometimes curious, deeds (cf. Judg. 6:34; 13:25; 14:6, 19; 1 Sam. 10:10; 11:6; 16:13), we might assume that here, too, Yhwh's spirit inspires Jephthah's victory over the Ammonites. The vow interferes, so to speak, with the logical progression of cause and effect; its position between the coming of the spirit of Yhwh upon Jephthah and the victory renders it impossible to determine whether victory comes as the result of the spirit, or the vow, or both.[7]

More important, it is not the making of the vow that is so disturbing but its content. Had Jephthah said, "If God will be with me, and give me victory, so that I come again to my house in peace, then I shall set up an altar" (cf. Gen. 28:20–2), we should probably not be troubled by the presence of a vow. Even the vowing of a person to the deity need not unduly upset us, as Hannah's vow to give Samuel to Yhwh "all the days of his life" shows. Thus not until Jephthah utters the last two words of his vow do we encounter anything particularly unusual, do we realize how dangerous, and scandalous, the vow is. The text lingers over details, postponing the crucial element of the vow until the very end, where it has maximum effect: "If you will only give the Ammonites into my hand, then the one coming forth who comes forth from the doors of my house to meet me, when I return in peace from the Ammonites, shall be Yhwh's, and [now come only two words in the Hebrew] I will offer him [generic] up as a burnt offering (*weha'alitihu 'olah*)." Debates over whether Jephthah has in mind a person or an animal are pointless.[8] The fact is "the one coming forth" could be – and *we know it will be* – a human sacrifice, and so we confront in Jephthah's vow a sinister dimension we are hardly prepared for, even from a former outcast and a companion of worthless men. Jephthah, however, seems blind to the implications of his vow. Interestingly, he does not say "the first one," but simply "the one coming forth" (*hayyotse'*), as if not considering the possibility of being met by more than one. It is odd that he speaks of only one, and odder still that only one comes to greet him, and that, as his response makes clear, he had not expected it to be his only child.

The irony, the tragic irony, rests in the exact correspondence between the ill-chosen terms of Jephthah's vow and the subsequent events. We do not know what provokes Jephthah to set these particular terms or what determines this particular outcome, what accounts for the chilling coincidence between the vow and the daughter's appearance. The fact is their connection cannot be explained; it has no cause, at least not one we can name, and that is the source of its terror. James Joyce called it the "secret cause" of suffering.[9]

Victory marks the height of Jephthah's fortune; the vow signals his descent into tragedy. It would be enough for us to hear, "and Yhwh gave them into his hand" (11:32), but the text elaborates, as if to leave no doubt about the scope and significance of the victory, "And they smote them from Aroer to the neighborhood of Minnith, twenty cities, and as far as Abel-keramim, an exceedingly great slaughter, and the Ammonites were subdued before the Israelites" (11:33). Unqualified victory demands performance of the vow, and we dread the recognition scene, for we know who will be the only one to greet Jephthah upon his return to his house. As noted above, the terror and the tragedy lie precisely in the coincidence between what is vowed and what occurs, a correspondence underscored on the verbal level by an almost exact repetition of terms. "If you will only give the Ammonites into my hand...and Yhwh gave them into his hand." "The one coming forth from the doors of my house to meet me... I will offer up...Jephthah came to Mizpah to his house and his daughter came forth to meet him" (literally, "and behold his daughter coming forth to meet him"). At this point the narrative pace becomes agonizingly slow, pausing over a poignant description of the relation of daughter and father: "and only she – alone – he did not have, except for her, son or daughter." The description inevitably reminds us of another sacrificial victim, "your son, your only son, whom you love, Isaac." But there, in a wonderful comic resolution, a ram was sacrificed instead of the child. The redundancy here emphasizes the daughter's singularity and, simultaneously, Jephthah's isolation. Jephthah, the outcast, the marginal figure, who tends to act independently even when representing others, faces his tragic moment alone. Where are all the Israelites who have returned with him victorious from battle? Jephthah's isolation is all the more striking when we perceive the contrast with his daughter, who has companions with whom to share her grief.

As in the case of the vow, vv. 30–1, the text of v. 34 delays until the last possible moment the crucial information that this daughter is Jephthah's only child, and thus only now makes clear that for Jephthah, her death means the tragic extinction of his family line.[10] His tragedy – though not hers – would be less if he had other children. The moment he sees her, Jephthah realizes what will be required of him, and both his nonverbal response, rending his garments, and his outcry, "*'ahah*, my daughter, you have indeed brought me low," convey a combination of grief, dismay, shock, and consternation.

In the entire narrative, only this scene furnishes any insight into Jephthah's emotional state, portrays an inner conflict, and thus it is the one scene in which his character approaches anything like tragic proportions. Unlike Saul, whose tortured personality finds ample expression, Jephthah faces an internal dilemma only briefly portrayed. But brief as it is, this "confrontation with extremity"[11] is essential to a tragic presentation, for tragedy demands an awareness on the part of the protagonist that the situation is impossible, that there is no way out. Jephthah becomes a tragic figure insofar as he realizes that he has no alternative,[12] that he is caught in a situation both of his own making and, paradoxically, an accident of fate. His situation helps illuminate the import of his words to his daughter. "I have opened my mouth" acknowledges his role in setting into motion this terrible course of events. "You have indeed brought me low, and have become my trouble" blames the victim, as others have pointed out, but it also, it seems to me, strives to convey his sense of being not wholly responsible for this horrible, unexpected result. It points beyond itself to the "secret cause." Oedipus did not intend to kill his father and marry his mother; he does so only because he does not know their identity. Jephthah did not intend to sacrifice his daughter; he speaks his vow without knowing the identity of "the one coming forth." The experience of being trapped in an intolerable situation for which one is unintentionally, yet still somehow responsible gives rise to tragic awareness.

The vow is irrevocable and unalterable, and verbal allusions grimly underscore its tragic irony. Jephthah *returns*, "brought back" (*meshibim*, 11:9) by the elders, as leader against the Ammonites and subsequently *returns* (*beshubi*, 11:31) victorious from battle; only his words cannot be *returned* (*lashub*, 11:35). They have *gone forth* (*yatsa'*, 11:36) from his mouth, claiming as their victim his daughter who *came forth* (*yotse't*) to meet him. After her brief period of lamentation, she *returns* (*wattashab*, 11:39) to her father for the vow to be fulfilled.

The narrative describes the sacrifice summarily, without detail, a striking contrast to the story of Abraham's near sacrifice of the young Isaac in Genesis 22. But there, because we know the favorable outcome, know that Abraham will pass this test of faith, we could tolerate the details – the building of the altar, the touching dialogue between father and child, the raising of the knife – and the pathos they bring to the scene. Here we could not. Though no *deus ex machina* saves the daughter, a countermovement of resolution and repair tempers her tragedy: she shares her last months in lamentation with female companions, and after her death the women of Israel remember her in a yearly ritual.

In Chapter 1 I spoke of the downward movement of tragedy and its irreversible catastrophe. Clearly Saul's story illustrates this movement. Although acts of human kindness ameliorate the tragedy (the medium at En-dor, 1 Samuel 28; the men of Jabesh-gilead, 1 Samuel 31), any relief remains overshadowed by the reality of divine rejection. In the sacrifice of his daughter, Jephthah reaches his nadir. To what extent he rises above his personal catastrophe is difficult to decide. Does Israel's victory over Ammon compensate for the loss of his only child? Surely the large number of descendants attributed to Yair, Ibzan, and Abdon, judges before and after Jephthah – with an escalation that first includes daughters and daughters-in-law and then grandsons – draws attention to Jephthah's death without progeny.[13]

Jephthah's story does not end with the tragic sacrifice. No attempt is made to smooth over the abrupt transition between the story of the sacrifice and that of the war with Ephraim which follows. We find, however, subtle ironic reminders of the tragic events, both in the words of the Ephraimites and those of Jephthah. The Ephraimites' threat to burn Jephthah's house over him with fire rings hollow now that his daughter, his "house" since he has no other children, has already been burned as a sacrifice. In terms that have been forced to bear heavy weight, Jephthah reminds us, "Yhwh gave them into my hand" (12:3, cf. 11:30, 32), and perhaps "When I saw that you were not going to save me, I took my life in my hand" is a veiled reference to the vow and its consequences. (Note, too, that only the presence of one letter, the *kaph*, prevents our reading, "I took my life in my mouth.") Finally, the danger of uttering what turn out to be the wrong words is reflected in the deadly consequences of mispronouncing the word "shibboleth."

Jephthah fails to avert open conflict between Gilead and Ephraim, and we must ask ourselves how hard he tries. Gilead is victorious, but what meaning has victory when Israelite fights against Israelite? The Gileadites repeat Jephthah's deed on a tribal scale, slaughtering their own flesh and blood.[14] The verb used of the slaying, *shahat*, most often appears in sacrificial contexts (cf. Gen. 22:10); symbolically the Ephraimites too become Jephthah's sacrificial victims. We are told that Jephthah judged Israel six years, died, and was buried in Gilead (or if we accept the Masoretic text, in the cities of Gilead, a burial of uncertain location for a former exile from his father's house, forced by events to destroy his own).[15] That the end of his career leaves problems unresolved, that disorder reigns in spite of his military victories, that ambiguity surrounds his "successes" – all these things foster a tragic vision. Two important and related issues are left open: how, finally, to evaluate Jephthah, and – because it is the reason for our difficulty in doing so – how to regard the silence of God.

What manner of man is Jephthah? Does he have the makings of a tragic hero? Like Saul, he holds a privileged position of leadership, which thrusts upon him the necessity of facing demanding decisions. We have already seen that he embraces contraries: as "the son of another woman," he is cast out (11:1–5); as a "mighty warrior," sought after (11:1–11). When his story begins, he appears as a fugitive, a marginal figure who lives over against his brothers, a man who demonstrates his leadership abilities by raiding with worthless followers. Against a background of crisis, he rises to a position of authority, in which he customarily appears in adversary situations. Disputation brings to light the trait that most clearly defines his character: he is a negotiator. But as a negotiator he has a curious record; there is something excessive about him, which disposes him to tragedy.

In his first speech, when the elders of Gilead approach him to enlist his aid, Jephthah reveals his penchant for negotiation. He aspires to more than what is first offered and succeeds in getting the elders to accept his terms. The negotiations develop along interesting lines and merit careful scrutiny. Initially the elders formulate their offer in a way that assures maximum benefit for themselves, while leaving their obligation to Jephthah somewhat vague:

> Come and be our leader
> that we may fight the Ammonites.

Jephthah responds neither "yes" nor "no," but with rhetorical questions that reveal appropriate wariness, "Did you not hate me and cast me out from my father's house? Why do you come to me now when you are in distress?" Placed on the spot, the elders state their terms differently:

> ...that you may fight the Ammonites
> and be our chief over all the inhabitants of Gilead.

If "leader" (*qatsin*) is a temporary military leadership and "chief" (*ro'sh*) a permanent civil one, the stakes are higher than they were initially;[16] but correspondingly the fighting has been individualized, no longer "that we may fight" but "that you may fight." What remains unclarified is whether Jephthah will be chief only during the conflict with the Ammonites or also after. Jephthah now puts the proposition yet another way:

> *If* you are bringing me back to fight the Ammonites
> *and* Yhwh gives them to me,
> (then) I will be your chief.

This response accomplishes two things with impressive economy. First, it makes explicit that Jephthah will be chief of the Gileadites after the battle, assuming he wins (if Israel loses to the Ammonites, the issue becomes a moot one anyway). Second, it lends divine sanction to the negotiations by making Jephthah's appointment as chief contingent on divine favor. I shall return to this point later. The elders accept the terms, and the people make Jephthah chief and leader; that is, he is appointed for the present crisis and for the future if he succeeds in ridding Israel of the Ammonite threat.

Jephthah's negotiating skills are soon put to another test, and this time they prove inadequate. His extensive negotiations with the king of the Ammonites (11:12–28) do not succeed in averting warfare. A long and contorted effort to present his case, with all sorts of appeals to history and divine intervention, Jephthah's argument is a curious example of rhetoric with a sense of *déjà vu* about it. His appeal to the example of a failed attempt at negotiation and its outcome becomes yet another failed attempt at negotiation with the same outcome. Interestingly enough, neither the Ammonite king nor Jephthah benefits from the lesson in history Jephthah recounts. Jephthah describes Israel's attempts to reason with earlier kings (the kings of Edom, Moab, and Sihon, king of the Amorites), their failure to listen, and Yhwh's subsequent dispossession of them in favor of Israel. Similarly, the king of Ammon refuses to listen (cf. 11:17 with 11:28), and the Ammonites will meet the same fate in the ensuing battle: Yhwh gives them into Israel's hand (cf. 11:21 with 11:32). Jephthah's confidence in divine disposition, "all that Yhwh our God has dispossessed before us, we will possess," and his conviction that right and God are on his side ("I have not sinned against you, but you are doing me wrong to fight against me; Yhwh, the judge, judge today between the Israelites and the Ammonites," v. 27) should

afford him sufficient assurance that Yhwh will give him victory in the
upcoming battle, and thus, from another angle, point to something
excessive about the vow.

Against this background of negotiation, Jephthah's vow does not
appear out of character. Moreover, it is very much in context. When
we compare the historical situation Jephthah relates with the account
of the same events in Numbers 20–1, we find the Israelites vowing to
God complete destruction (*ḥerem*) of Canaanite cities in return for
victory (Num. 21:2). Israel's vow may be considered warranted by
the circumstances, and since Jephthah's situation clearly resembles,
and in a sense repeats, Israel's, his vow is not altogether unexpected.
In fact, the two vows are strikingly similar in their protases:

> "If you will indeed give this people into my hand..."
> (Num. 21:2)
> "If you will indeed give the Ammonites into my hand..."
> (Judg. 11:30)

Only with the apodoses do we note the dissonance in Jephthah's vow.
Whereas Israel promises to devote to God whatever they conquer in
battle, Jephthah does the excessive: he vows a special offering to God,
a personal sacrifice from his own household. All too soon he will
discover that his vow demands the ultimate sacrifice on his part –
"you have indeed brought me low and have become my trouble"
(11:35, with verbal similarity, *hakreʿa hikraʿtini* and *ʿokray*, emphasizing his misfortune). In other instances of biblical vows a relationship
exists between what is asked for and what is promised in return.[17] The
similar situations and similar language in Num. 21:2 and Judg.
11:30 reveal clearly that Jephthah does not vow the obvious thing,
an offering to God of Ammonite spoil. That he vows the ultimate
rather than the obvious (and perhaps even the logical?) lends further
poignancy to his tragedy.

By the end of the narrative, negotiation, if it can be called that,
breaks down completely. Again Jephthah fails to prevent the
outbreak of hostilities. Indeed, his exchange with the Ephraimites
(12:1–3) seems lame in comparison with his laborious reasoning with
the Ammonite king. The Ephraimites' anger at not having been
called to join Jephthah in fighting the Ammonites meets with
Jephthah's insistence that he sought their aid in vain, and thus we
have conflicting versions of events not reported in the narrative.
Surprisingly, Jephthah does not try reasoning with the Ephraimites.

The Ephraimites threaten Jephthah's house, already destroyed in the only sense that really matters, but do not announce full-scale war with Gilead. Here particularly Jephthah reveals a tendency towards excess. Without waiting for the Ephraimites' response to his explanation (v. 3), he assembles the men of Gilead for battle. Not only is he less patient and less persistent than with the Ammonites, where twice he sent messengers to plead his part, but his dealings with the Ephraimites stand in sharp contrast to the way an earlier judge handled the same situation. With some clever rhetoric, Gideon succeeded, where Jephthah does not, in averting the Ephraimites' wrath (Judg. 8:1–3). Jephthah, the mighty warrior, is a man of bloodshed. His "diplomatic" failures result in fighting, and in one case needless slaughter; his faithfulness to his vow costs his daughter's life.

The characterization of Jephthah as a negotiator whose virtue is also his weakness shows his potential for tragedy, but does not define him as a tragic figure. Jephthah, in contrast to Saul, fails to attain genuinely tragic proportions. To be sure, the makings are there: the *hamartia*, the incautious vow – but except for the scene when his daughter comes to meet him and he comprehends his destiny in one consuming and agonizing moment, there is no inner struggle, no wrestling against his fate. Unlike Saul, who knows he has lost the kingship yet multiplies his efforts to hold on to it, Jephthah does not grapple to find a way out of a situation for which there is no way out. I said of Saul that a lesser man might merely accept his fate. Jephthah does just that. He lacks *hubris*, and therefore no significant tragic development occurs within his character. His would be a tragedy of a different order, of a greater magnitude, if, like Agamemnon, he resisted; or, if like Jephthah in Amos Oz' short story, "Upon This Evil Earth," he displayed a desperate clinging to the hope that God would intervene, "I have not withheld my only daughter from you. Grant me a sign, for surely you are tempting your servant."

Much has been made of the satisfaction we experience in witnessing the strength of the human spirit as it rises to meet calamity.[18] We admire in tragic heroes their ability to confront misfortune head-on, when, like Saul, they expend the full range of their human powers before they are broken by necessity. We pity Jephthah, but we do not at any point admire him.

The agony and grandeur of tragic heroes lie in their isolation. Jephthah faces his cruel destiny essentially alone, for although his daughter accepts what he must do and urges him to carry out his vow, she does not share in his tragedy so much as she shares her own personal tragedy with her female companions – away from him and away from the company of men. Nor do the people, exulting in victory, step in to ransom Jephthah's daughter, as the people ransomed Jonathan from the oath of his father Saul (1 Samuel 14). No solace comes from God either, no ram in the thicket.

The daughter, too, lacks the development that makes for a genuinely tragic personality. She accepts her fate so willingly and obediently that it is shocking (and the narrative does not tell us how she knows or surmises the terms of the vow). She places her communal importance – her role as sacrificial victim that the vow may be performed – over her individual life, and because she does not fight her fate, she does not attain the kind of tragic stature that we find, for example, in the Iphigenia of Aeschylus. Her tragedy lies in the sacrifice itself, an outrageous, violent act, and in life cut off in its promise, a doleful theme of "incompleteness" well established in literature, from the Greek tradition of the young woman who dies on the eve of her wedding to Wordsworth's "Lucy Poems." In the space of a few brief verses, she moves from mirth and celebration of her father's victory to lamentation, and just as quickly she passes into death and celebration in communal memory. In particular the juxtaposition of her joy and Jephthah's dismay in the scene when she comes to meet him upon his return from battle is striking. A negotiator like her father, she asks for time to engage in lamentation with her companions. Yet she is not isolated in sorrow; and as we have seen, the company of her women companions and the yearly commemoration of her fate by women ameliorate her tragedy.

The heart of Saul's tragedy may be located in what Paul Ricoeur describes as the Aeschylean paradox of human guilt and hostile transcendence.[19] Saul is guilty and yet punished beyond measure by an unforgiving deity. In the story of Jephthah, ambiguity shrouds both sides of the paradox. Jephthah, too, is guilty. His suffering is not imposed on him; he opens his mouth (11:35, 36). But, like Saul, he is not really wicked. His vow is not a sign of insufficient faith. Rather it illustrates his piety, his confidence in Yhwh, for he has consistently invoked Yhwh in his other undertakings (11:9, 27). Ironically, his piety precipitates his disaster, and again we see signs of the excessiveness that disposes Jephthah to tragedy, transforming his virtue into *hamartia*. Jephthah's "guilt" remains particularly am-

biguous. No negative judgment attends either the making of the vow
or its performance. The loss of his daughter is not presented as
punishment for a rash vow made either in over-zealous piety or lack
of trust. The aftermath of the sacrifice, its effect on Jephthah's inner
life or his standing within the community, is passed over in silence,
and its effect upon his outward performance of his duties is, at best,
only hinted at in the account that follows, where he so clearly fails to
prevent tribal hostilities. Saul had the kingship torn from him,
experienced the terror of divine rejection, but still dies a king.
Jephthah dies a judge, but without suffering the indignity of rejection
or the curse of divine abandonment, and this absence of censure not
only makes us uncertain how to understand Jephthah's guilt, it also
leaves us in doubt about the role of the deity.

The source of the tragic in the story of Jephthah is not divine
enmity, as in Saul's case, but divine silence. Beginning with the
refusal to continue to deliver the Israelites in their distress (10:13)
through the elders' choice of Jephthah and negotiations with him, the
deity remains strangely aloof from the affairs of Israel and Jephthah.
Jephthah, on the other hand, regularly refers matters to the deity
(and here we may recall Saul's constant seeking after the divine will).
He involves Yhwh in the decision to make him chief over Gilead,
"if... Yhwh gives them to me, I will be your chief" (11:9). Setting
this condition may be Jephthah's way of seeking divine affirmation:
Jephthah will be chief only if Yhwh shows it should be so. The elders
follow suit, binding themselves to Jephthah's words by an oath to
Yhwh (11:10). Furthermore, Jephthah – and the narrator supplies
this bit of information – speaks all his words before Yhwh at Mizpah.
In his negotiations with the Ammonites, in addition to testifying to
Yhwh's past action on Israel's behalf, Jephthah appeals to Yhwh as
the final judge of the conflict between Israel and Ammon. "May
Yhwh, the judge, judge today between the Israelites and the
Ammonites" (11:27). Even his daughter brings the deity into the
picture, citing Yhwh's granting of victory to Jephthah as the ground
for observing the vow (11:36).

That the spirit of Yhwh affects Jephthah (11:29) offers a sign that
Yhwh intends to come to Israel's aid through him. But we have
already seen how the imposition of the vow raises questions about the
role of the spirit. Apart from this curious animation of Jephthah, the
only time Yhwh acts directly (as opposed to being spoken of) is to give
the Ammonites into Jephthah's hand (11:32, 36; 12:3). If not a tacit

acceptance of Jephthah's vow, this action nevertheless implicates the deity and helps determine Jephthah's tragic fate. That fate is sealed when Jephthah's daughter comes to meet him. "I have opened my mouth to Yhwh and I cannot take it back" (11:35); "You have opened your mouth to Yhwh; do to me according to what has gone forth from your mouth" (11:36) – thus he and his daughter accept the inevitability of the sacrifice. To speculate why Yhwh does not intervene at this point in the story gets us nowhere. The account of Abraham's near sacrifice of Isaac shows one possible direction our narrative could have taken, a last-minute intervention by the deity to save the child. Euripides' *Iphigenia in Aulis* shows us another, where the gods are without pity.[20] But in Judges 11, God neither requires nor rejects human sacrifice. Silent transcendence, if not a form of hostile transcendence, clearly raises questions about divine benevolence. Jephthah does not experience Saul's sense of separation from Yhwh, but, like Saul, he cannot depend on the goodness of Yhwh. He makes no final, urgent appeal to Yhwh which Yhwh refuses to answer, as in Saul's case. Rather, as in Greek tragedy, Jephthah faces alone a fickle world, a world where seemingly unrelated events conspire to overwhelm, where a victorious warrior returning from battle can meet tragedy at the threshold of his house. His story does not call into question the underlying causes of his misfortune; its tragedy lies in that "secret cause."

EXCURSUS I: THE AWFUL AND SUSTAINING POWER OF WORDS

A particular power resides in words of blessing and curse, oaths and vows.[21] "I have blessed him – yes, and he shall be blessed" (Gen. 27:33). Isaac cannot alter his blessing of Jacob, even though he has been tricked into giving it. "I have opened my mouth to Yhwh, and I cannot take it back" (Judg. 11:35). The vow is irrevocable, irreversible, and unalterable.[22] Thus Jephthah, who has elsewhere shown a propensity for negotiation, though not with particularly impressive results, does not make any attempt to modify its terms, by which he is bound to sacrifice to God his only child. Nor does his daughter challenge the inviolability of the vow, but asks only for a two months' reprieve, after which the vow is carried out. The word kills.

A father's sacrifice of his only child in fulfillment of an unfortunate vow bears witness to the pernicious power of words. But if words can kill, they can also heal. The corrosive power of language, its destructive aspect, is counterbalanced in this tale by its antipodal movement, the healing and sustaining capacity of words. Jephthah's daughter asks that one thing, *haddabar hazzeh*, "this word," be done for her, that she be given a period of two months during which to grieve with her companions. After her death, the women of Israel commemorate Jephthah's daughter in a yearly ritual. Whether we translate *letannot* as "lament" or "mourn," with the Septuagint and Vulgate or, more likely, "recount" (as in its only other occurrence, Judg. 5:11), we are speaking of a memorial event that is in some sense a linguistic act, not a silent vigil. To recount the story of Jephthah's daughter is to make her live again through words. This communal commemoration by women is an act of identification and integration, mitigating the wrong done by the word of the father. It cannot undo that word, just as Isaac could not undo his blessing given to the wrong son and give it to the rightful heir, but it prevents that word from extinguishing memory along with life. More than this, both the women's response and the father's unholy deed belong to a larger world of words. Because it contains within its formal and linguistic boundaries both the tragedy and the human courage to face and rise above it, the story itself provides a palliative for the wound this terrible deed inflicts on our sensibilities. Jephthah's daughter finds life through communal recollection, though different, of course, from the life she might have had through family and children, the life her father took away. The recounting of the daughter's courage and the women's refusal to forget is not just a balance to, but a transcendence of the tragedy of the daughter's death. The word heals.

A concern with words, their power and their importance, forms an important theme in the story of Jephthah. Speech exiles him, "You shall not inherit in the house of our father" (11:2). But speech, in the form of some rather contrived negotiations, also beings him back. What is interesting about these negotiations is the subtle changes in the way things are formulated. As we have seen, at first the leaders of Gilead offer to make Jephthah their leader and then they mention fighting the Ammonites; when they reiterate their offer in response to Jephthah's sarcastic retort, they speak first of fighting, and then offer Jephthah the position of chief. Jephthah, who has just been offered the position of leadership, now places a condition on it where none has appeared before, "if Yhwh gives them to me, I will be your chief." Now the elders do a significant thing: they bind themselves to Jephthah's words by an oath to Yhwh, "Yhwh is hearing between us, if we do not do according to your *word*." These negotiations between Jephthah and the elders afford our first sample of the nature of Jephthah's words, words that appear to complicate matters.

Jephthah returns (11:11) to become both chief and leader and we find the interesting statement that "Jephthah spoke all his *words* before Yhwh at Mizpah." Perhaps this refers to a ratification of his agreement with the elders, but it also points to a fatal association of Jephthah's words with Mizpah. Mizpah, where, according to 11:34, Jephthah makes his home, is a marginal place, at the boundary between Israel and Ammon, just as Jephthah is a marginal figure, an outcast from the familial hearth, who goes raiding with worthless fellows.[23] It is apparently from Mizpah that Jephthah carries out negotiations with the Ammonites; passing over Mizpah, he offers his vow, and there he fulfills it. (Note the play on *mitspah* and *patsiti* ["I have opened "].) All his words are thus through extension associated with Mizpah, and they are useless and destructive words – useless in that they fail to achieve peace, destructive in that they cost him his only child.

Jephthah's negotiations with the Ammonites represent what David Jobling has aptly described as "verbal combat preliminary to the military combat."[24] Verbal violence temporarily displaces physical violence, which, however, soon erupts. To the Ammonite king, Jephthah sends messengers who speak in his name ("thus says Jephthah," v. 15). His long speech presents a circuitous argument that fails to persuade. Certain curious elements of the speech lead Jobling to conclude that "Jephthah is dissatisfied with his case, and that he is disingenuously avoiding reference to the real basis of Ammon's claim." For example, Jephthah neglects to mention that Israel avoided Ammonite territory when it took possession of the promised land (cf. Deuteronomy 2; Numbers 21). His point about divine disposition (11:24) works both ways: perhaps Ammon has been given the disputed territory by its god. Finally, his argument that, having laid no claim to the land during the 300 years of Israelite occupation, the Ammonites have no right to dispute it now suggests that Ammon has a legitimate claim.[25] Even the precedent Jephthah cites – the speech within the speech, where Jephthah recounts Israel's earlier attempts to negotiate entry into the promised land – is not successful in averting conflict (vv. 17–20). Like the kings before him, "the king of the Ammonites did not heed the *words* of Jephthah which he sent to him" (v. 28). Battle is imminent, when Jephthah opens his mouth and out comes the vow. Even as the words are spoken, they arouse anxiety. Just who or what might come out from Jephthah's house to meet him? Whereas verbal combat was unsuccessful, the military combat is a success because words have been taken further. Jephthah has promised the ultimate in return for victory.

Now words are out of Jephthah's control. The vow cannot be retracted and both Jephthah and his daughter are caught up in its immutable course toward fulfillment. Granting her request for a two-month reprieve, he sends her away with one word, "go," the last recorded word he speaks to her (11:38). Between his first words to her, denoting their intimate relationship, "ah, my daughter" or "alas, my daughter," and his last, "go," without any accompanying mollifying particle (such as the customary particle of politeness, *na'*, usually translated "please" or "I pray you"), a distancing occurs, a separation now complete, a severing of familial integrity, which spells the extinction of Jephthah's family. Similarly, the young woman's speech to her father echoes this crucial metamorphosis:

She said to him,
   "My father, you have opened your mouth to Yhwh;
   do to me according to what has gone forth from your mouth,
   now that Yhwh has vindicated you against your enemies,
   the Ammonites."

And she said to her father,
   "Let this thing be done for me,
   let me alone two months
   that I may go and wander upon the hills
   and lament my nubility,[26]
   I *and my companions*."

Judg. 11:36–7

Only at the conclusion of her speech does the young woman reveal that, unlike her father, she has companions with whom to share her grief. Her last spoken word in the narrative is *ra'yotay*, "my companions"; *'abi*, "my father," was her first. Symbolically, through speech, she journeys from the domain of the father who will quench her life to that of the female companions who will preserve her memory.

The vow is carried out in the absence of dialogue, a pain too deep for words. There is a sinister play of words and silence in the text. Most disquieting, there is no word from the deity; no "Do not put forth your hand against the child or do anything to her" (cf. Gen. 22:10).

The text is silent about God's and Jephthah's reactions to the deed. It proceeds to narrate a final incident that illustrates vividly the power of words and the danger of speaking the wrong words. The Gileadites capture the fords of the Jordan and slaughter any Ephraimite who attempts to cross. "And the men of Gilead said to him, 'Are you an Ephraimite?' And he said, 'No.' And they said to him, 'Say "shibboleth."' And he said, 'Sibboleth,' for he could not pronounce it" (*ledabber*, to speak it, to word it). The correct word preserves life; the wrong word (the incorrect pronunciation) brings death. The power of language to destroy and redeem, so eloquently at work in the story of Jephthah and his daughter, is here reduced to its barest form: one word – one letter of one word – holds the power over life and death. Verbal violence is now at one with physical violence, and we recognize that their identity has heretofore been only thinly disguised. This is violence entirely out of control. For a second time Jephthah fails to prevent the outbreak of hostilities, but this time he seems less inclined to rely on words to help him. We saw above how his heated exchange with the Ephraimites (12:1–3) contrasts starkly with his laborious reasoning with the Ammonite king. Words fail Jephthah repeatedly. He, like his daughter, is the victim of words – his own words. In this final incident, there is no healing or mitigating word. Thus we might say that the daughter's tragedy is redeemed but the father's is not. Her memory is kept alive by the community of women, but ultimately, of course, through the story, since otherwise the women's ritual is unattested. And her story keeps Jephthah's memory alive, with the remarkable irony that perhaps the most memorable thing about him is not the kind of thing one wants to be remembered for. Jephthah is remembered and later hailed as a deliverer (1 Sam. 12:11), but human sacrifice and needless shedding of blood within Israel mark his record as a judge – a judge caught up in the escalating cycle of violence to which the book of Judges bears witness.

Geoffrey Hartman, in an essay on "Words and Wounds," suggests that we can associate the healing influence of words with a sense of closure. It seems to me that the story of Jephthah's daughter, with its resolution in the women's ritual of remembrance, indeed illustrates "closure [as] a sealing with healing effect."[27] On the other hand, no healing takes place in the Ephraim incident, where closure is, at best, awkward and abrupt. The aftermath of the battle between the tribes of Gilead and Ephraim is not recounted; Jephthah judges for six years and dies. The absence of healing/closure here prefigures the absence of closure to the book of Judges as a whole and is paradigmatic of the chaos and dissolution with which the book of Judges ends.

EXCURSUS 2: JEPHTHAH AND HIS DAUGHTER: A FEMINIST READING

Having recognized the connection between verbal violence and physical violence, let us consider how that violence is directed against women. The story of Jephthah's daughter presents us with a literary murder, and literary murder is different from the real thing, which may explain why the perpetrators have gotten away with it for so long.[28] The ritual act of sacrifice transforms murder in this story into a socially acceptable act of execution.[29] As we have seen, words make potent murder weapons in this narrative. Not only are the words spoken by the male protagonist deadly instruments of power over a woman, but the storyteller also uses the young woman's own words against her. How does Jephthah's daughter speak against herself? By neither questioning the man who consigned her to death nor holding him accountable:

She said to him, "My father, you have opened your mouth to Yhwh; do to me according to what has gone forth from your mouth now that Yhwh has granted you vindication against your enemies, the Ammonites." (Judg. 11:36)

The daughter submits to the authority of the father. His word is not to be countermanded but simply postponed: she asks only for a two-month respite before the vow is carried out. In encouraging her father to fulfill his vow, she subordinates her life to the communal good. The seriousness of the vow is upheld, the need for sacrifice is satisfied,[30] and paternal authority goes unchallenged.

After reporting the daughter's sacrifice, the text adds, "She had not known a man" (11:39). Particularly striking about this statement are the facts that it appears at the end of the story as a kind of closure sealing the woman's fate; it is stated categorically, as if it were an entirely neutral observation; and it is necessary. As sacrificial victim, Jephthah's daughter must be a virgin for reasons of sacrificial purity.[31] Since one lived on through one's progeny, having offspring

– many offspring, especially sons – was important both to men and to women (witness, for example, Abraham's concern over his childlessness). Understandably it mattered significantly to women, since women did not have other opportunities, open to men, to leave their mark on the world.[32] Without children, the woman is somehow incomplete; she has not fulfilled her role as woman. If to have no children means to die unfulfilled, it also means that the young woman has no one to stand up for her, no *go'el* to plead her case. She can be eliminated without fear of reprisal.[33]

The young woman inhabits a narrative world that, like her father, seeks to subordinate, and finally control, her. She accepts her fate with alarming composure. The vow is carried out, but the unnamed young woman who leaves behind no children as a legacy is not forgotten. Her memory is kept alive by the ritual remembrance of women. Because she does not protest her fate, she offers no threat to patriarchal authority.[34] And because she voluntarily performs a daughter's duty, her memory may be preserved:

It became a custom in Israel that the daughters of Israel went year by year to commemorate Jephthah the Gileadite's daughter, four days each year. (Judg. 11:39–40)

Patriarchal ideology here co-opts a women's ceremony in order to glorify the victim. The androcentric message of the story of Jephthah's daughter is, I suggest, submit to paternal authority. You may have to sacrifice your autonomy; you may lose your life, and even your name, but your sacrifice will be remembered, indeed celebrated, for generations to come. Herein lies, I believe, the reason Jephthah's daughter's name is not preserved: because she is commemorated not for herself but *as a daughter*. If we translate the difficult *wattehi ḥoq beyisra'el* at the end of v. 39 as "she became an example in Israel"[35] rather than "it became a custom in Israel," her value to the patriarchal system as a model is underscored.

The women of Israel commemorate Jephthah's daughter for four days each year. Exactly what their ritual involves is not clear, but as I have indicated, the verb *letannot* suggests that the women recount Jephthah's daughter's story. These women, however, do not actually speak in the narrative. They remember, and their yearly ceremony is used by the narrator to keep alive the memory of the victim. Jephthah and the women of Israel represent two poles: he blames his daughter, 11:35; they praise her through memorializing her. Praising the victim can, however, be as dangerous as blaming the victim. The problem lies in the victim–victimizer dichotomy, a way of structuring experience that ignores the complicity of the victim in the crime.[36] If we make Jephthah the callous victimizer and his daughter the innocent victim, we fall into a patriarchal pattern of thinking. If we allow the women's ceremonial remembrance to encourage glorification of the victim, we perpetuate the crime.[37] How do we reject the concept of honoring the victim without also sacrificing the woman? We must recognize that guilt and innocence are not clearly distinguishable. As I indicated above, Jephthah, like his daughter, is a victim of forces beyond his control; he utters his vow in a critical situation and is not responsible for the fact that his daughter appears rather than another. Nor is the daughter innocent; she did not resist. She speaks on behalf of the sacrificial system and patriarchal authority, absolving it of responsibility. And the women of Israel cooperate in this elevation of the willing victim to honored status.

It has frequently been suggested that the story of Jephthah's daughter is aetiological, aimed at explaining a women's annual observance.[38] There is, however, no evidence of such a ritual in ancient Israel apart from this story. Recently both Mieke Bal and Peggy Day have argued that the ritual involved is a rite of passage that signifies a young woman's physical maturity, her preparation for marriage.[39] Indeed, it is likely that the word *betulay* in the phrase usually translated, "to bewail my virginity," does not mean "virginity" but rather refers to a stage in the female life-cycle.[40] *Betulah* is a liminal stage, marked by insecurity and danger, a point of transition symbolizing the death of one phase in a young woman's life and the preparation for a new one.[41] Jephthah's daughter does not go to the mountains for two months to lament her childlessness, her lack of fulfillment, but rather to engage in a rite of passage with her friends. Bal thus reads the young woman's request for a two-month delay as "the accompanying ritual speech-act of the vow which gave her away."[42] But whereas, for the daughter, virginity is not the issue, for the androcentric narrative it is: "she had not known a man."[43]

Another possibility of reading a different meaning into the phrase "to bewail *betulay*" presents itself if we suppose the young woman's familiarity with the sacrificial system; that is, her better knowledge than ours about human sacrifice in the ancient Near East. She laments the brutal fact of imminent death, recognizing that if she were not a virgin daughter, her father could not sacrifice her.[44] Such an argument, informed by anthropology and Girardian theory, involves the same kind of retrospective reasoning as the rabbinic objection – what if the "one coming forth" had been a camel, a donkey, or a dog (_Bereshit Rabbah_ 60:3; _Wayyiqra Rabbah_ 37:4) – based on purity laws. I suggested above that narrative necessity determines the outcome. The daughter's tragedy is that she, not another, is the one to come forth to meet Jephthah, and that she is an (I would even say, the) acceptable sacrificial victim. This takes us back to my earlier remarks about the coincidence between the terms of the vow and the daughter's appearance, a conjunction of events beyond human control.

The androcentric bias of the narrative is clear in the way it presents the tragedy both from Jephthah's perspective (his family line comes to an end: "apart from her he had no son or daughter") and from his daughter's (the patriarchal concern with her virginity and the denial to her of motherhood). The narrative does not acknowledge female sexual pleasure. Indeed, patriarchal literature, and thus the Bible in general, reflects the underlying attitude that woman's sexuality is to be feared and thus carefully regulated.[45] Patriarchy severs the relationship between eroticism and procreation. As Julia Kristeva observes, it affirms motherhood but denies the mother's _jouissance_.[46] Jephthah's daughter is denied not just motherhood, the patriarchal mark of female fulfillment, but also the pleasure of sex, the right of passage into autonomous adulthood that opens the eyes with knowledge (cf. Genesis 2–3).

The father's name is remembered but the daughter's is not. Ultimately the text withholds autonomy from Jephthah's daughter. It confines her voice within patriarchal limits, using it to affirm patriarchal authority, but it does not succeed in fully suppressing it. The two parts of her speech pull in different directions. In the first part (v. 36), she surrenders volition. In the second (v. 37), within the boundaries set by her father's vow, boundaries she accepts, she attempts to define herself, to lay some claim to her own voice: she asks for a period of two months in which to grieve, accompanied by her female companions. As we have seen, her speech that begins "my father" and ends "my companions" transports her to a point of solidarity with her female friends and with other daughters, the "daughters of Israel," who refuse to forget. The resultant image cannot be fully controlled by androcentric interests. The (androcentric) text segregates women: the daughter spends two months with female companions, away from her father and the company of men; the ritual of remembrance is conducted by women alone.[47] But, as Gerda Lerner points out, when women are segregated ("which always has subordination as its purpose"), they transform such patriarchal restraint into complementarity and redefine it.[48] One way to read this story differently is by exposing its valorization of submission and glorification of the victim as serving phallocentric interests, and by redefining its images of female solidarity in an act of feminist symbol-making. If we approach the story as resistant readers, mistrustful of the dominant (male) voice, or phallogocentric ideology in the narrative, we can give the victim a voice that protests her marginalization and victimization – one that claims for her a measure of that autonomy denied her by the narrative which sacrificed her to the father's word.

CHAPTER 4

The fate of the house of Saul

When the gods shake a house, misfortune pursues the multitude
of its descendants without respite.

Sophocles, *Antigone*

In Chapter 2 we observed that Saul's tragedy affects not just Saul but
also the members of his house, all of whom come to unhappy, often
violent, ends. Here we shall investigate the fates of the more important
members of Saul's house, his daughter Michal, his sons Jonathan and
Ishbosheth, his cousin Abner, and, finally, his wife Rizpah and the
harrowing tale of the sacrifice of seven of Saul's descendants in an act
of expiation for Saul's crimes against the Gibeonites. As we shall see
in greater detail in the next chapter, the members of David's house
also suffer for David's sins. That the sins of the fathers are visited
upon the children is a painful reality well attested in literature
shaped by a tragic vision,[1] and commonly acknowledged in the Bible
(Exod. 20:5; cf. Jer. 31:29; Ezek. 18:2; Lam. 5:7; Ps. 79:8). Both
royal houses suffer, the Saulide and the Davidic, but with a subtle
difference. David's children contribute directly to their father's
tragedy by reenacting his sins – all as part of David's punishment. In
contrast, suffering befalls Saul's children simply because they belong
to a fated house. Theirs is hereditary guilt, a guilt that, as
Kierkegaard observes, involves the contradiction of being guilt and
not being guilt.[2] Saul's relations are all caught up in a process that,
once begun, cannot be halted – the inevitable working out of nemesis
within Saul's house.

Like Saul's tragedy, the tragic tales of the remaining members of
his house are embedded within the larger narrative of the vicissitudes
of David's kingship. But unlike the well-developed account of Saul's
demise, portraying events that transpire over a period of time and
taking up a major portion of the book of Samuel, the fate of his house
is presented as a series of poignant vignettes. Michal, Jonathan,
Ishbosheth, Abner, and Rizpah are not well enough developed as

characters to become genuine tragic figures (in this respect they resemble Jephthah's daughter). The tragic awareness, the masterful struggle against his destiny that sets Saul apart as tragic hero, is not to be found among the members of his family. We know almost nothing of their inner lives, of their perception of the events that close in upon them, or their comprehension of the fate that awaits them. We observed that Jephthah experienced this kind of tragic awareness in only one brief but crucial moment: seeing his daughter coming to meet him and realizing what would be required of him. In contrast we may consider Jonathan, about whom we have more material than any other member of Saul's house. We never learn how he perceives his situation – caught between filial loyalty and covenant friendship with his father's rival – nor is it apparent *why* he loves David. Similarly, with Michal, we must fill in the gaps surrounding her actions. That she loves David because he is a successful young warrior favored by her father's court is plausible. That her love turns to hatred out of jealousy and resentment aroused by her treatment at David's hands is equally plausible. Whereas the gaps in the text are highly suggestive and meaningful, Michal's inner turmoil remains a repressed dimension of the text (though, as we shall see, it surfaces in another form in 2 Samuel 6). Although the members of Saul's household do not present us with studies in developed character-ization or full-blown tragedy, their fates – and the narrative silences surrounding their fates – contribute importantly to, and complete, the tragedy of the house of Saul. It is in this sense that their lots are tragic.

MICHAL AND JONATHAN

Michal, Saul's younger daughter, and Jonathan, his son and heir, have much in common. In a narrative world where everyone loves David, as he steals the hearts of "all Israel and Judah" after his defeat of Goliath (1 Sam. 18:16), their love for David stands out as exceptional. It leads them to defy their father by helping David escape Saul's plots against him, and Saul's knowledge that his own children support his rival greatly intensifies his tragedy. Jonathan's two interventions on David's behalf, in which he tries to dissuade Saul from seeking David's life, frame Michal's deliverance of David by letting him down through the window of his house when the king's messengers come to take him. Like their father Saul, both Michal and Jonathan meet tragic fates. Jonathan must die and Michal cannot have children in order that Saul's house, rejected by Yhwh, come to its necessarily tragic end. Because he dies on the battlefield with his father, Jonathan remains true both to Saul and to David. His death at Saul's side, fighting for Israel, demonstrates that he is not a traitor, in spite of the fact that he supported David against Saul:

Jonathan, Saul's son, went to David at Horesh and strengthened his hand in God (1 Sam. 23:16),

and his father had accused him of treachery:

"No one discloses to me when my son makes a covenant with the son of Jesse; none of you is sorry for me and no one discloses to me that my son has stirred up my servant against me, to lie in wait as at this day" (1 Sam. 22:8).

Death conveniently removes him as an obstacle to David's rise to kingship – for giving David the kingship symbolically, as Jonathan does, is different altogether from achieving the transition in reality, as the opposition of Abner and Ishbosheth and the "long war between the house of Saul and the house of David" (2 Sam. 3:1) illustrate. Jonathan accordingly remains David's friend to the end.

In contrast to her brother's "ideal" relationship to David, where no conflict occurs, Michal's love for David turns to hatred, which she vents in a veritable emotional explosion when he brings the ark of Yhwh to Jerusalem. David responds in kind, and thus an easy resolution to the transfer of the monarchy, the uniting of the two rival houses through a child of Michal and David, is precluded. Like Jonathan's death, Michal's childlessness is convenient, if not necessary, since a child of Michal and David would only create problems in view of Yhwh's rejection of Saul's house.[3] A descendant of Saul cannot sit upon the throne of Israel.

Kingship over Israel is mediated to David through Jonathan, not Michal; that is, through friendship with the king's son, and not the more common means, marriage to the king's daughter. Jonathan represents the uncomplicated transfer of kingship to David, whereas Michal's is one of the few voices of resistance raised by the house of Saul to David's assumption of royal prerogative after Saul's death. Viewed from David's perspective, Jonathan is portrayed positively, and Michal negatively. Adele Berlin has observed in the roles of Jonathan and Michal a certain kind of reversal; however, to ascribe to Jonathan feminine characteristics and to Michal masculine ones, as Berlin does,[4] is to look in the wrong direction for the male/female dynamics of the story, as well as to risk reinforcing gender stereotypes.

Jonathan replaces his sister as love-object. This "love" is not eros but *male bonding*, and it explains, I suggest, Jonathan's near-absorption into David, what David Jobling aptly describes as his identification with and self-emptying into David.[5] Male bonding characteristically excludes and undervalues women.[6] Thus David says of Jonathan, "Your love for me was wonderful, more than the love of women" (2 Sam. 1:26). I take the most natural meaning of this statement to be that Jonathan loved David (nothing is said of the converse) more than women love men.

In the case of Michal the issue is *male rivalry*, where woman is frequently victim. The rivalry is that between David and Saul, and after Saul's death, its intensity diminished, between David and Ishbosheth, as Saul's successor and king of the northern tribes. Whereas Jonathan functions to mediate the kingship from Saul to David,[7] Michal mediates relations between the two men, Saul and David, who, on the evidence of 1 Samuel 16 and 18, appear in a classical Freudian Oedipal relationship of rivalry and love. Saul intends to use Michal as a "snare," as a means to rid himself of David (1 Sam. 18:21). Marriage to the king's daughter will bring David closer to the kingship. The text suggests his political ambitions by stating, "it pleased David to be the king's son-in-law"; it does not say whether or not it pleased him to have Michal as his wife.[8] Whereas the men are motivated by considerations of politics and power, the woman responds on a personal level:[9] "Michal Saul's daughter loved David," we are told quite simply (1 Sam. 18:20). Her desire can find expression only in the context of the men's political machinations, to which she unavoidably falls victim.

After Saul's death, Ishbosheth replaces him as David's rival, though it is a role he is too ineffectual to sustain. In asking for the return of his wife Michal, whom Saul had married to Paltiel apparently to deny David claim to the throne, David again appears politically motivated.[10] Paltiel's weeping as Michal is taken away from him (2 Sam. 3:16) draws attention to the textual silence surrounding both David's and Michal's emotions. The rivalry here involves Ishbosheth as much as Paltiel, which is why David asks *Ishbosheth* for her.[11] The Saul–David rivalry reappears in David and Michal's final confrontation, where at last it effectively humiliates and eliminates the woman.

Connected to the themes of male bonding and male rivalry is the issue of autonomy. Michal expresses autonomy *vis-à-vis* her father

Saul when she defies him by helping David escape and then lying to conceal her involvement. She reveals her autonomy from David when she criticizes his behavior before the ark. Michal's difficult position between the two men becomes even more apparent in the alternating descriptions of her as "David's wife" or "Saul's daughter" which we shall examine more closely below. Autonomy proves to be very costly, indeed, ultimately impossible and thus self-destructive, for Michal. Jonathan's autonomy from Saul is problematic, as Jobling shows in his discussion of Jonathan's identification with and independence of Saul.[12] Jonathan's lack of autonomy from David is most clearly attested by the fact that, with two exceptions, Jonathan appears in the narrative only in relation to David. The exceptions are when he is introduced (which takes place before David is introduced) and at his death. Lack of autonomy, especially from David, involves a curious kind of self-preservation through effacement for Jonathan. In order to investigate the dynamics at work in the corresponding roles of Michal and Jonathan, we must probe more deeply into the way the nemesis that falls on Saul works itself out in their lives.

JONATHAN

It is for this men pray they may beget
households of dutiful obedient sons...
Sophocles, *Antigone*

Whereas Saul is the king unwilling to relinquish the kingdom, Jonathan is the crown prince ready to hand it over to David. Jonathan's acceptance of the inevitable replacement of Saul's house by David's dramatizes Saul's refusal. It also turns Saul's house into a house divided. Had Saul so acquiesced in his fate, had he accepted his rejection by Yhwh, he would not have attained tragic proportions. Jonathan, who lacks *hubris*, is tragic only insofar as he participates in the tragic fate of Saul's house. In structuralist terms, Jonathan is a mediating figure.[13] His gesture of giving David his robe, armor, bow, and girdle functions as a symbolic giving-over of the kingdom, and he progressively acknowledges David's claim to the throne from early avowals of support (19:3; 20:9, 12–16) to his climactic, "you shall be king over Israel and I shall be your second-in-command" (1 Sam. 23:17). He dies, of course, before that vision of the future can be tested, and his concern with the place of his progeny under David's rule appears well justified in light of subsequent events.

Jobling analyzes the structure of 1 Samuel 13–31 according to alternating sections of David–Saul material and Jonathan material, arguing convincingly that the theological problem of the transfer of kingship from Saul to David is resolved in Jonathan. He observes that Jonathan does not appear in the sections dealing with the relationship of David to Saul, and suggests that "with the single exception of 22:8, there seems to be nothing in them that would be different if Jonathan did not exist."[14] Both Jobling and Edmund Leach draw attention to Jonathan's identification with David, an "equation [that] implies that David ultimately replaces Jonathan as Saul's 'rightful' successor."[15] The scenes in which Jonathan appears occur in chiastic order; and apart from his first and final scenes, Jonathan appears only in association with David. This narrative pattern of forward movement and then reversal (here, a kind of retreat) suggests something static about Jonathan's role. He carries out the important function of mediating the kingship from Saul to David, but accomplishes little else of lasting significance.[16]

A Jonathan fights with Saul against the Philistines: victory (1 Samuel 13–14)
B Jonathan makes a covenant with David; gives him the trappings of kingship (1 Sam. 18:1–4)
C Saul seeks David's life; Jonathan effects a reconciliation (1 Sam. 19:1–7)
C' Saul seeks David's life; Jonathan fails to achieve a reconciliation (1 Samuel 20)
B' Jonathan recognizes David as future king; makes a covenant with David (1 Sam. 23:15–18)
A' Jonathan fights with Saul against the Philistines: defeat (1 Samuel 31)

Jonathan is introduced in 1 Samuel 13 as fighting with his father against the Philistines. According to v. 3, Jonathan killed the Philistine prefect at Geba, whereas v. 4 attributes the deed to Saul. The house is united, harmonious, and the accomplishments of father and son are indistinguishable. In 1 Samuel 14, Jonathan shows his bravery as a warrior and becomes a popular hero when he and his armor-bearer cross over to the Philistine camp and throw the enemy into a panic, thereby inspiring an Israelite victory. He acts without his father's knowledge; the royal house no longer acts in unison and the division hinted at by Jonathan's independent action will end in a fateful confrontation between father and son.[17] In the ensuing battle, Israel defeats the Philistines, but the victory is marred, and the fault is perhaps not Saul's alone. Complications arise when Saul imposes an oath upon the people: "Cursed be the man who eats food before evening and I am vindicated against my enemies" (14:24). Jonathan, unaware of the oath, eats some wild honey, and consequently God is silent when Saul inquires about pursuing the Philistines by night. When Saul seeks to discern where the fault lies, the sacred lot falls on Jonathan, and Saul sentences him to death for this ritual infraction.

Why does Saul place such an oath upon the people? It is not unlike Jephthah's vow in several respects. Like Jephthah, Saul appears to be genuinely pious, and, after his recent encounter with the prophet Samuel who has announced Yhwh's rejection of his kingdom, he is no doubt especially anxious to gain the divine favor. But if Saul intends to ensure a great victory, the oath seems to have the opposite effect. "The people were faint," the text twice reports (v. 28, "very faint," v. 31); and the people sin by falling upon the spoil with such rapacity that they do not slaughter it properly before eating.[18] Jonathan's criticism is especially severe, "My father has troubled the land (*'kr*, the same word Jephthah uses of his daughter) ... How much better if the people had eaten freely today from the spoil of their enemies which they found, for now the slaughter among the Philistines has not been great" (vv. 29–30). Moreover, and again the similarity with Jephthah is noteworthy, the object of Saul's oath turns out to be his own child. Like Jephthah, Saul speaks words that mean more than he knows, "Though it [the sin] be in Jonathan my son, he shall surely die" (v. 39).[19] The people know Jonathan is guilty and therefore say nothing. Jonathan is taken by lot and Saul is prepared to carry out the death penalty, just as Jephthah was prepared to carry out the sacrifice. Like Jephthah's daughter, Jonathan is ready to die as a consequence of his father's words. Saul swears another oath, this time an apparent self-imprecation,[20] "God do so to me and more also, you shall surely die, Jonathan" – an imprecation that becomes self-fulfilling since Jonathan does not die. Whereas there was no one to speak up for the life of Jephthah's young daughter, the people step in to ransom their deliverer Jonathan.

If Saul is to be blamed for imposing an oath upon the people – and Jonathan, for one, blames him – and for his willingness to have his son executed for its violation, Jonathan, too, bears some responsibility for the unsettling events. One might question Jonathan's tactical wisdom in launching a surprise attack on the Philistine garrison without telling his father. "We are given the general impression that this is not a well-considered plan of Jonathan's, but a sudden idea," observes H. W. Hertzberg.[21] And even if Saul was wrong to impose the ban on eating, what useful purpose does it serve to criticize his father's judgment publicly? Furthermore, Jonathan's point of view is not unbiased and his claim (v. 30) that the victory was not so great as it might have been is challenged by the narrator's statement in the next verse, "They struck down the Philistines that day from Michmash to Aijalon," indicating a major victory.[22] Diana Edelman, who sees in this material evidence for a three-part kingship installation ritual, argues that Jonathan fails his "test" as a suitable candidate for kingship. Through the sacred lot Yhwh declares Jonathan's guilt and unworthiness as candidate for king-elect.[23]

According to 1 Samuel 13, Yhwh would have established Saul's kingdom forever, but because Saul disobeyed, it will not endure. Jonathan belongs to a fated house, and even if it were the case that he has done nothing wrong,[24] he cannot escape his tragic destiny. The issue is not whether or not Jonathan is worthy of the kingship, for it is simply not to be his. If Saul had not imposed the ban, perhaps the victory would have been greater. If Jonathan had not violated the ban, perhaps Yhwh would have answered Saul's inquiry. The direct cause of Yhwh's silence is the violation of the ban, not the imposition of it, and not, apparently, the people's improper slaughter of the spoil, which Saul's altar seemingly rectifies.[25] The effect of all these unfortunate occurrences is cumulative. Saul, for all his effort, cannot do the right thing. And what of Jonathan? Jonathan violated his father's ban unwittingly. His eating the honey has a coincidental quality about it reminiscent of the "coincidental" appearance of Jephthah's daughter as the only "one coming forth" to meet him. If the honey simply were not "there," accessible, readily edible – Jonathan has merely to reach out his staff to taste it – the infraction probably would not have occurred.

Like Jephthah's daughter, Jonathan is a victim – a victim, however, not just of his father's oath but, more pointedly, of his father's rejection by Yhwh. The account of Jonathan's heroism and military success is framed by the two accounts of Saul's rejection, dismissing from the start any prospect Jonathan might have had as Israel's future leader. The young soldier who so boldly faced a

Philistine garrison with only his armor-bearer to back him up is strikingly absent when Goliath issues his challenge for an Israelite to meet him in hand-to-hand combat. It is left for David to take up that challenge, with words of confidence in Yhwh similar to Jonathan's (compare 17:47 with 14:6). Before Jonathan appears again in the narrative, we meet David as the man chosen by Yhwh after his own heart, and we witness his secret anointing (1 Samuel 16). From this time on, until his death, Jonathan is effectively subordinated to David; he (re)acts in relation to David, to support him against his father Saul and against his own interests as heir apparent.

Immediately following David's defeat of Goliath, Jonathan appears on the scene, entirely won over by the young hero (1 Sam. 18:1). His love for David is sudden, unexplained, and inexplicable. Not only will it induce him to yield his rightful claim to the throne without so much as a protest, but it will also lead him to conspire against the incumbent king, his father. Because he loves him as himself,[26] Jonathan makes a covenant with David, the nature of which is not yet revealed to us, and he hands over to David the trappings of kingship, his robe, his armor, his sword, his bow, and his girdle. Though he earlier refused Saul's armor (17:38–9), David accepts from Jonathan these royal symbols – a sign that what he could not _take_ from Saul, who wants to retain the kingship, he can _receive_ from Jonathan, who is willing to give it up. Jonathan, the popular hero of 1 Samuel 14, recedes into the background. Saul places David, not Jonathan, in command of the troops (18:5), and the women's victory song (v. 7), destined to become so widespread that even Philistines quote it (1 Sam. 21:11; 29:5), praises Saul's and David's heroism, not Jonathan's (though to Saul's dismay, David receives greater acclaim).

When next we hear of Jonathan, Saul has made known his intention to kill David: "Saul told Jonathan his son and all his servants that they should kill David" (1 Sam. 19:1). Initiative is entirely on Jonathan's part, whose affection for David is again singled out for attention, "Jonathan, Saul's son, took much delight in David." David does not speak in this scene. At Jonathan's suggestion, he hides in the field while Jonathan intercedes with Saul on his behalf, pleading his innocence ("Why will you sin against innocent blood by killing David without cause?") and citing his service to Saul ("for he took his life in his hand and he slew the Philistine").[27] Jonathan successfully reconciles his father to his friend. Saul "listened to [or obeyed] the voice of Jonathan," a phrase that recalls his rejection as king because he "listened to [or obeyed] the voice of the people" and did not "obey the voice of Yhwh."

Not surprisingly, the reconciliation is short-lived. The text says that David was in Saul's presence "as before"; but "before," Saul had tried to kill David while under the influence of an evil spirit from God (1 Sam. 18:10–11), and this happens again (19:9–10). A further attempt by Saul on David's life is thwarted by Michal, and David flees to Samuel at Ramah.

Corresponding to the scene where Jonathan achieves a reconciliation between Saul and David, we have in 1 Samuel 20 an episode where he fails to do so. The incidents are similar in that again Jonathan pleads David's cause and argues his innocence, and David hides in the field to learn the outcome. Here, however, David initiates the action. He returns from Ramah to confront Jonathan with his anxiety over his safety. Jonathan's love for David continues to play a deciding role. Once more the narrator informs us that Jonathan loved David as he loved himself (1 Sam. 20:17).[28] In the only dialogue that ever takes place between them, David invokes Jonathan's friendship ("I have found favor in your eyes," 1 Sam. 20:3) and their covenant ("You have brought your servant into a covenant of Yhwh with you," v. 8) in order to encourage Jonathan's support. His overriding concern is his own welfare. Jonathan's responses reveal his concerns and indicate for the first time his awareness (a presentiment, perhaps, of his tragic destiny) that David's future kingship poses a threat to him and his house. In return for the throne, as it were, Jonathan wants a promise. He adjures David to show loyalty to him while he lives and to his house after he is dead (v. 14). And he calls on Yhwh as witness, "Yhwh is between me and you forever" (v. 23).

Jonathan tries but fails to achieve a reconciliation between his father and his friend. Furious at Jonathan for taking David's part, Saul puts bluntly what Jonathan must now know and accept, "For as long as the son of Jesse lives upon the earth, neither you nor your kingdom shall be established." When Jonathan protests David's innocence, as he had earlier ("Why should he be put to death? What has he done?"), Saul casts his spear at Jonathan, as he had cast it before at David. As Jobling points out, Jonathan's identification with David is here complete.[29] Saul's dramatic gesture and Jonathan's fierce anger widen the rift between father and son.

When Jonathan reveals Saul's evil intentions to David, they part dramatically amid kissing and weeping. Overcome by emotion, Jonathan still manages to reiterate his concern for his house, "Yhwh shall be between me and you and between my descendants and your descendants for ever." That David speaks no parting words is characteristic of him in the account of his rise to power, where we know little, if anything, about his feelings and intentions.[30]

Is Jonathan entirely altruistic, or is his support of David partially motivated by anxiety over the fate of his progeny under a Davidic king (an apprehension that future events will show to be well-founded)?[31] The biblical narrator places in his mouth two statements that further complicate the portrayal of Jonathan. "May Yhwh be with you as he was with my father" (1 Sam. 20:13) sounds a discordant note, given Yhwh's treatment of Saul. But Jonathan also says, "May Yhwh requite the enemies of David" (v. 16). Since we know "Saul was David's enemy continually" (1 Sam. 18:29; cf. 19:17), is Jonathan, knowingly or unintentionally, calling down divine wrath upon his own father?

A mere three verses describe the next, and final, encounter between Jonathan and David, with speech attributed only to Jonathan:

Jonathan, Saul's son, went to David at Horesh and strengthened his hand in God. He said to him, "Do not be afraid, for the hand of Saul my father will not find you; you shall rule over Israel and I will be your second-in-command. Moreover, Saul my father knows this." The two of them made a covenant before Yhwh. David remained in Horesh, and Jonathan went to his house. (1 Sam. 23:16–18)

Whereas in the corresponding scene, 1 Sam. 18:1–4, Jonathan symbolically gave David the kingship, here he verbally acknowledges David's future rule, with himself second in rank to David (*mishneh*). As in 1 Samuel 18, the two men make a covenant. This is the first we hear of Jonathan's role under David's rule, and it sounds as if Jonathan is attempting to secure a place for himself, unless we take "your second" to be totally devoid of political implications.[32] Jonathan's behavior seems to confirm his father's worst suspicions, "my son has stirred up my servant against me, to lie in wait as at this day" (1 Sam. 22:8).

But Jonathan is no traitor. In 1 Samuel 31, we find him once again fighting at his father's side, as he did when he was introduced in 1 Samuel 13–14. Their earlier battle against the Philistines ended in victory, though as we saw, a marred one. Death was threatened for Jonathan, but averted. The battle on Mount Gilboa ends in defeat for Israel and death for Saul and his sons, Jonathan, Abinadab, and Malchishua. Jonathan's allegiance to the house of Saul is symbolically affirmed. At the same time, his death removes the danger he represents, actual or potential, to David's advancement.

MICHAL

For a woman silence and discretion
are best, and staying inside quietly at home.
Euripides, *Heraclidae*

Saul and Jonathan die violent, bloody deaths on the field of battle, deaths befitting heroes. Saul's suicide has particularly tragic force as his last desperate attempt to control his destiny. His daughter Michal meets a woman's tragic end, denied children and voice (and thereby narrative presence) in one fatal stroke. Her heated quarrel with David over his behavior before the ark of Yhwh ends in David's having the last word, a cruel rebuttal that is followed by the narrator's laconic comment: "Michal, Saul's daughter, had no child to the day of her death." Yet, like her brother Jonathan, she loved David. Whereas Jonathan's love remained constant, Michal's turns to bitterness and rage. How are we to understand her passage from love to hatred, recounted as it is in snatches and obscured by narrative silences? We may begin with an overview of Michal's place in the narrative, where she plays a minor but significant role in the tragedy of Saul's house:

1 Samuel 14   Michal is introduced in the list of Saul's children.
1 Samuel 18   *Saul's daughter Michal* loves David; Saul uses her as a "trap," in the hope that David will be killed trying to meet the bride price of one hundred Philistine foreskins. She becomes David's *wife*.
1 Samuel 19   *Michal, David's wife*, allies herself with David against her father, saves David's life by orchestrating his escape through the window, and lies to Saul to conceal her involvement.
1 Sam. 25:44   Saul had given *Michal, his daughter, David's wife* to Palti.
2 Samuel 3   David tells Abner he must bring *Michal, Saul's daughter* to him; tells Ishbosheth to return "*my wife Michal,*

whom I betrothed at the price of one hundred Philistine foreskins." Michal is sent to David.

2 Samuel 6 *Michal, Saul's daughter*, sees, through the window, David and "all the house of Israel" rejoicing before the ark. She and David quarrel. Michal has no children.

2 Sam. 21:8–9 David hands over the five sons of *Michal* [or Merab?], *Saul's daughter*, to the Gibeonites for execution.

Michal is introduced as Saul's younger daughter in 1 Sam. 14:49. That "Michal Saul's daughter loved David" is significant for our understanding of Michal, not least because it is the only time the Bible tells us that a woman loves a man. When he learns of his daughter's love for David, Saul is pleased and uses the opportunity to dangle a desirable prize before his rival: "become the king's son-in-law." He hopes that David will be killed trying to meet the bride price of a hundred Philistine foreskins. But why should it matter to Saul that Michal loves David? What do the woman's feelings have to do with it? Saul had already tempted David with his older daughter Merab – where love is not mentioned – but he gave her to another (1 Sam. 18:17–19). Even earlier, the reward for killing Goliath was rumored to be marriage to the king's daughter (1 Sam. 17:25). Thus, for the charmed third time, David has a chance at what Saul seems unwilling to let him have. From Saul's perspective, Michal's love for David may be convenient but otherwise largely gratuitous. It would be much more to Saul's advantage if David loved Michal – but that is precisely what the text leaves unsaid, suggesting, as I indicated above, that David's motives, like Saul's, are purely political. Saul even appears to recognize the threat Michal's love for David poses for him:

When Saul saw and knew that Yhwh was with David, and that Michal Saul's daughter loved him, Saul was still more afraid of David.[33]

And rightly so, for in the next chapter, Michal defies her father by helping David escape Saul's attempt on his life (1 Sam. 19:11–17).

In saving David from Saul, Michal loses him, for he leaves his house-within-Saul's-house, his advantageous position as the "king's son-in-law," never to return. He does return to meet Jonathan and to conspire with him to discover Saul's intentions (1 Samuel 20) and he hides for three days until Jonathan brings him news – but all this time, he apparently makes no effort to see Michal. His leave-taking from Jonathan is tearful and dramatic, unlike his exit in 1 Samuel 19,

where he practically bolts out the window. He has no parting words
for Michal, in fact, no words at all.[34] Nor does David include his wife
Michal when he arranges refuge for his parents with the king of Moab
(1 Sam. 22:3–4). He thereby consigns her proleptically and
permanently to Saul's house, for she will not again be "David's wife"
in any real sense.

David becomes a fugitive and an outlaw, futilely pursued by Saul,
and he manages to gain not one, but two wives while roaming about
the countryside (1 Sam. 25:42–3). At this point we learn that Saul
had given Michal to Palti, the son of Laish (1 Sam. 25:44).[35] Time
passes, Saul is killed in battle at Gilboa (1 Samuel 31), and David is
anointed king over Judah. About Michal we hear nothing further
until David is offered the opportunity to become king over the
northern tribes. (In the meantime David has acquired more wives
and many children, 2 Sam. 3:2–5.) Then he does precisely what Saul
had sought to prevent; he demands the return of his wife Michal in
an apparent move to lay claim to Saul's throne. The actual reunion
is not reported, a highly significant textual gap that suggests a
volatile subtext.

Michal appears as an agent in her own right in two important
scenes, 1 Samuel 19, where she allies herself with David over against
her father Saul, and 2 Samuel 6, where she takes the part of her
father's house over against her husband David. Apart from these
scenes, she neither speaks nor initiates action, but rather is the object
of the political machinations of the two men, who are locked in bitter
rivalry over the kingship. The account of her loyalty to David and
defiance of Saul is framed by occasions where Saul uses her for
political ends at David's expense. His motive is stated in 1 Samuel 18,
"Saul thought to make David fall by the hand of the Philistines,"
whereas in 1 Samuel 25:44 it is reasonable to assume that he gives
Michal to another man to prevent the fugitive David from claiming
the throne through her. Michal's confrontation with David and
identification with her father's house is preceded by the account of
David's using her to bolster his title to the throne (2 Samuel 3) and
followed by that of David's complicity in the execution of Saul's –
Michal's or Merab's? – descendants (2 Samuel 21), a step that
removes any remaining Saulide claimant to the throne (his sparing of
the lame Mephibosheth has dubious significance). The use of epithets
for Michal is especially revealing.[36] When passed back and forth
among men for political purposes, she is referred to as both Saul's

daughter and David's wife (1 Sam. 18:20, 27, 28; 25:44; 2 Sam. 3:13, 14) – an indication of her political importance to both houses. The nature of the Saulide–Davidic rivalry, however, the exclusiveness of the claim of each to the throne, makes it impossible for Michal to belong to both houses at once.

Michal is "hemmed in" narratively – the scenes where she is a subject are surrounded by scenes in which she is "acted upon," first by her father, then by her husband – just as she is hemmed in by the men's political maneuvering. Significantly, the scene in which Michal acts autonomously as "David's wife" is surrounded by accounts in which she is "acted upon" by her father Saul; and the scene in which she acts autonomously as "Saul's daughter" is framed by accounts where she is "acted upon" by her husband David. This narrative imprisonment underscores the impossibility of autonomy for Michal and represents, in the surface structure of the text, the confinement we shall explore below in the image of the woman at the window.

As a woman, Michal is not free to choose between conflicting allegiances in an open, political way – in the way, for example, Jonathan is free to align himself with David against his father's will. Her father even exploits her love for David to serve himself. He marries her off to David, but he also takes her back and gives her to another. In the struggle over the kingship, Saul is destined to fail, while David, supported by Yhwh, emerges as victor. David's demand for Michal's return indicates his readiness to use her to further his political ambitions and shows how futile was Saul's attempt to thwart him by giving Michal to another man. David buttresses his demand by referring to the bride price he paid for Michal, doubtless a way of stressing the legitimacy of his claim.[37] The last reference to Michal, if indeed it refers to her – some ancient witnesses read "Merab" for the Masoretic text's "Michal" in 2 Sam. 21:8 – calls her "Saul's daughter," for the rival claims to the throne have been resolved in favor of David, and Michal has forfeited her role in the Davidic house.

Although she cannot act with political autonomy, in the scenes where she is the subject of action Michal exercises the freedom to take sides denied to her elsewhere, supporting first her husband, but ultimately representing her father's house. Significantly, Michal is called "David's wife" when she defies her father and orchestrates David's escape, and "Saul's daughter" when she challenges her husband. Thus it is as rival's wife – not daughter – that Michal confronts her father, the king, in 1 Samuel 19, and as rival's daughter – not wife – that she confronts her husband, the king, in 2 Samuel 6. The tension between Michal's lack of autonomy and her attempts to assert her will intensifies her tragic plight, particularly in view of the fatal nature of her final attempt. Like her father Saul, she wrestles against her limitations, protests her fate, but whereas the king's struggle is depicted against the grand backdrop of affairs of state, his daughter's is given a "domestic" context. She cannot avoid her tragic fate as a member of Saul's house; she can only protest it, and that she does forcefully in 2 Samuel 6.

In 2 Samuel 6, David twice seeks to bring the ark of the covenant of Yhwh to Jerusalem, a move that lends religious authority to his newly established kingdom. The first attempt fails when Yhwh strikes Uzzah for touching the ark and David is afraid to bring the ark into the city. The second attempt succeeds, though here, too, an unexpected event disturbs the mood of jubilation: a conflict between Michal and David that remains unresolved. The rift is not only inevitable, given the resentment Michal must surely feel over the way she has been treated, but also essential, since any possibility that Michal and David might have a child, who as a scion of both royal houses might someday reign, must be ruled out – otherwise Saul's tragedy would not be complete. Saul's house no longer stands in David's way: Ishbosheth and Abner have been treacherously murdered, and David has just been anointed king over the northern tribes, making him king of a united Israel and Judah. The account of Michal and David's quarrel and Michal's childlessness appears in a context where the crucial concerns are royal progeny and succession. It is preceded by a list of David's many children born in Jerusalem (2 Sam. 5: 13–16), adding to those born in Hebron (2 Sam. 3: 2–5), and followed by the famous dynastic oracle to David in 2 Samuel 7, promising the kingship to David's descendants forever. The events of 2 Samuel 6 resolve a potential political problem by guaranteeing that a descendant of Saul, a member of the rejected house, will not rule.[38]

The key issues in 2 Samuel 6 are the "house" (David comes to bless his house), the kingship (both Michal and David refer to it), and the blessing (the ark conveys blessing to Obed-edom's house; David blesses the people; he comes to bless his house, but no blessing ensues for Michal, who represents Saul's house within David's). Verse 16 is pivotal:

As the ark of Yhwh entered the city of David, Michal the daughter of Saul looked down from the window and saw King David leaping and cavorting[39] before Yhwh. And she despised him in her heart.

For the first time since telling us Michal loved David, the text permits us access to her feelings. Why does she despise him? Robert Alter offers a perceptive analysis of the considerable pent-up jealousy, anguish, and fury that must lie behind Michal's emotional explosion.[40] That her love has turned to hatred serves as a pointed indication of her suffering at David's hands. Berlin alerts us to the narrative subtlety of v. 16 that allows us to see things from Michal's point of view. Michal sees David "leaping and whirling" (*mepazzez umekarker*), more exaggerated behavior, claims Berlin, than the narrator's portrait of David's "whirling with all his might" (*mekarker bekol 'oz*, v. 14) or David's own perspective, "dancing" (*wesihaqti*, v. 21).[41] But Michal sees more than this. What makes the leaping and cavorting so offensive? Is it not that "David the king," who has replaced her father, dances triumphantly "before Yhwh," who brought about the downfall of her father's house, while Michal remains inside, watching "all the house of Israel" celebrate? Verse 16 makes no mention of Michal's reaction to the way David was clad; that is revealed when she ventures outside to confront the king:

David returned to bless his house, and Michal the daughter of Saul went out to meet David. She said, "How the king of Israel has honored himself today, exposing himself today in the eyes of his subjects' women servants as one of the worthless fellows flagrantly exposes himself." (2 Sam. 6:20)

It doesn't take a psychologist to recognize that Michal's complaint about David's attire, or lack of it, is not the real issue. That the real issue in this dramatic domestic dispute is the kingship can be seen from Michal's speech, in which she refers to David as the "king of Israel," and in David's retort, which takes up first the subject of kingship, stressing Yhwh's preference for him over the whole of Saul's house, and only then turns to the matter of his comportment:

David said to Michal, "Before Yhwh who chose me over your father and over all his house to appoint me king-elect over the people of Yhwh, over Israel – I will dance before Yhwh. And I shall dishonor myself even more than this and be abased in my eyes, but among the women servants of whom you have spoken, among them I shall be held in honor." (2 Sam. 6:21-2)

Surely the emphasis on Saul's rejection – "over your father," "over all his house" – and on the magnitude of David's kingdom – "over the people of Yhwh," "over Israel" – ensures that the effect

will not be lost on Michal.[42] And divine sanction is accentuated by
the repetition of "before Yhwh" (*lipne yhwh*) at the beginning and
end of the first part of David's rebuke, the part dealing with the
kingship. We see in David's response to Michal what was so neatly
concealed in his relationship with Jonathan, and resolved by
Jonathan's death: David's taking the kingship from Saul's house. We
recall, also, that though Saul repeatedly sought to kill David, David
refused to strike out against "Yhwh's anointed" (1 Samuel 24 and
26), choosing instead to become a fugitive and outlaw until the time
was right. The hostility one would have expected David to express
toward Saul, who sought his life, and toward Jonathan, who as heir
to the throne stood in David's way, is directed toward Michal, where
it offers less of a threat. The problem at the political level is
symbolically resolved by foregrounding a less consequential level, the
domestic one. The resolution is simply a displacement. The animosity
between the house of David and the house of Saul is played out in
2 Samuel 6 as a marital conflict, complete with sexual insinuations
and implications. Michal accuses David of sexual vulgarity, of
displaying himself flagrantly. The consequences strike her at a sexual
level; she has no child.

There is no evidence David ever had any real feeling for Michal,
anything resembling her love for him. In discussing Michal's
understandable metamorphosis from love to hatred, commentators
allude to Michal's feelings of anger and humiliation at being used by
David for political purposes and particularly at being neglected by
him as a wife practically since the beginning of their relationship.[43]
That sexual jealousy plays a role finds support in the sexual
innuendos. It is tempting to speculate about Michal's feelings and
motivations throughout the narrative. The supplying of motivation,
however, can go in all directions, as Peter Miscall demonstrates in his
literary commentary on 1 Samuel; and it is not always a useful
pursuit.[44] Encouraging such speculation by means of what Alter calls
"the 'overdetermined' nature of [Michal's] contemptuous ire"[45]
belongs to the narrative's strategy of displacement. Focusing on the
domestic scene takes our attention away from the political issue that
is quite clearly at stake: the end of perhaps the most important
branch of Saul's line. The politics of gender serve the politics of
state.[46]

David the king wields the power and has the last word. They are
also his only words to Michal. The final word of his retort, "I will be
honored" (*'ikkabedah*), picks up Michal's first words, "How he has

honored himself (*nikbad*) today, the king of Israel!," as if to demonstrate, in Humpty-Dumpty fashion, that the one in power decides the meaning of honor. But David also speaks of the reverse: *uneqalloti*, "I will make myself light (dishonored)," is the opposite of *'ikkabedah*, "I will be heavy (honored)." How will he abase himself? I suggest the next verse hints at the answer: by ceasing to have sexual relations with Michal, by putting aside the woman who earlier saved his life.[47] If we follow the Septuagint in reading "be abased in your eyes," then David equates dishonor in Michal's view with public honor. If, on the other hand, we accept the Masoretic text's "in my eyes," perhaps David reveals his discomfort with this necessary solution to the issue of succession. The juxtaposition of David's rebuke and the narrative comment that Michal had no children invites the positing of a causal connection.[48] That the text is not explicit, however, renders Michal's childless plight more poignant in that we cannot specifically locate its cause. I spoke above of narrative displacement. We could also borrow from psychoanalytic literary theory the concept of repression. The silence surrounding the reason for Michal's childlessness may hint at the text's uneasiness about the precise location of responsibility. Have we here a case of male solidarity between the narrator and David? Or since it is Yhwh who opens and closes the womb (Gen. 20:18; 29:31; 30:2, 22; 1 Sam. 1:5, 6; Isa. 66:9), does the textual reticence point to the deity, yielding a situation of cruel coincidence reminiscent of the "secret cause" of Jephthah's tragedy?[49]

Possibly it is Michal who refuses to have sexual relations with David, for refusal would not be out of character for her. Given the cultural, and also here the political, context, it is most likely that Michal is the object of her husband's whim. The fact, however, that commentators do not even raise the possibility of Michal's refusal once again robs Michal of autonomy and is an example of what Esther Fuchs calls reinscribing patriarchal ideology.[50]

To appreciate more fully the tragically cruel reversal of Michal's fortunes, replaying the reversal of her feelings for David, let us look more closely at the relationship between 1 Samuel 19, where she is disloyal to Saul to save her husband, and 2 Samuel 6, where she represents a voice of protest from her father's house when she criticizes David. In 1 Samuel 19, Michal saves David's life by letting him down through the window when Saul's messengers come to kill him. She deceives the messengers, and gains time for David to escape, by disguising an image in his bed and claiming that David is ill. When Saul discovers the ruse and questions her, Michal lies to conceal her accountability, claiming that David threatened her life. Judging from Saul's response to Jonathan in 1 Samuel 20, when he casts his spear at him for abetting David, Michal's life might have been in jeopardy had she not fabricated a clever alibi.[51]

In 1 Samuel 19 David flees his house; in 2 Samuel 6 he comes to bless his house. He has come a long way, from fugitive to king of a united Israel. And what of Michal, whose journey has also been considerable, though of a different nature, from love to hate? Her watching through the window as David and the people celebrate the ark's procession recalls her saving David by letting him down through the window, and the recurrence of the phrase "through the window" (*be'ad haḥallon*) draws attention to Michal's place inside, confined. The text provides our window on Michal, offering us only a glimpse, the kind of view a window gives, limited in range and perspective. We are, as it were, outside, watching her, inside, watching David. The woman at the window is a well-known ancient Near Eastern motif, for which we have both archaeological and textual evidence.[52] The woman looks out upon the world to see what men have accomplished. In 2 Kings 9:30, for example, Queen Jezebel, having painted her eyes and adorned her head, looks out the window for the insurgent Jehu's arrival, apparently knowing what ferocity to expect from him. And Sisera's mother peers out the window, watching in vain for her son's return from battle laden with spoil (Judges 5:28).

The house is frequently in literature a metonymical symbol of woman. By letting David out the window – and Michal is the subject of all three verbs, *wattored* ("let [David] down"), *watteshalleḥi* ("let [my enemy] go"), *shalleḥini* ("let me go") – Michal figuratively births David into freedom. David, in 1 Samuel 19, passes through the vagina/window into the larger world, so to speak, to meet his destiny. Michal stays behind, inside, attending to matters innocently domestic – making the bed, caring for the sick. She manages David's escape through deception, frequently, though not exclusively, a woman's way of exercising power.[53]

In 2 Samuel 6, Michal remains inside while "David and all the house of Israel" (v. 15) are outside celebrating the ark's arrival in Jerusalem. References to "all the people, the whole multitude of Israel, both men and women" and "all the people" in v. 19

underscore Michal's isolation. When she goes outside to confront David (2 Sam. 6:20), she triggers a conflict that ends in disaster. In Euripides' *Heraclidae*, Macaria, before she embarks on her tragic fate as sacrificial victim, observes that it is best for a woman to remain inside her house. Whereas Michal was able to exercise power "inside" in 1 Samuel 19, David has the power "outside," in society – reflecting the conventional notion that women hold sway over domestic matters but men rule the world.[54] The emotional tension unleashed in 2 Samuel 6, when Michal vents her frustration, makes 1 Samuel 19, where she remains "domesticated," almost claustrophobic by comparison. Michal has stepped outside her "place"; she has seen fit to criticize the king, and she does so not as the king's wife but, what is worse, as the representative of the rejected house, as "Saul's daughter." As a consequence of her bold outspokenness, Michal becomes a victim. Ironically she had presented herself as a potential victim in 1 Samuel 19, claiming that David threatened, "Why should I kill you?"[55] The last word of that account is *'amitek* ("kill you"), and it reappears hauntingly as the last word of 2 Samuel 6, "until the day of her death" (*motah*).

Who are the "women servants of his male servants" (*'amhot 'abadav*), who, according to Michal, have relished David's sexual display, and by whom David avows he will be held in honor? These women are doubly subordinated – by sex, to all of David's male subjects or servants, and by class, to the royal couple, whose mutual rebukes derive their sting from the imputation of inferior status to these women. Whether or not Michal means to include the "(primary) wives of the free Israelites" in her reproach,[56] by implying that these women are below her dignity, she aims to disgrace the king, who turns her words around ultimately to shame the queen. A class issue intrudes to set the women over against each other.[57] Michal's privilege as a king's daughter and a king's wife isolates her from these women. By having her oppose herself to them, while David professes (at least) solidarity with them, the narrative leaves her to stand alone against the authority of her husband the king. Her isolation, so clearly signified by the picture of her inside watching the public spectacle from the window, is now complete.

Depriving her of children is a symbolic way of killing Michal. Denying her a reply to David kills her off as a narrative presence, except for her unexpected reemergence in 2 Samuel 21 as the mother of five sons. What are we to make of that reference?

The king took the two sons of Rizpah the daughter of Aiah, whom she bore
to Saul, Armoni and Mephibosheth; and the five sons of Michal, the
daughter of Saul, whom she bore to Adriel the son of Barzillai the
Meholathite; and he gave them into the hand of the Gibeonites, and they
dismembered them on the mountain before Yhwh. (2 Sam. 21:8–9)

The usual solution is to read "Merab" instead of "Michal" with a
number of ancient manuscripts, since Merab, Saul's older daughter,
was the wife of Adriel the Meholathite (see 1 Sam. 18:19).[58] Thus
Michal's suppression and humiliation become complete: she loses her
name to a variant. Does the confusion of the names reflect the easy
confusion of women in general: Michal and Merab are both
daughters of Saul, so what difference does it make whose sons are
sacrificed? Or might we view the appearance of Michal's name as a
sign of her refusal to be written out of the story, as undermining the
claim in 2 Sam. 6:23 that she had no children? If so, her attempt to
gain control of her story is once again tragically thwarted: the
narrative gives her children only to take them away again.

Whereas the window plays an important role in both accounts, the
bed, a key term in 1 Samuel 19, is conspicuously absent in 2 Samuel 6.
Jan Fokkelman discusses the window and bed in 1 Samuel 19 as
indices of movement and standstill, representing life versus death for
David.[59] Whereas this symbolism may fit David's (male) perspective,
neither image has positive meaning for Michal, for David's escape
through the window is his departure from the conjugal bed. Michal's
ruse in disguising the image involves the difference between
appearance and reality. David was not in his bed, though Saul's
messengers believed him to be there. After their angry confrontation
does David no longer share Michal's bed? 2 Samuel 6 leaves us with
a situation not unlike the illusion created in 1 Samuel 19 for the
guards, only this time *we* are the ones who do not know whether
David is in his bed or not.

Like her brother Jonathan, Michal has only one dialogue with
David. His only words to her are words of rebuke.[60] By alienating
David, Michal forfeits the recognition she might have received as
queen. But the fact that she is inside and plays no role in all Israel's
celebration of the ark reveals her exclusion and already suggests that
she will likely not fill this role. She might have gained status as
mother, and eventually queen mother, a part resourcefully played by
Bathsheba, but after her confrontation with David, this role is also
denied her.[61] Her losses, then, are many and significant: David,

whom she loved; Paltiel, who appears to have loved her; royal status and recognition; and, finally, offspring a woman of her time so desperately needed.

I observed earlier that Jonathan replaces his sister as love-object. The converse also holds true: Michal replaces Jonathan as object of David's hostility. As we have seen, where conflict should have taken place – between David and the rightful "heir" to the throne – there is harmony. The conflict arises between David and his wife from the royal line, where a suitable *political* resolution (though one impossible theologically) could have occurred. A political problem (David's accession to the throne and, implicitly, his dealings with Saul's house) becomes an individual, "family" matter that, in its turn, only thinly disguises the issue of gender and the dynamics of sexual politics. The narrative amalgamates the public and the private, national concerns and individual tensions, and foregrounds conflicts at other levels: relation by blood versus relation by marriage, male versus female. In the handling of these complex issues, the daughter of Saul is sacrificed that the son may be honored.

The fates of Jonathan and Michal are gender-specific.[62] The young prince dies a hero's death on the battlefield. Because he dies early, he will not have to witness the progressive debasement of his father's house. He mediates the kingship to David on an ideological level, but he does not live to face the actual problem of transition. He is spared, in other words, the indignities Michal must endure. For her there is no graceful exit in honorable death by the sword, death that exalts male courage. A woman's tragic fortune is to survive, to remain on the scene, watching as others benefit from her family's losses. To live in the victor's house as an outsider, as "Saul's daughter," excluded from celebration that includes "all the people, the whole multitude of Israel, men and women," is a grievous injury. Michal protests, but, as is frequently the case in a protest that issues out of weakness, to no avail, and to her detriment.

Because he has no direct role in Jonathan's death, David can lament it; he is strongly implicated, however, in Michal's tragic fate. Male rivals are honored publicly. David laments the deaths not only of Saul and Jonathan but also of Abner, and he has words of esteem for Ishbosheth, whose death he avenges. The issue is not whether or not his sentiments are genuine but that they are given public expression. One can easily posit political motives for David's display of grief over the deaths of members of the rival house, which, no doubt, still had its loyal supporters. Even David's lament over Jonathan is not without its ambiguities. There is, for one thing, the issue of who loved whom. D. N. Freedman construes the anomalous verb form *npl'th* in 2 Sam. 1:26 as *nipla' 'attah*, and translates, "You were extraordinary. Loving you, for me, was better than loving women,"[63] a sentiment that suggests David loved Jonathan more than David loved women, or, that David preferred male bonding to involvement with women – an appropriate commentary on David's less-than-ideal relationships with women. It may also suggest David gained more from his relationship with Jonathan, though he gained substantially through his liaison with Abigail. But nowhere is it unambiguously stated that David loved Jonathan, whereas it is frequently mentioned that Jonathan loved David. If we take *npl'th* as an archaic form for the sake of assonance, as W. L. Holladay suggests, we may translate, "your love for me was wonderful, beyond the love of women," a reading also supported by the Septuagint.[64] Jonathan loved David more than women loved David – or, as I proposed above, more than women love men in general. After all, it is a magnanimous gesture to give up a throne for one's friend.

Another curious point in David's lament over Saul and Jonathan concerns v. 23. Again, there is disagreement over the proper division and translation of the verse, but if we follow the Masoretic text and translate, "Saul and Jonathan, beloved and beautiful, in their lives and in their deaths they were not divided," we can only marvel at David's poetic liberty. Saul and Jonathan were acutely divided in life – over David! David's lament, a moving public tribute to the king and his heir, is not to be accepted uncritically, and we should not allow its beautiful cadences and lofty sentiments to obscure its ironies and ambiguities.

In conclusion, we might consider the relation between autonomy and gender, and between discourse, autonomy, and progeny. Jonathan, who as a man could be autonomous without censure, cannot be truly autonomous because of his role as mediator. Michal, as a woman, ought not to act autonomously, and because she dares to try, we should not be surprised to see her put in her place by an angry and dismissive husband. Both Michal and Jonathan have only one dialogue with David; Jonathan, however, speaks in a number of scenes. His speeches offer no resistance to David: on the one hand, they encourage him; on the other, they seek to ensure the welfare of Jonathan's descendants. Michal's one speech voices resistance and dissatisfaction. Her angry words are a claim for attention, ineffectively challenging David on behalf of her father's house. David's reply abruptly cuts off her protest, and her childlessness cuts off a branch of the Saulide line.

Saul's line continues in Jonathan's progeny, also marked for misfortune. Jonathan's young son Mephibosheth is crippled as the result of being dropped by his nurse, who hastily flees with him when she hears the news of the deaths of Saul and Jonathan (2 Sam. 4:4). Lameness renders him an unlikely candidate for the throne, and thus less of an obstacle to David's accession. And what, we might ask, comes of the promises Jonathan extracted from David to deal loyally with his house? David claims to show loyalty to Mephibosheth "for Jonathan's sake" (2 Sam. 9:1), and he spares Mephibosheth's life "because of the oath of Yhwh which was between them, between David and Jonathan," when the Gibeonites demand blood for blood (2 Sam. 21:7). But perhaps Mephibosheth eats at the king's table so that David can keep an eye on him. We know incidentally from 2 Sam. 5:8 that David hates the lame and the blind. That no trust binds David to Jonathan's son seems clear from 2 Samuel 16:1–4 and 19:24–30, where David appears unable to evaluate Mephibosheth's loyalty. Jonathan does not live to become David's "second-in-command" (1 Sam. 23:17), nor is a place of honor held by a descendant of Jonathan. Mephibosheth plays no real role in David's kingdom, and his son Mica (2 Sam. 9:12; "Micah" in 1 Chr. 8:34) simply drops out of the picture. Jonathan, it appears, cannot guarantee a future for his descendants, even at the price of autonomy. Saul's house is fated, and none of its members remains untouched by tragedy.

Michal's outburst, together with Shimei's curses (2 Sam. 16:5–13), Sheba's revolt (2 Samuel 20), and Rizpah's silent resistance (2 Samuel 21), protest against David's royal privilege at the expense of the house of Saul. David's dealings with Saul's house are complex and open to question. He is loyal to "Yhwh's anointed"; on two occasions he spares Saul's life, but robs him of any dignity by pointing out Saul's impotence (1 Samuel 24 and 26). He treats Jonathan well, for the two of them have a covenant; but the covenant appears to be Jonathan's idea, and serves chiefly to protect Jonathan's descendants. David is exonerated in the deaths of Abner and Ishbosheth, but the circumstances cast suspicion on him: his general Joab kills Abner in cold blood, and the murderers of Ishbosheth come to David for a reward. Though proclaimed innocent, David benefits from their deaths. Toward Michal he behaves cruelly; his treatment of Mephibosheth is questionable; and, after the painful experience of losing sons of his own, he hands over seven of Saul's "sons" to the Gibeonites for execution. David had earlier sworn to Saul that he would not cut off his descendants (1 Sam. 24:21–2). As we shall see below, Rizpah's silent protest at this last act, her appeal beyond the reach of language, is more effective than Michal's emotional outburst. With Saul's house essentially destroyed, Rizpah's deed will bring its tragedy to closure.

ABNER AND ISHBOSHETH

> In der Tragödie wird leicht der Anschein erweckt,
> als müßte der Untergang des Einzelnen irgend ein gestörtes
> Gleichgewicht der Dinge wieder herstellen.
> [In tragedy, the impression is readily created
> that the fall of the individual necessarily redresses
> some kind of imbalance in things.]
>
> Franz Rosenzweig

Unlike Saul and Jonathan, who perish heroically in battle, Saul's general Abner and Saul's son Ishbosheth die unworthy deaths, unseemly deaths for an army commander and a king. The violent and ignominious ends they meet provide yet another gruesome episode in the troubled history of Saul's house. Both men are murdered in cold blood, struck in the belly, caught off-guard and unsuspecting. Believing he and David have formed an alliance, Abner leaves David's presence "in peace" (2 Sam. 3:21, 22, 23). But why, rather than becoming suspicious when messengers summon him back, does he unhesitatingly turn aside to speak privately with Joab, who was not present during his negotiations with David and who had good reason to hate him? Joab's brutal assassination of Abner, later described by David as shedding blood of war in time of peace (1 Kings 2:5), occurs almost effortlessly, facilitated by Abner's lack of caution and by circumstances favoring Joab. Where, for example, are the twenty men who had accompanied Abner on his mission (3:20)? Not long after Joab kills Abner, Ishbosheth is ruthlessly murdered in his sleep, that most peaceful state of total vulnerability. Like his father Saul, whom the Philistines decapitated when they found his body on Mount Gilboa (1 Sam. 31:9–10), Ishbosheth is beheaded, and the assassins, his own officers, journey all night with their trophy to present David this gory token of victory over his "enemy." The two men tell David that "Yhwh has vindicated my lord the king this day against Saul and against his offspring" (2 Sam. 4:8), and though David takes offense, their words ring true.

No familial tomb accommodates Abner's body; his burial takes place in David's territory, and Ishbosheth's head is later interred in Abner's tomb. The severed head of Ishbosheth affords a violent image of the painful and drawn-out severing, the gradual but unrelenting removal and destruction, of Saul's house. In bitter irony, Saul's heir finds uneasy – partial – accommodation alongside the man who betrayed him and whose treachery led to the end of Saulide rule over Israel. The dead of Saul's house frequently suffer bodily desecration. The Philistines beheaded Saul and displayed his body and those of his three sons, Jonathan, Abinadab, and Malchishua, on the wall at Beth-shan (1 Samuel 31). Perhaps because the idea of desecration is so abhorrent, the text repeatedly leaves details dangling and obscure.[65] The men of Jabesh-gilead rescue the bodies of Saul and his sons and bury their bones, but what of Saul's head? And what becomes of Ishbosheth's body? The extreme example of abuse of the dead and the final resolution of this theme will come in the ritual killing and exposure of the bodies of seven of Saul's descendants (2 Samuel 21), a tale we shall consider later in this chapter. In this case, too, it is not unambiguously stated that the bones of Saul's two sons and five grandsons receive burial along with the bones of Saul and Jonathan. This uncertainty regarding the reparation for the dead poses a problem that cannot be easily dismissed. It is symptomatic of the larger problem of the innumerable ills suffered by Saul and members of his family that qualify Saul's house as tragic.

As was the case with Michal and Jonathan, the fates of Abner and Ishbosheth are sketchily related as background to David's spectacular rise to kingship over all Israel. Since their destinies are inextricably intertwined, it is fitting to consider Abner and Ishbosheth together. The power vacuum created by the deaths of Saul and his heir apparent thrusts them into prominence (2 Samuel 2–4). While Saul still reigns and Jonathan lives, Abner plays a minimal role and Ishbosheth is ignored by the biblical writers. Abner is introduced in the list of Saul's relations (1 Sam. 14:49–51) as Saul's cousin[66] and commander of his army, and he is close enough to the royal family to share their new moon feast at the king's side (1 Sam. 20:25). He appears briefly, in an ancillary role, in 1 Sam. 17:55–8, after David has slain Goliath, and in 1 Samuel 26, where, with Saul and the army, he pursues David in the wilderness of Ziph. Apart from 1 Samuel 26, Saul seems to lead his own troops, be it chasing David in the wilderness or doing battle against the Philistines. We know nothing of Abner's or Ishbosheth's activities during the fateful battle of Gilboa, where Saul and three of his sons are slain.[67] Upon Saul's death, David becomes king over Judah, but Abner preserves Saulide rule over the northern tribes by making Ishbosheth king.[68] This is Ishbosheth's first appearance in the narrative, unless he is to be identified with Ishvi in 1 Sam. 14:49, Ishbosheth ("man of shame") being a euphemism for Ishbaal ("man of Baal"), and Ishvi a form of Ishyo ("man of Yhwh").[69]

We have seen how, in terms of narrative poetics, the tragedy of Saul's house requires Jonathan's premature death and Michal's childlessness. Similarly, as obstacles to David's kingship and as remnants of a doomed house, Abner and Ishbosheth must be eliminated. Ishbosheth's identity is bound up with, and subordinated to, Abner's. Abner establishes Ishbosheth's kingship (2 Sam. 2:9), sustains it (2 Sam. 3:8), and sows the seeds of its destruction (2 Sam. 3:17–21). Ishbosheth's soldiers are Abner's soldiers (2 Sam. 2:12–31). Abner and Ishbosheth are linked with the same woman, Rizpah, and their quarrel over her divides them (2 Sam. 3:7–11). David demands Michal's return from both Abner and Ishbosheth (2 Sam. 3:13–16), and, not insignificantly, both participate in her return. Abner's assassination paves the way for Ishbosheth's, neither man prepared for the treachery that brings about his disgraceful death. Though the bond between them is broken by betrayal, they are joined in death, in Abner's tomb in Hebron (2 Sam. 4:12).

Unlike Jonathan, who sides with David but in the end remains faithful to his father's house, Abner is a traitor to the house of Saul. He, too, mediates the kingship to David, though differently from Jonathan. He offers to do it by betraying Saul's house, but he accomplishes it by his unanticipated death, his betrayal by Joab (and possibly David?). Like Saul, Abner, for a time at least, opposed God's plan to transfer the kingship from Saul's house to David's. Ironically, when he proposes to help David, death prevents him. Does he deserve to die a fool's death?[70] David's question echoes provocatively throughout the chapters dealing with Abner.

If Saul may be characterized as a man driven by his daemon, and

Jephthah as a negotiator trapped in a terrible dilemma by his own words, Abner is best described as a man surrounded by questions. Consider the following questions addressed to him:

> Whose son is this young man, Abner?
>> 1 Sam. 17:55
> Will you not answer, Abner?
>
> Are you not a man?
> Who is like you in Israel?
> Why have you not kept watch over your lord the king?
>> 1 Sam. 26:14–15
> Why have you gone in to my father's wife?
>> 2 Sam. 3:7

And these questions spoken by him:

> Who are you that calls to the king?
>> 1 Sam. 26:14
> Is that you, Asahel?
> Why should I smite you to the ground?
> How could I lift up my face to Joab your brother?
>
> Shall the sword devour forever?
> Do you not know that there will be bitterness in the future?
> How long will you delay ordering the army to turn back from
>   pursuing their brothers?
>> 2 Sam. 2:20, 22, 26
> Am I a dog's head of Judah?
>> 2 Sam. 3:8
> Whose is the land?
>> 2 Sam. 3:12

And finally, questions spoken concerning him:

> What have you done?
> Why have you sent him away, and he has indeed gone?[71]
>> 2 Sam. 3:24
> Should Abner have died a fool's death?
> Do you not know that a prince and great man has fallen this
>   day in Israel?
>> 2 Sam. 3:33, 38

Abner is first addressed in the story with a question. After David slays Goliath, Saul asks, "Whose son is this young man, Abner?" Commentators have long noted the difficulty Saul's question, repeated three times, poses, since David has already been introduced as Saul's armor-bearer, and earlier in the same chapter David told

Saul that he would fight the Philistine. Robert Polzin offers a plausible explanation of the discrepancy in psychological terms: Saul seeks from David an affirmation of sonship, of his complete allegiance, and thereby, I would underscore, of his subordination.[72] But what of Abner, who claims not to know the answer to Saul's question? Is David too far away for Abner to recognize him?[73] Or is Abner unwilling to identify David to Saul since Saul, who ought to know his armor-bearer, seemingly refuses to? Since Abner swears by the king's life, one hopes his ignorance is genuine or that the question has a deeper meaning. Perhaps, as Edelman suggests, it is a test of loyalty which Abner passes by refusing to identify David.[74]

The second time Abner is addressed, again with a question, David chides him for sleeping while he and Abishai slipped into Saul's camp and took Saul's spear and water jug. To David's taunt, "Will you not answer, Abner?," Abner responds with a question of his own, "Who are you that calls to the king?" Once more Abner does not identify David. Earlier Saul pressed the question of David's identity/ allegiance, but in the meantime he has come to "recognize" David for who he is, a threat to his throne. Thus his question in 1 Sam. 26:17, "Is this your voice, my son David?," can be viewed as another desperate attempt to lay claim to David's sonship/allegiance/ subordination.[75] Abner provides not simply a contrast to Saul in these two encounters with David; he also embodies Saul's refusal to surrender the kingship. In the parallel 1 Samuel 24, Saul verbally relinquishes the kingship to David, "Now I know that you will indeed be king" (1 Sam. 24:21). Nevertheless, after Saul's death Abner perpetuates the reign of Saul's house over Israel.

In 1 Samuel 26, David mocks Abner with questions that accuse him of negligence in guarding the king. But we know that Abner could not have been vigilant, for the entire army has been rendered impotent by a *tardemah*, a deep sleep, sent by Yhwh. The deep sleep recalls the evil spirit Yhwh sent to torment Saul; like Saul, Abner is at God's mercy. David's words foreshadow both Saul's and Abner's fates. Refusing to lift his hand against Yhwh's anointed, David predicts, "As Yhwh lives, Yhwh will smite him, whether his day comes and he dies or he goes down into battle and is swept away." To Abner and the army he says, "As Yhwh lives, you are dead men, because you have not kept watch over your lord, over Yhwh's anointed." David's words point ahead to Saul's death in battle at Gilboa. Whether Abner was absent or escaped from that battle –

another unanswered question – clearly he was not at Saul's side and thus for a second time he fails to protect his sovereign.[76] If he cannot safeguard the king against David, and later against the Philistines at Gilboa, neither can he save himself from the fate that awaits him.

Questions concerning Abner become more persistent in 2 Samuel 2–4, alerting us to the highly ambiguous, severely gapped nature of the text. In his monumental and controversial study of biblical narrative, Meir Sternberg shows how questions have a way of echoing, functioning to fill gaps by eliciting information or to deepen them by bringing into play the disparity between our knowledge and that of the characters.[77] In 2 Samuel 2–4, questions do not lead to answers; they point rather to further questions, leaving us with an excess of questions and compounding the difficulty of determining what "really happened." Amid the political subterfuge and conspiracy, noting is so straightforward as it seems.

The struggle between the houses of Saul and David is represented literarily through a balanced series of events in 2 Samuel 2–4. The struggle is gradually resolved in these chapters and concluded in 2 Sam. 5:1–5, with David's kingship over a united Israel and Judah. First, in the battle scene of 2 Samuel 2, each action has its counteraction, each scene its counterpart, until the struggle expectedly shifts in David's favor. Next, Abner and Ishbosheth's quarrel over a woman (2 Sam. 3:7–11) has its counterpart in Abner and David's negotiations over a woman (2 Sam. 3:12–16): the one undermines Ishbosheth's rule, the other strengthens David's claim to Saul's throne. These events are followed by two assassinations: Abner's, then Ishbosheth's, and the way is opened for David's accession.

In 2 Samuel 2, the forces of David and Ishbosheth meet at Gibeon. Gibeon is the source of much misfortune for Saul's house. In his zeal for Yhwh, Saul sought to destroy the Gibeonites, leaving them with a claim of bloodguilt against his house (2 Samuel 21). Rechab and Baanah, the assassins of Ishbosheth, are from Beeroth, a town associated with Gibeon (Josh. 9:17), and perhaps were among those who fled Saul's persecution. The journey of Abner and the servants of Ishbosheth to Gibeon is matched by the same movement on the part of Joab and the servants of David. They meet at the pool at Gibeon and square off, one on one side of the pool and the other on the other side of the pool. Twelve men go forth into hand-to-hand combat from Ishbosheth's men; twelve from David's. Each catches his opponent by the head and thrusts his sword into his side so that they fall down together. Only after fighting breaks out and Abner's forces are roundly defeated is the balance broken, both militarily and literarily, in David's favor.

Several details remain unclarified, however. Abner, in his first independent speech – that is, a speech that does not respond to a question addressed to him – initiates the action by suggesting a contest between representatives of the rival forces, "Let the young men arise and serve as amusement for us" (2 Sam. 2:14). We do not know for certain what kind of fighting he means. Is it a mock duel that turns fatal,[78] or actual combat to decide who is king, a contest like that between David and Goliath,[79] which similarly did not decide anything? The verb used, *tsaḥaq* in the piel, can indicate playing or merry-making, but a person who is made to perform for someone else's pleasure rarely enjoys it. We have encountered the verb before in the description of Samson's serving as amusement for the Philistines (Judg. 16:25, 26), but also of David's rejoicing before the ark of Yhwh when he brings it to Jerusalem (2 Sam. 6:5, 21). The contest turns out to be in dead earnest, and regardless of what Abner may or may not have intended, a major battle ensues in which Abner's forces suffer severe defeat.

Abner retreats, pursued by Asahel, Joab and Abishai's brother. With a series of rhetorical questions, Abner tries to persuade the swift-footed son of Zeruiah to turn aside, but Asahel refuses, and Abner kills him. Again details are hazy, giving rise to questions. How, precisely, does Asahel die? Does he run into the shaft of Abner's spear when Abner stops suddenly,[80] or does Abner attack him with a backward thrust of his spear?[81] Does Abner intend to knock him out, but instead the blow kills him? Abner's questions indicate he does not want to kill Asahel. Whatever the circumstances, Asahel's death at Abner's hands motivates Joab's assassination of Abner (2 Sam. 3:27, 30). Or does it? Are causes so clear-cut?

Joab and his men pursue Abner's forces. Whereas he failed to persuade Asahel, Abner succeeds with Joab, ending the pursuit with his eloquent rhetorical questions. Why one brother listens and the other does not is not clear.[82] Abner's questions call for Joab to end the hostilities, but Joab holds Abner accountable for allowing things to go so far, "If you had not spoken, it would have been morning before the men gave up the pursuit of their brothers."[83] Abner refers to bitterness in the future and the sword's lust for blood, and, indeed, it will be bitter for Abner when Joab's sword devours him. After Joab calls a halt to the fighting, Abner and his men march all night to reach Ishbosheth's base in Mahanaim, while Joab and his men march all night to return to David's stronghold in Hebron. Though the retreating movement of the two armies reinforces the sense of balance in 2 Samuel 2, Abner's many casualties underscore David's advantage: Joab's losses are 19 men besides Asahel, whereas Abner's are 360.

The struggle between the houses of Saul and David continues to provide the backdrop for 2 Samuel 3 – "there was a long war between the house of Saul and the house of David" – but the shift in David's favor is pronounced: "David grew stronger and stronger while the house of Saul became weaker and weaker." Abner, in the meantime, is also growing stronger (v. 6). Since he clearly wields the power in the weak house of Saul, the implicit question becomes: what will be his place in the strong house, that of David? The text leaves this question unanswered.

The event that occasions Abner and Ishbosheth's rift also remains unexplained. Did Abner take Rizpah, Saul's wife of secondary rank, as Ishbosheth alleges, or not (2 Sam. 3:7)? And why is the question important? Does sex with the former king's concubine amount to a claim to the throne? Abner answers Ishbosheth's question with a question, and the narrator sheds no light on the explosive situation. The scene does, however, provide our one insight into Abner's emotions, "Abner was very angry over the words of Ishbosheth" (v. 8). Abner threatens to deliver Israel to the house of David. Does anger drive him to such lengths? His words indicate both confidence in his own strength and disdain for Ishbosheth. Particularly striking in Abner's rejoinder to Ishbosheth's question is the discrepancy between Abner's professed knowledge that Yhwh has given all Israel to David, and the fact that Abner has up to now been opposing Yhwh by supporting Saul's house against David. Is he, for this obstinacy, destined to die a fool's death?

This day I keep showing loyalty to the house of Saul your father, to his brothers, and to his friends, and have not given you into the hand of David; and yet you charge me today with a fault concerning a woman. God do so to Abner, and more also, if I do not do for David what Yhwh has sworn to him, to transfer the kingdom from the house of Saul and establish the throne of David over Israel and over Judah, from Dan to Beersheba. (2 Sam. 3:8–10)

Abner accomplishes what he proposes, the transfer of the kingdom to David. The events he initiates will lead to the elimination of the rival claims of Saul's house. But he will have no control over these events.

Further questions attend Abner's negotiations with David. What does Abner stand to gain by helping David establish his kingship over a united Israel and Judah? Merely the satisfaction of his anger at Ishbosheth? Ishbosheth owed his throne to Abner; does Abner want David similarly indebted?[84] An appropriate reward for Abner would be Joab's position as commander of David's army, yet the text says nothing about Abner's future role in David's service.

Abner's overtures to David begin with a question, "To whom does a land belong?" McCarter considers the question intrusive, and omits it from his translation, though admitting that its source "is as difficult to surmise as its meaning."[85] But the question should not be so easily dismissed; like most of the questions surrounding Abner, it is highly ambiguous. Perhaps Abner means to suggest that a country belongs to the one who holds power over it – in this case, Israel belongs to Abner – and if David will make a covenant with Abner, then the whole land can belong to David. David poses a condition, however: "You shall not see my face unless you bring Michal Saul's daughter when you come to see my face" (2 Sam. 3:13). Abner withdrew his support from Ishbosheth because of Rizpah, Saul's wife; he will join forces with David by means of Michal, Saul's daughter and David's wife. In both cases, a woman serves as a token of kingship, as a pawn in the power struggle between men. Later in the narrative Michal and Rizpah will have their literary revenge, when, on behalf of Saul's house, they will protest David's (ab)use of power. As we have seen, Michal's protest in 2 Samuel 6, her verbal castigation of David, is ineffective, except insofar as it exposes a problematic side of David. Rizpah's silent protest, her vigil of 2 Samuel 21, will finally bring a measure of dignity to Saul's beleaguered house.

When David demands Michal's return from Abner, he refers to her as "Saul's daughter." He follows up his charge to Abner with a message to Ishbosheth calling for the return of "my wife Michal." The different epithets for Michal indicate not David's attitude to her but rather David's relationship to, and assessment of, Abner and Ishbosheth. From Abner, David wants a token of good faith, a sign that Abner's offer is genuine; thus Abner must bring David something that belongs to *Saul's* house. With Ishbosheth, the issue is ownership and David offers proof of his claim by referring to the bride price he paid for "my wife."[86] Ishbosheth's compliance reveals his weakness. At stake is *Abner*'s cooperation in what is clearly a claim to Saul's throne on David's part. Since, however, both Ishbosheth and Abner cooperate in returning Michal to David, it is not yet apparent that Abner has betrayed Saul's house. (One may wonder, of course, whether or not Ishbosheth suspects something is amiss, when Abner not only permits, but participates in, Michal's return.)

Clear signs of betrayal appear in 2 Sam. 3:17-19, when Abner confers with the elders of Israel and the house of Benjamin regarding David's kingship, raising the question: does Ishbosheth now know of Abner's treachery? Some curious features stand out in Abner's speech to the elders:

Abner's word to the elders of Israel was, "For some time you have been seeking David as king over you; now bring it about. For Yhwh said concerning David, 'By the hand of my servant David I will deliver my people Israel from the hand of the Philistines and from the hand of all their enemies.'"

Have the elders of Israel sought David as their king? If so, Abner has not only stood in God's way, as he revealed in his angry words to Ishbosheth, he has also opposed the will of the people. Or is Abner manipulating the elders, using a conventional rhetorical ploy to identify their interests with his? – and with God's! We are not told the elders' response or the reaction of Benjamin, Saul's tribe, only that Abner goes to David to report "all that was good in the eyes of Israel and in the eyes of the whole house of Benjamin" (2 Sam. 3:19). What was good in their eyes? Has Saul's own tribe forsaken Saul's heir?[87] The focus on Abner, at the expense of other characters and their reactions, shows his control over the situation, power that will prove tragically illusory.

Why does Joab kill Abner? The questions he hurls at David indicate another possible interpretation of Abner's behavior:

What have you done? Abner came to you; why have you sent him away, and he has indeed gone? You know Abner the son of Ner, that he came to deceive you, to know your going out and your coming in and to know all that you do. (2 Sam. 3:24-5)

Does Joab believe that Abner came to deceive David or does he dissimulate to mask his jealousy for his position? These questions point to another, more problematic issue, that of the narrator's reliability. The text makes no mention of Joab's concern for his position as commander of David's forces, though commentators are quick to point it out;[88] the only motive it gives for Joab's assassination of Abner is blood vengeance. The problem arises when one considers the discrepancy between two statements:

When Abner returned to Hebron, Joab took him aside within the gate to speak with him privately, and there he smote him in the belly so that he died for the blood of Asahel his brother. (2 Sam. 3:27)

So Joab and Abishai his brother slew Abner, because he had killed Asahel their brother in the battle at Gibeon. (2 Sam. 3:30)

The motive remains consistent, but who killed Abner, and under precisely what circumstances?[89] Is v. 30 simply an elaboration of v. 27? Are we to assume that Joab and Abishai together take Abner aside to speak with him, yet Abner suspects nothing? In view of the high degree of textual ambiguity and the many questions surrounding Abner, it is not surprising that the account of his assassination should be so equivocal.

Before killing Asahel, Abner protested, "Why should I smite you to the ground? How could I lift up my face to Joab your brother?" Now he goes willingly and unsuspectingly to face Joab in private. Do the twenty men who accompanied him to his meeting with David not return with him? Do they stand by helplessly? Or do they wait at the cistern of Sirah, and if so, what do they do when he does not return? Another nagging question cannot quite be put to rest: is David really innocent in the death of Abner, or does the text protest too much? The apologetic nature of the narrative has long been noted.[90] As in the negotiations with the Israelite elders, so too in the negotiations with David, only Abner's words are reported. Of David we learn only that he sent Abner away and Abner went in peace.[91] When he learns of Abner's murder, David curses Joab, but he does not punish him.[92]

Abner, it seems, would have given David authority over the northern tribes without a struggle. Yet in spite of appearances, Abner's death benefits David. David will not owe his kingdom to the hot-headed general who has already betrayed one king, and Abner will not live to cause problems for David in the future. Ishbosheth's death comes swiftly, inevitably, and anticlimactically. David attains the throne of a united Israel without a struggle *and* without Abner. Consequently he can well afford to lament Abner's death, and to blame Joab. David's response casts him in a favorable light; indeed, "everything the king did was good in the eyes of all the people" (2 Sam. 3:36). But how genuinely does David grieve over Abner's death? Like his lament over Saul and Jonathan (2 Samuel 1), David's words about Abner are not without their irony. And his lament is appropriately couched in the form of a question: should Abner have died as a fool dies?

How does a fool die? The word for "fool," *nabal*, recalls that quintessential fool, Nabal, who lost his life and his wife by crassly refusing hospitality (or, depending on one's perspective, protection money) to David (1 Samuel 25). Abner's question to Ishbosheth in 2 Sam. 3:8, "Am I a head of a dog (*keleb*) in Judah?," draws an implicit connection between him and the Calebite Nabal. Nabal dies when Yhwh strikes him down in punishment for his stubbornness, for standing in David's way. Nabal functions as a substitute for Saul, and the placement of the story about him between the two accounts of David's sparing Saul's life serves to dramatize Saul's folly in opposing David.[93] In 1 Samuel 26, after David chides Abner for not protecting the king and predicts Saul's and Abner's deaths, Saul refers to himself as acting foolishly (*hiskalti*). Abner too, for a time, has stubbornly blocked David's way, delaying David's reign over the northern tribes. Like Saul and Nabal, he must be removed.

How does a fool die? David's lament supplies one answer, with hands bound (*'asurot*) and feet in fetters (*linehushtayim*), a sober reminder of Samson who was bound by the Philistines in bronze fetters (*wayya'asruhu banehushtayim*, Judg. 16:21), and whose folly was the design of Yhwh. The Philistines had Samson brought to Dagon's temple for their amusement (*tsahaq*); in 2 Samuel 2, Abner suggested combat to provide amusement (*tsahaq*). If the purpose of that combat had anything to do with deciding who should be king, the issue has finally been settled. Abner's death, like Samson's, serves God's plan; God will give the kingdom to David. "As one falls before sons of iniquity you have fallen" – so David concludes his lament. Abner falls before the sons of Zeruiah, violent and blood-thirsty men whom David labels "too hard for me" (2 Sam. 3:39).[94]

Many questions surrounding Abner remain unanswered. In conclusion, what can we say about him? Less tragic than enigmatic, Abner is a prime example of *hubris* that never comes to know its limits: sure of himself with Ishbosheth, confident in his negotiating position with David, not anticipating Joab's revenge. He is presented sympathetically – in 2 Samuel 2, Abner does not want to kill Asahel, and he recognizes, like a good general, the bitterness of battle – though not favorably. Abner the army commander does not know David's identity when the youth kills the formidable Philistine Goliath (1 Samuel 17); he does not protect his king (1 Samuel 26); he suffers embarrassing losses in battle against Joab (2 Samuel 2); he betrays the man he made king (2 Samuel 3); he falls prey to Joab's ploy, showing none of the wariness one would expect of a seasoned warrior, and thus is assassinated (2 Samuel 3). Finally, if we take his words at face value, he knowingly acts both against God's plan and against the wishes of the elders of Israel in maintaining the rule of Saul's house over against David. It appears that Abner was a fool, as Nabal was, and that he deserved a fool's death.

Paradoxically, Abner's power matches his vulnerability to circumstance. Whereas God sends the *tardemah* that comes upon Abner and the army, there is no indication that God inspired Abner's carelessness. Divine and human causes operate simultaneously, with Yhwh using the opportunity to establish David's kingship. As an obstacle to the divine plan, Abner must be removed, for David will owe his kingship to God alone. Abner invokes Yhwh's name twice, and both times he refers to Yhwh's plan to give David the kingdom:

God do so to Abner and more so, if I do not do for David what Yhwh has sworn to him: to transfer the kingdom from the house of Saul and to establish David's throne over Israel and over Judah... (2 Sam. 3:9–10)

...for Yhwh said concerning David, "By the hand of David my servant I will deliver my people..." (2 Sam. 3:18)

How ironically tragic and fitting that his own death should serve that purpose.

Association with Saul taints Abner, but, like Saul, he bears responsibility for his failures. Ishbosheth, in contrast, is caught in a web of intrigue outside his control. How should we assess this last king of Saul's line, heir to an ill-fated throne? He is so completely identified with, and dependent upon, Abner that he can be said to have almost no life apart from him. No wonder, then, that he panics upon learning of Abner's death; his fate is sealed, and already he is a dead man. Ishbosheth's only speech is an accusation of Abner in the form of a question, an accusation that arises out of weakness: "Why have you gone in to my father's wife?" The question receives no answer and it triggers his downfall. This one scene in which he speaks stresses his inability to speak: "Ishbosheth could not answer Abner another word because he feared him" (2 Sam. 3:11). His only action is to give Michal to David, a concession that undermines his own kingship. On two different occasions, he displays the same reaction: fear. Such revelation of a minor character's feelings is striking, and thus defines him; he lacks the resolve to function on his own.[95] He cannot answer Abner's rebuff to his question about Rizpah, and when he hears of Abner's death, "his hands became weak"; that is, his courage failed (2 Sam. 4:1). He is killed at his most passive, lying in his bed.

Ishbosheth's death is much like Asahel's and Abner's, but under increasingly villainous circumstances: Asahel was struck in the belly in time of war; Abner, in time of peace; and Ishbosheth, in his sleep. How the assassins entered Ishbosheth's bedchamber unnoticed is, like so much in the narrative, not clear. According to the Hebrew text, Rechab and Baanah went inside the house fetching wheat and struck Ishbosheth in the belly while he was taking his noonday rest. According to the Septuagint, which has a less redundant reading than the Hebrew, the doorkeeper, who was cleaning wheat, became drowsy and fell asleep, thus allowing the assailants to slip by. Regardless of how it was carried out, the foul deed and its aftermath are clear enough. When confronted with the evidence, David does not lament Ishbosheth's death, as he had Saul's, Jonathan's, and Abner's, but he avenges it. The scene between David and Ishbosheth's assassins recalls David's treatment of the Amalekite who brought him the news of Saul's death (2 Samuel 1) in a double sense, by referring to it and by repeating it. It is only fitting that David's last words about the man who stood in Abner's shadow should take the form of a question:

The one who told me, "Saul is dead," thought he was bringing good news. But I seized him and slew him at Ziklag, which was the reward I gave him for his news. How much more, then, when wicked men have slain a righteous man in his house upon his bed! And now, shall I not seek his blood from your hand and destroy you from the earth? (2 Sam. 4:10–11)

David avenges the death of Saul's successor, as he had earlier avenged Saul's death. Later in his career, however, he will collaborate with the Gibeonites to wipe out Saul's house.

Ishbosheth's reign is so inconsequential and transitory that its length is open to doubt;[96] and Ishbosheth so insubstantial that even his name has not come down to us unambiguously. Not only does Chronicles, probably rightly, attest the name of Saul's heir as Eshbaal; there is also the question whether this is the same man as Ishvi in 1 Sam. 14:49. To complicate matters further, conflicting manuscript evidence exists regarding the name in 2 Samuel 3–4. In some ancient witnesses the name Mephibosheth appears instead of Ishbosheth,[97] a confusion not unlike the one we saw earlier regarding the names Michal and Merab in 2 Sam. 21:8. Mephibosheth is the name of Jonathan's lame son in 2 Sam. 4:4, and also the name of a son of Saul who is ritually executed in 2 Samuel 21. This arresting and apparently ancient confusion of Saul's descendants, the interchangeability of their names, emphasizes their common destiny as members of a fated house who share indiscriminately in its ruin.

RIZPAH'S VIGIL AND THE TRAGIC END OF THE HOUSE OF SAUL

> Auch die Juden haben ihre ewige Antigone,
> auf ihre, jüdische Art.
> [The Jews too have their eternal Antigone,
> in their own, Jewish way.]
> Martin Buber

Second Samuel 21:1–14 brings to a close the chain of tragic events which has beset the house of Saul. Seven of Saul's "sons" are brutally sacrificed – to Yhwh – as atonement for crimes against the Gibeonites. Thereafter no one remains of Saul's house except the crippled Mephibosheth, a pathetic figure hardly capable of staging a glorious renewal of the Saulide dynasty. (And of Mephibosheth's son, Mica, we hear nothing further.) The brief, laconic account of the execution of Saul's descendants and Rizpah's silent vigil over their exposed bodies is, to be sure, far removed from the fully developed tragedy of Saul, with its impressive handling of the dialectics of fate and freedom. Six verses, devoted primarily to dialogue, disclose the reason for the famine that afflicts the land and recount David's negotiations with the Gibeonites in an effort to end it. A shift from dialogue, so characteristic of Hebrew narrative style, to narrative report occurs with v. 7, when the sacrificial victims are selected, so that the tragic reaches us through the authoritative narratorial voice, gaining objectivity, and in this case propriety, but losing the immediacy, subtlety, and ambiguity that reported speech imparts to the telling.[98]

The tragic arouses our empathy by drawing us into sympathetic participation in the tragic hero's struggle against fate, as the story of Saul well illustrates. We see some of the internal dilemma, but none of the outward struggle against his nemesis in the story of Jephthah, and for this reason Jephthah emerges as less a tragic figure than Saul. The account in 2 Samuel 21, because it offers no insight into feeling or motivation after v. 7, lacks the element of heroic defiance. It scandalizes us without showing us directly the personal anguish of the characters. Neither Rizpah nor David – even less so the seven victims – seeks to avert the inevitable, though Rizpah's action serves as a powerful protest against the fate of Saul's sons. Not that anguished cries, impassioned pleas, or emotional outbursts would contribute to the force of the story: its tragedy derives from the shocking events, events that evoke a sense of outrage at the unremitting demands of destiny and the deity against Saul's house, and at the seemingly mechanical way in which these demands are met.

The tale is strange and disturbing in many ways. It verges on a world of elemental terror, the point of contact between the realm of the living and the realm of the dead, a place where human actions are undertaken in response both to perceived supernatural demands and to a sense of primal obligation of the living to the dead. Its themes are more familiar to us from the literature of ancient Greece than from Israelite tradition, with its reluctance regarding the chthonic sphere:[99] we encounter questions of bloodguilt and atonement, blessing and curse, honor and dishonor, divine displeasure and appeasement, pollution of the land and its purification. But an essential causal connection is never made clear: what is the precise relation between human sacrifice, the reverence for the dead exhibited in Rizpah's behavior, and the eventual appeasement of the deity?

Bloodguilt on Saul's house infects the land. Its cause lies in the past. In violation of the treaty made between Israel and the Gibeonites in the days of Joshua (Joshua 9), Saul sought to exterminate the Gibeonites, possibly because the presence of this non-Israelite enclave posed a threat to his nascent kingdom in its struggle with the Philistines.[100] The famine of three years' duration (21:1) is a sign of divine displeasure and a tangible indication that the land is out of synchrony with the normal cosmic order of seedtime and harvest, life and death, renewal and destruction. Atonement (*kpr*, v. 3) is sought through the sacrifice of members of the guilty house.

Regardless of the exact nature of the death they suffer – ritual dismemberment seems likely, though hanging, impalement, crucifixion, being broken on the wheel or cast down from a height have all been suggested – clearly at issue is exposure of the corpse.[101] And it is surely not fortuitous that the seven victims suffer a fate hauntingly reminiscent of the Philistines' desecration of Saul's and Jonathan's bodies (1 Samuel 31). Whereas ritual execution such as we find here constituted punishment for treaty violation in the ancient Near East, the disrespect of the elemental right of the dead to burial complicates the narrative by posing a danger as serious as the taint of blood-guilt.[102] The implicit question raised – whether natural order can be reestablished through a sacrifice which itself transgresses the natural order – receives only an indirect answer.

The causal nexus between divine displeasure, atonement, and anticipated divine appeasement set up by the story is abruptly broken by Rizpah's awesome display of the proper reverence due the dead. Up to this point, the narrative has given detailed attention to the problem of famine and the initiative of David and the Gibeonites to solve it; now the focus shifts to one action, presented with minimal commentary, but decisive in the resolution of the crisis. Rizpah's long and solitary vigil outwardly dramatizes her private tragedy in a public action that commands David's attention. She is not an Antigone, persevering in defiance of a royal command not to bury the dead; but like Antigone, she symbolizes the demands of familial loyalty as over against the power of the state. Authority rests with the royal house of David: "the king took [Saul's descendants] and he gave them into the hand of the Gibeonites," vv. 8–9; "they did all that the king commanded," v. 14. Because Rizpah has no authority of her own – she is, after all, a woman, a wife of secondary rank now widowed, and a member of the deposed house – she can only react to David's decrees as familial obligation dictates. The bonds of kinship determine the roles to be played out within Saul's house; blood ties mark Saul's descendants for doom and compel Rizpah to watch over the dead. Her deed forces the king to act: when he learns of her vigil, David has the bones of the dead interred. God hears supplications for the land "after that."

The tragic story of the end of Saul's house has its tempering elements. The first sign of relief comes in David's compassion, v. 7, an ironic reminder that David's own personal tragedy began because he did not have compassion (*we‘al 'asher lo' ḥamal*, 2 Sam. 12:6).

Appearing as they do immediately after the king's agreement to hand over Saul's sons to the Gibeonites for execution, the words, "the king had compassion" – in Hebrew the order is the reverse, *wayyaḥmol hammelek* – hold out for a brief moment the possibility that the king might not comply with the Gibeonites' demand. David's faithfulness to his oath to Jonathan is singled out as motivating his decision to spare Mephibosheth. The irony here is brutal: Saul's descendants are killed because Saul broke an oath sworn by Israel to the Gibeonites (v. 2), yet one of his descendants is saved by an oath, the oath of friendship between David and Jonathan. The comparison conveys the impression that, unlike his predecessor, David is faithful to an oath once taken. Yet the fact that one descendant of Saul is spared heightens by contrast the sacrifice of seven others, and this contrast receives further emphasis in the word-play on "oath" (*shebu'at*) and "seven" (*shib'ah*). The crucial problem of the dishonorable deaths of these seven Saulides remains unresolved until some months later when David gives orders to bury their bones. The burial, with its focus on the burial of the bones of Saul and Jonathan – indeed, to the surprising exclusion of explicit reference to the burial of the seven – provides both the resolution to Saul's tragedy, which broke off in 1 Samuel 31 with his burial outside his native territory, and the final resolution to the tragedy of his house, which has been gradually destroyed through events connected with the rise of the house of David.

In 2 Samuel 21, David appears in a characteristically ambiguous role. Although he delivers Saul's sons to the slaughter, he does not emerge as a villain. A crisis from Yhwh in the form of a natural disaster and a solution supplied by Yhwh and the Gibeonites relieve David of direct responsibility for wiping out Saul's house, a politically expedient outcome. David's effort to alleviate the crisis posed by the famine, his compassion on Mephibosheth, and his command to bury the bones of the dead, all reflect favorably on the king. Significantly, however, the resolution to the dishonor suffered by Saul's house and, implicitly, the divine receptivity to human supplication are not brought about at David's initiative but rather triggered by Rizpah's deed.

David's actions, which decide the course of events, are directed by others. David's handing over of Saul's sons for execution is determined by what the Gibeonites *say* ("What do you say I should do for you?" v. 4). His decision to have the bones of the dead buried comes in response to what Rizpah *does* ("David was told what Rizpah had done," v. 11). The shift in attention from words to deed corresponds to the transition from dialogue in vv. 1–6 to narrated action in vv. 7–14. Although it is the focal point of the story, Rizpah's deed receives the least amount of narrative space. Rizpah never speaks; nor would speech serve her, since her dealings are with the dead, not the living. The fact that she and David never interact reflects the division between the house of David and the house of Saul. But more than this, her isolation symbolizes her "otherness," her alliance with the dead. Her silence gives her preternatural magnitude and underscores the gravity of the ritual she performs. To follow her action with reported speech would lessen the effect by detracting attention from the deed itself. Whereas the Gibeonites and David are shown actively discussing and deciding the fate of Saul's house, Rizpah's silent vigil ultimately determines it. David and the Gibeonites offer a sacrifice of atonement, aimed at cleansing the land of evil; Rizpah prevents a horrible sacrilege. In the end the deity is appeased.

Martin Buber connects the deity's openness to supplication to the reconciliation between the houses of Saul and David symbolized in the burial and accomplished through Rizpah's deed.[103] The role of the deity is slightly more ambiguous, however, and we shall explore this ambiguity below.

Like the tragedies of Saul and Jephthah, our story opens against a backdrop of crisis: "there was a famine in the days of David, three years, year after year." The repetition, *shalosh shanim shanah 'aḥare shanah*, and the striking alliteration underscore the severity of the curse upon the land. "And David sought the face of Yhwh" (why, we might wonder, has it taken him three years?). The divine oracle at the beginning of the tale states the problem; it does not offer the solution: "against Saul and against his house there is bloodguilt because he sought to kill the Gibeonites." This condemnation is particularly jarring, for it adds to the list of Saul's transgressions one unknown to us from the earlier narrative in 1 Samuel. In fact, throughout 2 Samuel 21 attention is continually directed to Saul, to his culpability, and to the working out of nemesis within his house. For one thing, there are the curious speeches of the Gibeonites. Their audience with David, reported in vv. 2–6, provides the only direct speech in the narrative besides Yhwh's in v. 1. The Gibeonites' speeches reinforce Yhwh's and elaborate upon it by offering a solution. Their words also contrast suggestively with David's, for while the Gibeonites aim their accusations at Saul, David makes no direct reference to him. Though he knows through the divine oracle that Saul and his house are the source of the problem, David focuses the issue on how he, as king, can make expiation and thus bring a blessing upon his polluted kingdom, "What shall *I* do for you and how may *I* make atonement that you may bless the inheritance of Yhwh?" The Gibeonites state their initial response to the king's question provocatively, "It is not a matter of silver or gold between us and *Saul* and *his house*, nor is it our place to cause the death of a(ny) man in Israel." As resident aliens in Israel, the Gibeonites apparently do not have the right to exact bloodguilt, and thus the king must take responsibility, "What do you say I shall do for you?"[104]

Again the Gibeonites refer to "Saul" and "his sons" (v. 6). Though they avowed earlier, "it is not for us to cause *a man* to die in Israel,"[105] now they single out "*the man*" against whom they seek redress through the sacrifice of "*seven men* from his sons." These they will offer to Yhwh in a public ritual "at Gibeah of Saul, the chosen of Yhwh." This last phrase is often emended to read "at Gibeon, on the mountain of Yhwh" (cf. v. 9), but the cruel irony of the Masoretic text should not be too readily dismissed. "Saul, the chosen of Yhwh," standing as it does amid repeated references to David as "the king," provides yet another pointed reminder of the rejection of the Saulide house in favor of David. A terrible finality resides in the starkness of David's terse reply, "I will give (them)," though as we have seen, its harshness is somewhat mitigated by the next word, *wayyaḥmol*, "but the king had compassion" (v. 7). "I will give (them)" are the last words spoken in the narrative; in a sense, nothing more need be said.

It seems only appropriate that Saul, though dead, should dominate the account. His crime must be atoned for, and this explains the inordinate emphasis on kinship ties to Saul. Whenever Hebrew narrative style departs from its usual terseness in favor of redundancy, the purpose is usually emphatic. Mephibosheth is called "Mephibosheth the son of Jonathan the son of Saul" (v. 7). Jonathan's name never stands alone; he is repeatedly identified as "Jonathan the son of Saul" (twice in v. 7) or "Jonathan his son" (vv. 12, 13, 14). Saul's sons Armoni and Mephibosheth are identified as "the two sons of Rizpah the daughter of Aiah whom she bore to Saul," and the other unnamed five as the "sons of Michal [Merab] the daughter of Saul whom she bore to Adriel the son of Barzillai the Meholathite."

Rizpah is called "Rizpah the daughter of Aiah, the (secondary) wife of Saul" (v. 11), and Michal (or Merab) is "the daughter of Saul" (v. 8). Such detailed attention to familial relationships makes painfully apparent the involvement of Saul's entire house in his tragedy; no one related to Saul – not even Jonathan's son, Mephibosheth, here singled out as spared – ultimately escapes a tragic fate. Similarly, the threefold repetition in vv. 12–14 of "the bones of Saul and [the bones of] Jonathan his son" stresses the tempering of the tragedy which the burial provides.

The narrative further reveals a preoccupation with Saul and his house by presenting information already known to us from earlier sources about events that have transpired within the house of Saul. Verse 7 reminds us of the oath of loyalty between David and Jonathan familiar to us from 1 Samuel 20. Verse 12 goes into detail about Saul's death. Not only does it underscore the similarities between Saul's death and the deaths of his seven sons – thus uniting Saul's house in its tragic fate – it also introduces Saul and Jonathan as the subjects of events now taking place – thereby also uniting Saul's house in the tempering of its tragedy. Reference is made to the day the Philistines slew Saul on Gilboa. Is this simply an abridged way of recounting Saul's death, or is it another, variant account, giving us now three possibilities: Saul died by his own hand (1 Samuel 31), an Amalekite killed him (2 Samuel 1), the Philistines in fact killed him? The abuse of Saul's and Jonathan's bodies by the Philistines is recalled, and we recognize it as tragically paralleled in the Gibeonites' contemptuous treatment of Saul's descendants. Correspondingly, the valor and loyalty of the men of Jabesh-gilead in stealing the bones of Saul and Jonathan from the wall of Beth-shan receives attention, finding its analogue in Rizpah's valor and loyalty. Finally, there is that crucial bit of information we had not heard before, the crime that explains the disaster about to befall the remnant of Saul's house: Saul in his zeal sought to detroy the Gibeonites, a blatant violation of treaty obligations.

The zealous side of Saul's nature comes as no surprise; we have seen before his ardor for Yhwh in driving the mediums and wizards out of the land (1 Samuel 28), and in constantly seeking divine counsel. His tendency to overzealousness in ritual matters played a role in his rejection as king (1 Samuel 13–15). We have also seen his ruthlessness in the slaughter of the priests of Nob (1 Samuel 22), as well as in his attempts to kill David. In 2 Sam. 21:2, Saul's zeal for

Israel and Judah contrasts with the Israelites' relation to the
Gibeonites, a relationship viewed ambivalently both here and
elsewhere. Verse 2 points out that the Gibeonites are not "sons of
Israel," the first occurrence of the word "son," which will play a
central role in the story. It goes on to identify them as "the remnant
of the Amorites" and to allude to the treaty Israel made with them
as a result of deception and without consulting Yhwh (Joshua 9).
Ironically, Saul is guilty of violating a treaty that should not have
been made. Whereas the Israelites should have been zealous, wiping
out the Gibeonites in the time of Joshua, Saul's zeal for the "*sons* of
Israel and Judah" (v. 2) wrongly leads him to crimes against people
protected by treaty. Consequently, "seven men of his *sons*" (v. 6)
must die in propitiation.

Whereas the greatest amount of narrative attention is devoted to
the dialogue between David and the Gibeonites, vv. 1–6, the handing
over of Saul's sons and their deaths, vv. 7–9, and the burial of the
bones of the dead, vv. 12–14, considerable narrative power is
concentrated in the account of Rizpah's vigil, vv. 10–11:

> Rizpah the daughter of Aiah took sackcloth
> and spread it out for herself on the rock
> from the beginning of the harvest until
> rain fell upon them from the heavens.
> She did not let the birds of the heavens rest upon them
> by day or the beasts of the field by night.
> It was told to David what Rizpah the daughter of Aiah,
> the wife of Saul, had done.

The account is brief and controlled. Its emphasis is temporal: first on
the length of the vigil, "from the beginning of the harvest until rain
fell upon them from the heavens," which appears to be from late
April until the fall rains (some suggest late spring or early summer
rain), and then on Rizpah's watchful attention day and night. Her
action on behalf of the dead tempers this gruesome tragedy by
restoring dignity to the house of Saul. It is also associated with
renewal in the realm of nature: "until rain fell upon them from the
heavens" (v. 10) marks the end of the famine and foreshadows the
divine appeasement (v. 14).

Rizpah's long and silent vigil bears eloquent witness to her valor,
determination, and tenacity. The heroism of the men of Jabesh-
gilead in rescuing the bodies of Saul and Jonathan from disgraceful
exposure finds a clear analogue in Rizpah's heroism, which prevents

the desecration of the bodies of Saul's sons and grandsons and brings to an end their disgraceful exposure. She achieves not only (apparently) the necessary burial of the executed Saulides, but also the return of Saul's and Jonathan's bones from Jabesh to the familial tomb. When one considers David's praise for the men of Jabesh-gilead (2 Sam. 2:5–7), his silence here becomes a telling commentary on his own ambivalent role in these events.

The tempering of the tragedy through Rizpah's action recalls another account of relief brought by a woman, the medium of En-dor's kindness to Saul the night before his death (1 Samuel 28). In both cases, a woman functions at the terrifying threshold between the realms of the living and the dead. Each faces as well a certain personal risk for her act of kindness.

In addition to her similarities to characters who bring relief in the tragedy of King Saul in 1 Samuel 9–2 Samuel 1, Rizpah presents significant contrasts to other figures active in 2 Samuel 21. Whereas the Gibeonites in this story bring death, the end of the Saulide dynasty, and disgrace upon Saul's house, Rizpah brings restoration and a measure of honor to Saul's house. Her vigil affirms familial loyalty and maternal bonds (note the twofold repetition of "the sons whom she bore to" in v. 8). Whereas the rain comes before the dead are buried, and offers a sign that expiation has been effected, the final resolution is reached only afterward, with the divine receptivity to supplications for the land. Rizpah's act of maternal devotion is somehow connected to the renewal of fertility in the land.[106] The normal cycle of nature, whose reestablishment is signaled in the onset of the rains, depends, in the final analysis, on the restoration of harmony between the human and divine realms, which Rizpah's deed helps achieve.

One of the master strokes of the narrative is the subtle contrast between Rizpah and David. Her behavior reflects his previous action and, more important, foreshadows his subsequent action. David *takes* (*wayyiqqaḥ*, v. 8) Saul's sons and *gives* them over (*wayyittenem*, v. 9) to the Gibeonites; Rizpah *takes* (*wattiqqaḥ*, v. 10) sackcloth to spread on the rock, from where she does not *give* (*natenah*, v. 10) either bird or beast an opportunity to desecrate the bodies. Only when David learns what Rizpah has *done* (*'et 'asher 'asetah ritspah*, v. 11) does he cause the appropriate thing to be *done* (*wayya'asu kol 'asher tsiwwah hammelek*, v. 14). After reporting the burial of the bones at the king's command, the narrative closes with the laconic observation, "God heeded supplications for the land after that." The questions it leaves unanswered are disquieting. In particular, how are we to understand the role of the deity in this tale? Divine displeasure initiates the crisis and divine appeasement resolves it. In between, humans struggle to deal with the terrible events that confront them. A natural disaster – famine, "three years, year after year" – sets events in motion. Like the plague that grips Thebes as the result of Oedipus' deed, the famine is a sign of continuing divine displeasure with Saul, now dead, and with his house, contaminated by his guilt. David seeks to alleviate the problem by consulting the wronged party, the Gibeonites, who emerge as a sinister force in the story, with their sevenfold call for vengeance.[107] Or perhaps the Gibeonites are simply performing the will of Yhwh, for we know Yhwh has been antagonistic toward Saul and his house from the start.

Atonement is made through a human sacrifice to Yhwh, and, as in the story of Jephthah's sacrifice of his daughter, no divine pronouncement condemns this practice. To make matters worse, the dead are exposed for a considerable period of time. Are we to assume that the divine receptivity to supplication referred to at the end of the narrative (v. 14) is achieved by the propitiatory sacrifice of Saul's sons? Clearly Yhwh has called for this: "there is bloodguilt upon Saul and upon his house..." The onset of the rain would thus be the sign that the expiation is effective, the famine is over, and David is now free to bury the dead. The burial of the dead would then have no direct relation to the divine appeasement; rather it is a human response that tempers the tragedy (just as in 1 Samuel 28 and 31 the tempering is found in acts of *human* kindness). On the other hand, the reference to divine receptivity at the end of the story – that is, after the burial and not before it – permits another reading. While the expiation perhaps produces the needed rain, is does not end the affliction of the land because of the sacrilege upon the dead. In this case, the ultimate source of divine appeasement is the burial of the dead, which Rizpah's deed has helped bring about. Clearly the resolution of the story, and of the whole, long tragedy of the house of Saul, occurs in the return of Saul's and Jonathan's bones to rest in their ancestral tomb and, as Buber maintains, in the reconciliation between the houses of Saul and David symbolized by the burial at David's command.[108]

Following closely upon this narrative, 2 Samuel 24 describes a similar situation. In this story, however, it is *David* who is punished, by means of a *plague*, not a famine. The crisis is resolved when David offers himself *and his house* in expiation, an interesting variation on the expiation theme of 2 Samuel 21.[109] In both cases, a sacrifice leads to divine appeasement, and the two tales end the same way, "and God [or Yhwh] heeded supplications for the land."[110] Like 2 Samuel 21, 2 Samuel 24 exposes the dangerous, demonic side of God: Yhwh incites David to commit the sin of taking a census in the first place.[111] Little wonder that 1 Chronicles 21 substitutes "Satan" for "Yhwh." Hostile transcendence figures prominently in the tragedy of King Saul. Important issues in 2 Samuel 21 also have counterparts in the tragedy of Jephthah: the centrality of a vow or an oath and its disturbing connection with human sacrifice; the ambiguous presentation of the deity especially in regard to human sacrifice; and the cloudy issue of reconciliation through death. In 2 Samuel 21, the precise meaning of the sacrifice and of the divine appeasement remains uncertain, and mystery surrounds the nature of their relationship. The dark fate of Saul's house is counterbalanced by Rizpah and the effect of her act on David. In this tragic end of the house of Saul, Rizpah's helpless yet heroic grief provides a measure of resolution and repair.

CHAPTER 5

David: the judgment of God

Never, never, never, never, never.

King Lear, Act V, Scene III

My son Absalom, Absalom my son, my son.

2 Samuel 19:4 [Heb. 19:5]

"Who is David? And who is the son of Jesse?" The answer to Nabal's question in 1 Samuel 25:10 remains complex and elusive (and that Nabal died for his lack of perception serves as a sobering warning to the adventuresome critic). The story of David, 1 Samuel 16–1 Kings 2, has the makings of tragedy: David's moment of *hubris* – his compound sin of adultery and murder – and the reversal of his fortunes as a result. But David defies easy categorization as a tragic figure, just as he defies Nabal's attempt to cast him as an ordinary outlaw. Modern critical assessments stress the multifaceted picture the text gives of David and the difficulty of unraveling his manifold personality.[1] At times he appears pious, trusting, and faithful, as when he faces Goliath armed with only sling and stone and bold words about Yhwh's protective power. But he may also be calculating and manipulative – in his first recorded speech, he inquires about the reward for slaying Goliath.[2] He can appear magnanimous, as in his dealings with Jonathan's son Mephibosheth. But then again, his decision to have Mephibosheth "eat at the king's table always" (2 Sam. 9:7, 13) could stem from a desire to keep an eye on the hapless Saulide. He inspires loyalty: Ittai, a non-Israelite, who has been in David's service only a short time, staunchly stands by the king in his darkest moment (2 Sam. 15:19–20). And he can be ruthless, on his deathbed calling down the sword upon Joab and Shimei. He bears much tribulation, yet he seems to lack true tragic greatness, choosing to compromise, to adjust to circumstances, rather than struggle heroically against his lot. Unlike Saul and Jephthah, whose guilt is uncertain, David's guilt is clear. His adultery with Bathsheba and murder of her husband Uriah are not crimes unwittingly committed out of ignorance or due to misjudgment, neither is his failure predestined, as Saul's seems to have been. Above all, and here the difference from Saul and Jephthah is noteworthy, God does not abandon him.

David's story makes an especially fitting conclusion to our investigation of the Bible's tragic dimension precisely because it both admits and resists interpretation along tragic lines. Thus, in what follows, my intention is not to argue that the story must be read as a tragedy, but rather to explore the possibilities and limits of a tragic reading. Specifically, I want to illuminate the tragic vision in 1 Samuel 16–1 Kings 2, and to examine how, in the final analysis, the narrative falls short of realizing its full tragic potential. There is no question the *story* is a tragic story – what happens to David, the "evil" that befalls his house, as the text puts it, is undeniably and profoundly tragic – but the protagonist, for reasons we shall explore below, does not measure up to the role of tragic hero.

In Chapter 3, I argued that the tragic dimension in Jephthah's story lies not so much in his character as in the events that enmesh him – although, to be sure, the manner of man he is bears directly on what happens to him. David's case is similar, though David's character is infinitely more complex, and consequently gives rise to perpetual uncertainty about cause and effect and about how exactly his strengths and weaknesses influence his fortunes. If, like Jephthah, David cannot achieve true heroism in his struggle against fate, he nonetheless undergoes hardships of tragic proportions, and for one anguished moment, when he learns of his son Absalom's death, he experiences tragic alienation at its extreme. In contrast to the account of Jephthah's vow and human sacrifice, where God neither condemns nor condones Jephthah's actions, God responds unambiguously to David's deeds. God is angry – "the thing David had done was evil in the eyes of Yhwh" (2 Sam. 11:27) – and punishes David by raising up evil against him out of his own house. The burden of divine judgment that David must bear, the working out of nemesis within his house, is what makes David's story tragic. David cannot prevent the disasters that, one after another, befall his house, and like Saul and Jephthah, he is the cause of them. To what extent he comes to terms with his responsibility is a question we shall consider later. As in Saul's tragedy, punishment seems out of proportion to guilt, though, as Jan Fokkelman observes, it is qualitatively fitting, if quantitatively excessive.[3] As with Saul and Jephthah, we shall discover that in David's story, too, Yhwh assumes an ambivalent role. Like Saul, David sins and confesses sin (2 Sam. 12:13). And though Yhwh never ceases to be involved in David's affairs, he is not with David in the same way as before.

Tragedy, according to Chaucer's monk, tells a story of a fall from prosperity into misery. This simple definition concisely and fairly accurately describes David's story.[4] David's fortunes, his "rise" and "fall," from his introduction in the narrative in 1 Samuel 16 to his death in 1 Kings 2, follow a tragic course.[5] The immediate background to David's rise is 1 Samuel 8–15, the inauguration of monarchy in Israel and the first king's failure. As early as 1 Samuel 13, the first account of Saul's rejection, we learn that Yhwh has chosen for himself a man after his own heart to replace Saul as king. In 1 Samuel 16 we discover David is that man. Like Saul, David is secretly anointed by Samuel in the context of a sacrifice. But whereas Saul's anointing took place against the backdrop of Yhwh's negative attitude toward kingship, David's occurs against the backdrop of Yhwh's negative attitude toward *Saul*. Thus, just as Yhwh was predisposed to reject Saul, he will look favorably on Saul's replacement. No antimonarchic sentiment taints David's election, and Samuel, who as champion of the perils of kingship opposed Saul, plays no real part in David's rise. David faces no opposition except Saul's, whose resistance proves ineffectual. The distinction between the anointed successor and the rejected king could not be greater: the spirit of Yhwh comes upon David (16:13) and departs from Saul (16:14).

To be appreciated in its terrible fullness, David's fall must be viewed against his dramatic rise. We saw in Chapter 2 how Saul serves as a foil to David, and how his dogged efforts to hold on to the kingdom throw into relief the comparative ease with which David acquires the throne from Saul's house.[6] David's success derives from Yhwh's unqualified support. Early in the narrative we are informed that "David was successful in all his undertakings, for Yhwh was with him" (1 Sam. 18:14), and repeatedly we hear the refrain, "Yhwh was with him,"[7] as David pursues an unhampered path to the throne. Although he encounters setbacks – for example, when Saul's envy forces him to flee the court, and when he puts his reputation with his people on the line by seeking refuge among the Philistines – everything works out to his advantage. There is no doubt that David will continue to succeed in whatever he does and will eventually reign over Israel, for Yhwh has promised him the kingdom. Eventually even Saul recognizes this: "Now I know that you shall surely be king, and that the kingdom of Israel will be established in your hand" (1 Sam. 24:20 [Heb. 24:21]); "Blessed are you, my son David. You will do many things and you will surely succeed" (1 Sam. 26:25).

David's famous double introduction in 1 Samuel 16 and 17 portends great things for him.[8] When Saul seeks out a musician to ease his tormented spirit, one of his attendants recommends David in terms both glowing and proleptic:

I have seen a son of Jesse the Bethlehemite, who is skilled in playing music, a man of valor, a man of war, prudent in speech, and a man of good presence; and Yhwh is with him. (1 Sam. 16:18)

Whereas we already know Yhwh is with David (16:13), only after he answers Goliath's challenge (1 Samuel 17) shall we encounter him as a man of valor, a man of war, and a man prudent in speech – qualities that will be manifested and tested in a variety of ways.[9] From the moment he prevails over the mighty Philistine champion, David becomes the people's hero: "Saul has slain his thousands, and David his ten thousands" (1 Sam. 18:7). Straightway all Israel and Judah love him (18:16), including Saul's children Michal and Jonathan, whose loyalty to David in defiance of their father intensifies Saul's desolation. When David flees Saul's court, he has no difficulty amassing a following that grows quickly to 400 men (1 Sam. 22:2) and then to 600 (1 Sam. 23:13).

David receives support from many quarters. Ahimelech the priest, though unaware of David's fugitive status, inquires of God for him, as he has done on other occasions. When Saul later questions him, Ahimelech defends David to the king, "Who is there among all your servants as faithful as David, the king's son-in-law and captain over your bodyguard and honored in your house?" (1 Sam. 22:14).[10] The king of Moab provides a refuge for David's parents (1 Sam. 22:3–4), Gad the prophet warns David (1 Sam. 22:5), Abiathar the priest joins his band (1 Sam. 22:23), and Saul's own son meets with David in the wilderness to encourage him (23:16–18). Even a Philistine raid on Israelite territory benefits David by prompting Saul to abandon the chase just when he has David cornered (23:25–8).

Not only do people he encounters seem well disposed to David and events so often work to his advantage (all contributing to his inevitable success), David's behavior toward those ill disposed to him, especially Saul, but also the churlish Saul-surrogate Nabal, makes him appear worthy of that success and of God's favor. Whereas Saul clearly means to rid himself of his rival, David undertakes no hostile action against Saul. He assumes the role of the wronged party, a faithful subject in spite of Saul's aggression (1 Sam. 20:1; 24:9–15 [Heb. 10–16]; 26:18–20). When Saul pursues David in the wilderness, in hopes of killing him, he ends up in David's power, not once but twice (1 Samuel 24 and 26). Whatever its motivation, David's refusal to kill Yhwh's anointed is one of those grand gestures that can only endear him to the people he will one day rule, even if his followers might prefer more immediate action.[11] Between the two accounts of David's sparing Saul's life, the virtuous reputation David has been building for restraint is tested. David comes close to attacking Nabal's household and taking vengeance with his own hands, but Abigail opportunely intercedes to stop him (1 Sam. 25:26, 33–4). Both Abigail and David attribute David's good fortune in avoiding a crime of bloodguilt to Yhwh. Indeed, our hero, as he moves ever closer to the kingship (which Abigail incidentally predicts, 1 Sam. 25:30), seems to lead a charmed life.

A source of David's success and a critical difference between David and Saul is David's ready access to divine counsel. David repeatedly inquires of God and repeatedly receives straightforward answers regarding the course he should take.[12] The fugitive David asks Yhwh about defending Keilah against the Philistines and Yhwh urges him on (1 Sam. 23:2). When his followers express reluctance, David inquires again, and God displays no sign of impatience with David's need for reassurance (23:4). To his further inquiries about the intentions of both Saul and the inhabitants of Keilah, David receives answers that convince him to flee the city. David's inquiries are never rebuked. At other times, Yhwh instructs him about pursuing the Amalekites when Ziklag has been pillaged (1 Sam. 30:7–8), about returning to Judah after Saul's and Israel's defeat at Gilboa (2 Sam. 2:1), and, on two different occasions after his anointing as king over a united Israel and Judah, about fighting the Philistines (2 Sam. 5:19, 22–4). How unfortunate by comparison was Saul, who tried but never quite succeeded in obtaining unambiguous divine guidance.

As we saw in Chapters 2 and 4, Yhwh more than once intervenes overtly on David's behalf: when he sends his spirit upon Saul's messengers and then Saul, rendering them helpless (1 Sam.

19:18–24), and when he causes a deep sleep to fall upon Saul's camp, allowing David and Abishai to enter undetected (1 Samuel 26). In 1 Samuel 26, as in 1 Samuel 24, David and his men acknowledge Yhwh for placing Saul in their power. As Yhwh's chosen, David is Yhwh's protected, and Yhwh delivers David from all harm, be it a man of war, Goliath, or a determined enemy, Saul, or something intangible, like bloodguilt.

It can scarcely be fortuitous that so many events work out in David's favor or that David makes such a favorable impression on everyone, even in potentially compromising situations. David's three-year sojourn among Israel's enemies, the Philistines, might have severely tarnished his reputation. But he avoids becoming a traitor in his people's eyes,[13] and at the same time he dupes Achish into believing "he has made himself utterly abhorred by his people Israel" (1 Sam. 27:12). Achish even brings David with him to fight against Israel, convinced that David is as innocent as an angel of God. It is essential that the Philistine lords succeed with their objection to David's presence among them, for David can neither oppose Saul, thereby betraying his people, nor cross over to Saul's side, since Israel must lose the battle and Saul must die. Another potentially dangerous situation for David occurs when his band returns from their rendezvous with the Philistines to discover that the Amalekites have pillaged and burned Ziklag in their absence: David's own followers speak of stoning him. The threat is resolved when they pursue the Amalekites, recapture their possessions, and, amazingly, "nothing was missing" (1 Sam. 30:19). There is even a positive benefit arising from the Amalekite raid: David is able to offer a present of Amalekite spoil to his "friends, the elders of Judah," who will soon in their turn offer him kingship over them (30:26–31). Perhaps nowhere is David more publicly appealing than when he laments the deaths of Saul and Jonathan, and, after quickly assuming kingship over Judah, when he protests his innocence of the deaths of Abner and Ishbaal, who blocked his ascent to the throne of Israel. David survives this remarkable series of dubious and compromising adventures without any opprobrium attaching to him, and the united kingdom becomes his without a struggle.

In 2 Samuel 5–8, David reaches the height of his fortunes as king over Israel and Judah. He extends his power, and, in a familiar refrain, the theme of his rise is reiterated: "David became greater and greater, for Yhwh God of hosts was with him" (2 Sam. 5:10). He makes Jerusalem his capital (2 Samuel 5) and the home of Yhwh's ark (2 Samuel 6). To crown his career, David receives from Yhwh the promise of an eternal dynasty (2 Samuel 7) – a dynasty distinguished from Saul's house by virtue of Yhwh's promise not to remove his covenant loyalty from David's house, as he removed it from Saul's. The divinely favored king succeeds both on the battlefield, as a warrior who subdues many nations, and at home, as one who dispenses justice to his people:

Yhwh gave David victory wherever he went. (2 Sam. 8:6 and 14)

David ruled over all Israel, and David administered justice and equity to all his people.[14] (2 Sam. 8:15)

One could hardly imagine a more thoroughgoing success story, and the descent from good fortune into adversity is equally spectacular. Often in tragedy the hero reaches undreamed of heights from which, blinded and spoiled by fortune, he or she displays the *hubris* that results in fortune's turn. David's compound sin of adultery and murder marks such a turning point. It initiates a tragic decline and a descent into suffering which will only occasionally be relieved by events in David's favor. David's wrongdoing involves not just an error of judgment, like Saul's and Jephthah's, but is a sin deliberately pursued. In an unguarded moment of royal indulgence, he has sexual relations with another man's wife, who consequently becomes pregnant. Then, to cover his guilt, David has the husband killed.

Both Saul and Jephthah appeared at a time of leadership crisis in Israel; under David that crisis has been resolved. If a leadership problem exists, it is of a vastly different order, the problem of a king who stays at home while others conduct his battles.[15] Unlike Saul and Jephthah, who make ill-fated choices under urgent circumstances, David sins at leisure: "It happened late one afternoon, when David arose from his couch and was strolling upon the roof of the king's house that he saw from the roof a woman bathing..." Saul and Jephthah incur guilt on the field of battle, in misguided, but apparently earnest, attempts to ensure victory. In 2 Samuel 11, war is, in fact, being waged, but David's absence is pointedly remarked upon: "In the spring of the year, the time when kings go forth to battle,[16] David sent Joab and his servants with him, and all Israel, and they ravaged the Ammonites and besieged Rabbah, while David remained in Jerusalem." By not going forth to war, David brings the war home. What began as a war against an outside enemy, Ammon, will become a war that divides the Davidic house, when David's own son leads a revolt against him. And it will culminate in war involving the whole family of Israel – civil war between the northern and southern tribes.

As we saw with Saul, the privileged position of kings, which enables them to break laws others must respect, disposes them to tragic treatment. David's abuse of royal power sets him on a tragic course.[17] His position allows him both the opportunity and the authority to summon another man's wife to his bed. Against a background of incriminating allusions to the king's idleness (his mid-day nap that stretches until late afternoon, and his evening stroll on the roof) and to his casual voyeurism (he spies a beautiful woman bathing), the deed itself is described briefly:

David sent messengers and took her. She came to him and he lay with her, while she was purifying herself from her uncleanness. Then she returned to her house. (2 Sam. 11:4)

A context of aggression and violence, war with Ammon, surrounds this act of sexual aggression, but the narrator plays down any suggestion of force.[18] The encounter is over as suddenly as it began. That is not, however, the end of the matter. Once the first sin is committed, two things happen – neither of which is a *necessary* consequence – which lead David to commit the second sin. First, though obviously not every act of sexual intercourse issues in pregnancy, as fate would have it, this one does: "The woman conceived and sent and told David, 'I am pregnant'" (v. 5). We know, and David knows, the child is his, for the small but hardly extraneous detail about Bathsheba's ritual purification in v. 4 has ruled out Uriah's possible paternity.[19] In response to the news, David decides to bring Uriah back to Jerusalem on a pretext, send him home where he will have sexual relations with his wife, and let it appear that the child is Uriah's. Clearly the king is not prepared for the second, more disastrous but still unnecessary, consequence: Uriah does not cooperate. The faithful soldier, unlike the king, refuses to enjoy sex with his wife while "the ark and Israel and Judah dwell in booths, and my lord Joab and the servants of my lord are camping in the open field" (v. 11).[20]

David is caught up by action he precipitated, now beyond his control. It is a classic tragic situation from which David can find no way out except a way that involves him more deeply in sin. David

does not have Uriah killed out of desire to have Bathsheba for himself
– for letting Uriah think the child his own would solve his problem
– but because he has no other way to conceal his adultery with
Bathsheba, since Uriah refuses to "go down to his house." The king
writes to Joab, telling him to arrange for Uriah to be killed in battle,
and even has the gall to send the letter by Uriah's hand. Surely this
is *hubris* almost unchecked, as well as a calculated act of desperation.
The murder requires yet another perpetrator and claims other
victims. Joab must arrange Uriah's death to look like a casualty of
war, and to do so he is forced to use bad military strategy. In addition
to Uriah, other faithful soldiers die as part of the cover-up.

Upon receiving the news of the deaths of some of his soldiers,
including Uriah, David sends a message back to Joab: "Do not let
this thing be evil in your eyes, for the sword devours now one and now
another…" (11:25). What is "this thing" – the military defeat? the
conspiracy to murder Uriah? the deaths of other valiant soldiers?
what the command to have Uriah killed says about David's
character? The whole business were better forgotten, suggests David,
but he cannot so easily escape the repercussions of his deed (not "this
thing" [*haddabar hazzeh*] but "the thing David had done" [*haddabar
'asher 'asah david*]): "The thing David had done was evil in the eyes of
Yhwh" (v. 27). David's *hubris* in violating the limits of kingship, his
failure to obey God's laws and to deal justly with his subjects, cannot
go unpunished.[21] Yhwh sends Nathan to chastise David, with the
accusation, "Why have you despised the word of Yhwh, to do what is
evil in his eyes?" (12:9). These key words of David's speech to Joab,
"evil" and "the sword," come back now to haunt him, for Nathan
promises that evil and the sword will be his nemesis. Nathan, who
speaks for nemesis, picks up the words:

"Uriah the Hittite you have slain with the *sword*, and his wife you have
taken to be your wife, and him you have killed with the *sword* of the
Ammonites. Now therefore the *sword* shall never depart from your house."
(2 Sam. 12:9b–10a)

"Because you have despised me and have taken the wife of Uriah the Hittite
to be your wife" – thus says Yhwh – "I am raising up *evil* against you out of
your own house, and I will take your wives before your eyes and give them
to your neighbor, and he shall lie with your wives in the eyes of this sun. For
you did it in secret, but I shall do this thing before all Israel and before the
sun."[22] (2 Sam. 12:10b–12)

David's "this thing," which Joab was to dismiss from his mind

(11:25), becomes Yhwh's "this thing" (*haddabar hazzeh*), which will be done openly.

It is no accident that punishment falls upon the house. Yhwh promised to build David a secure house (2 Samuel 7), now he says the sword will never depart from that house.[23] We saw in the tragedies of Saul and Jephthah that the sins of the fathers were visited upon the children, bringing down their houses in a tragic denouement. Jephthah's daughter had to die that his vow might be fulfilled. Saul's family all suffer as members of a fated house. In David's case there is an added twist, a tragic complication. Yhwh uses David's children as the *instruments* of their father's punishment. David's sins are not only visited upon his children but reenacted by them. Tamar's rape by Amnon and Amnon's murder by Absalom reflect David's sin with Bathsheba and murder of Uriah. In the reprise, the sexual crime is by contrast explicitly brutal,[24] while the murder might be considered more justified, since Absalom acts to avenge his sister. Absalom has his servants murder Amnon just as David had Joab murder Uriah, with the difference that this second murder is carried out openly (just as later Absalom will openly rape David's wives in the sight of all Israel, thereby fulfilling Nathan's prophecy).

Upon hearing Nathan's story about the rich man's crime against the poor man and his ewe lamb, David exclaims that the man should pay fourfold "because he did this thing."[25] David himself will pay four times over. Four of his sons die, the first three while he lives to see it: the unnamed first-born child of David and Bathsheba; Amnon, David's first-born son and heir; Absalom, for whom David would have given his own life; and Adonijah, the son next in line for the kingship before Solomon. As for the sword never departing from David's house, three sons (Amnon, Absalom, and Adonijah) meet violent deaths, not by the swords of outsiders, but at the hands of other members of David's house. Amnon is slain on his brother Absalom's orders; Adonijah, on those of his brother Solomon. Joab is responsible for Absalom's death, as well as Amasa's – sons, brothers, nephews, cousins, all being caught up in the cycle of violence. In accord with David's deathbed orders, Solomon has Joab struck down. The threat of the sword extends to the house of Israel, which ought to be under David's care ("I gave you the house of Israel and Judah," 2 Sam. 12:8). Rebellion almost tears the kingdom apart: first from within the Davidic house, when Absalom leads a revolt against his father; then from without, from Saul's tribe of Benjamin, when Sheba incites the northern tribes against the Davidic house (a reminder that David is not finished with the rival house of Saul).

The bitterness of David's tragedy is that he not only cannot spare his children misery, but he even plays an unwitting role in the tragic fates they suffer. The first son Bathsheba bears to David dies in David's place, as it were ("you shall not die; nevertheless ... the child that is born to you shall die"). Neither David's penitence nor his prayers can reverse Yhwh's decision (2 Sam. 12:15b–23). David figures prominently in Jonadab's scheme to help Amnon seduce his sister Tamar: Jonadab calculates that if Amnon feigns illness, the king will visit him and grant his request that Tamar be sent to prepare food for him. Indeed, David sends his obedient daughter off to Amnon's house, where she will be raped and then discarded (2 Sam. 13:7). David also sends Amnon with Absalom for the sheep-shearing where Absalom has him killed, although this time the king appears reluctant: "Why should he go with you?" But he sends him anyway after Absalom repeatedly presses him (2 Sam. 13:24–7). When Absalom returns to Jerusalem after a three-year exile, David's refusal to see his son (14:24, 28) and their eventual strained reconciliation symbolized by a ceremonial kiss[26] may well have intensified Absalom's hostility and contributed to his eventual rebellion. It is David who grants Absalom leave to go to Hebron, where he sets his insurrection in motion (15:7–12).[27] Finally, David's appointment of Solomon to succeed him spells death for Adonijah, who was next in line for the throne (1 Kings 2:15).

With Absalom's revolt and death, David's fortunes reach their lowest point. The evil Yhwh promised to raise up against David out of his own house is fully unleashed, and the divine judgment to give David's wives to another to lie with "before all Israel and before the sun" comes to pass in a tent pitched for Absalom on the roof. Now the tragic receives its fullest expression in a rare, intimate view of David. In his vulnerability the king becomes most sympathetic.[28] His conduct indicates a genuine inner conflict. This is not the first time he has shown ambivalence toward Absalom; he longed for Absalom after Absalom fled Jerusalem but refused to see him after his return. Now, however, his mood is more intense, as he wavers between desire to hold on to his kingdom and protectiveness toward his son who would take it from him forcibly. David's erratic behavior suggests confusing, conflicting emotions. He abandons Jerusalem without a struggle, but thereafter puts up a determined fight for his throne, and, when the crisis has been resolved, cares less about the battle's outcome than about his son's well-being.

In his flight from Absalom, David reaches true tragic status. This is made possible because we see him for the first time, like Lear cast out by his offspring, as unaccommodated man. Once loved by all the people (1 Sam. 18:16; 2 Sam. 3:36), David is forced to flee for his life by his son, who has found considerable support among David's subjects (2 Sam. 15:12). Not that David lacks a following: he withdraws from Jerusalem with his attendants, "all his household" (except the ten wives left to keep the house), "all the people," Joab (though we do not hear of him at this point), "all his servants," "all the Cherethites, and all the Pelethites, and all the six hundred Gittites," including the faithful Ittai.[29] As they cross the Kidron toward the wilderness, "all the country wept aloud as all the people passed by" (15:23). Others who would join the king are sent back: Abiathar and Zadok "with all the Levites," Ahimaaz and Jonathan, and Hushai. Yet despite the many people he can rely on, David's suffering has the effect of isolating him from them, for though they remain loyal to him politically, they cannot share his personal pain at his son's betrayal.[30] David's sense of isolation is revealed when he refers to Absalom as "the king," while the narrator and David's followers use that title for David (2 Sam. 15:19). Psychologically has he already abdicated? In a moving scene on the Mount of Olives, David stands out as a symbol of desolation among the people, who seem almost incidental:

David went up the slope of the Mount of Olives, weeping as he went, with his head covered, going barefoot. All the people who were with him covered their heads and they went up, weeping as they went. (2 Sam. 15:30)

That the people are no real source of comfort for the king will soon enough become apparent, when David's grief over Absalom's death will reveal that they mean less to him than his rebel son (2 Sam. 19:6 [Heb. 19:7]).

A further blow to David's already shattered spirit is the humiliation he suffers from Shimei's curses and stone-throwing, as his retreat continues. Abishai is eager to right the public disgrace to the king and his entourage by cutting off Shimei's head, but David sees the insult as a personal matter, one he accepts as related to Absalom's treason: "My own son seeks my life; how much more so may this Benjaminite!" (2 Sam. 16:11). Meanwhile, back in Jerusalem,

Ahithophel in his wisdom senses David's isolation and his tenuous bond with the people when he counsels Absalom:

I will come upon him while he is weary and disheartened, and throw him into a panic, and all the people who are with him will flee. I will kill the king alone, and I will bring back all the people to you. When all return [except] the man you seek,[31] all the people will be at peace. (2 Sam. 17:2–3)

Hushai is wrong when he counters Ahithophel's advice, but he too, interestingly, separates David from the people:

You know that your father and his men are mighty men, and that they are enraged, like a bear robbed of her cubs in the field. Your father is expert in war; he will not spend the night with the people. (2 Sam. 17:8)

The confused and hopeless state David has reached manifests itself in the exhaustion he and his followers have experienced by the time they reach the Jordan (16:14). On the other side of the Jordan, at Mahanaim, Shobi, Machir, and Barzillai meet the weary entourage with provisions (17:29). On both sides of the Jordan, David receives physical sustenance (Ziba had earlier brought supplies, 16:1–2), but what of emotional sustenance? Although he calls on Yhwh for help (2 Sam. 15:31), David cannot "strengthen himself in God," as he had in an earlier crisis, when at Ziklag his men had spoken of stoning him (1 Sam. 30:6). Perhaps he can no longer confidently rely on Yhwh's support. From David's perspective, it is tempting to believe that Shimei is now right when he says, "Yhwh has given the kingdom into the hand of your son Absalom" (16:8).

On his way to the kingship, when he fled before Saul, who actually was king, David was able both to act resourcefully and to turn to Yhwh for guidance. Now in his flight from Absalom, whom he dispiritedly calls "the king," he seems confused and irresolute.[32] When he hears of the rebellion, he instructs his followers, "Let us flee at once, or else there will be no escape for us from Absalom. Go in haste, lest he overtake us quickly, and bring down evil upon us, and smite the city with the edge of the sword" (2 Sam. 15:14). David's reference to "evil" and the "sword" echoes Yhwh's judgment against his house. Is he acquiescing in his fate or seeking to flee from it? Why does the king, a seasoned warrior, simply abandon Jerusalem to Absalom? Perhaps to spare the city.[33] But it appears he has no plan: to Ittai he protests, "Shall I today make you wander about with us, when I am going wherever I can go?" (2 Sam. 15:20). And

David seems so to have lost control of his future that it is Hushai who must counsel him to cross the Jordan during the night in order to escape Absalom's forces (2 Sam. 17:15–22).

Although David wages no heroic struggle against his fate, he does not yield completely. He appeals to Yhwh, but he also relies on his own cunning, suggesting ways Abiathar, Zadok, and Hushai can be of use to him (2 Sam. 15:27–36). But in spite of displaying some characteristics of the old David, he is no longer the mighty warrior of earlier fame. Tragic events have taken their toll. His soldiers advise him not to go out to battle, lest he be killed, and he meekly accepts "whatever is good in [their] eyes" (18:4; a contrast to the Ammonite war, during which David remained at home to do "evil in the eyes of Yhwh" when he should have gone to fight). The only command he gives to his troops as they go into battle is to "deal gently with the youth Absalom," a command heard by all the people (18:5, 12). Repeatedly he refers to his son as a "youth" (*na'ar*), as though he were only a child, and not a threat to his kingdom and his life (David, for example, was only a youth when he slew Goliath).

Joab and his armor-bearers kill Absalom (2 Sam. 18:15). Another seventeen verses pass before David learns that Absalom is dead. Our knowledge of Absalom's death long before David hears of it does not diminish suspense but actually heightens it, since it delays the moment of tragic recognition.[34] We know, but David does not know, and thus we watch him endure the agony of waiting. We are forced to wait while information about Absalom's pillar is given. A series of vivid scenes follows: two runners are dispatched to bring David news of the battle; the runners are observed by a watchman who tells the king what he sees; finally, each of the runners gives his battle report, with only the second willing to answer David's question about Absalom. The scene between Ahimaaz and Joab (2 Sam. 18:19–23), where Ahimaaz finally convinces Joab to let him run after the Cushite, is necessary to set the stage for the arrival of two messengers in vv. 28–32, and it introduces the concern with "bearing tidings" (*bsr*), a term repeated nine times in vv. 19–32. But what purpose does the exchange between David and the watchman serve (vv. 24–7) if not purely to retard the action and prolong the king's uncertainty?

David was sitting between the two gates and the watchman went up to the roof of the gate by the wall. When he lifted up his eyes and looked, he saw a man running alone. The watchman called out and told the king, and the king said, "If he is alone, there are tidings in his mouth." And he drew nearer and nearer. The watchman saw another man running, and the watchman called to the gate and said, "Look, another man running alone!" The king said, "He also brings tidings." The watchman said, "I see that the running of the foremost is like the running of Ahimaaz the son of Zadok." The king said, "He is a good man and comes with good tidings."

The very unnecessariness of this scene, the way time drags, lends pathos to David's situation. The king hangs on to hope, looking for signs that things will work out. Perhaps he recalls an earlier occasion, when the report that all the king's sons were dead turned out to be false, since soon thereafter it became apparent only Amnon was dead (2 Sam. 13:30–6). Clearly the king is anxious to learn what has happened, but his anticipation that Ahimaaz "is a good man and comes with good tidings" (*besorah tobah*, v. 27) raises the question: what tidings will the king consider good? Not, it turns out, the news that his forces have won the day.

In addition to delaying David's discovery of his son's fate, the narrative use of two messengers and two messages discloses most vividly what occupies David's mind. When Ahimaaz arrives with a cry of *shalom* and news of victory, David shows no interest in details of the battle or casualties among his troops, but only in the welfare of the rebel leader: "Is it well with the youth Absalom?" Ahimaaz' lie that he does not know further prolongs David's uncertainty. The Cushite arrives next with tidings of victory (*yitbasser*), and David asks him the same question, "Is it well with the youth Absalom?" Upon hearing the answer at last, David breaks down. The news transforms his anxiety into pain. Just as in Saul's tragedy, where the hero's fearful state was vividly depicted at the low point in his fortunes, his visit to the medium at En-dor, similarly here, at David's personal nadir, his grief is repeatedly exposed: "the king was deeply shaken"; "he wept" (18:33 [Heb. 19:1]). Joab is told "the king is weeping and mourning for Absalom" (19:1 [19:2]). The people hear, "the king is grieving for his son" (19:2 [19:3]). And again, "the king covered his face"; "the king cried with a loud voice" (19:4 [19:5]).

The shock reduces David to anguished repetition:

My son Absalom, my son, my son Absalom! If only I had died instead of you! Absalom, my son, my son! (2 Sam. 18:33 [Heb. 19:1])

So intense is the pain that he can do no more than repeat essentially the same outpouring of grief a few verses later:

My son Absalom, Absalom, my son, my son! (2 Sam. 19:4 [Heb. 19:5])

As an expression of utter loss, David's lament over Absalom, like Lear's fivefold "never" and Job's "cursed be the day I was born," touches the core of tragic despair. It threatens to render meaningless everything Yhwh has done for him. Yhwh gave David the kingdom as he had given it to Saul earlier, but unlike Saul, David never showed any sign of not wanting to be king. Although he does not want Absalom to be successful in his bid for the throne, he also does not want Absalom to be hurt. And he cannot have it both ways. This is the focus of David's tragic conflict. Political victory is a personal defeat. He wins the battle but loses his son and wishes he could give his life instead. Part of him seems to have died with Absalom. The part that survives will again be king – but a diminished king.

Lear dies of a broken heart. David endures, broken in spirit. His grief, so tragically excessive, demoralizes the people:

The victory that day was turned into mourning for all the people; for the people heard that day, "The king is grieving for his son." So the people stole into the city that day as people steal in who are ashamed when they flee in battle. (2 Sam. 19:2–3 [Heb. 19:3–4])

Circumstances could hardly be more inverted or catastrophic: a king so thoroughly absorbed in his personal tragedy that he gives no thought to the soldiers who have risked their lives for him.[35] Such irrational behavior provokes Joab to recall the king to his responsibility. Joab's accusation, "...you have made it clear today that commanders and servants are nothing to you...if Absalom were alive and all of us were dead today, then you would be pleased" (19:6 [Heb. 19:7]), may overstate the case, but it testifies to David's extremity. Joab warns David that the entire army could desert him by daybreak. And such an outcome, he avers, would be an even greater tragedy, "worse for you than all the evil that has come upon you from your youth until now" (2 Sam. 19:7 [Heb. 19:8]). Never before has David taken rebuke of this kind from a subordinate; perhaps he accepts it because he has already expended all emotion.[36] Without a word, he takes his place at the gate.

Unlike Saul, who is crushed by fate, David bears tribulation from this point forward with a certain acceptance. That, after Absalom's death, David's fortunes take an uncertain course becomes apparent in his journey back to Jerusalem, when he meets various people he had encountered during his flight. These encounters seem uneventful enough; they are not cases where one would expect problems to develop. But on closer examination they reveal a way things have of going awry – not necessarily *wrong*, but somehow out of kilter – for David as he regains his throne.[37] He pardons Shimei for cursing him and promises "you shall not die." One might expect Shimei to drop out of the picture, like so many minor characters, or at least no longer to be an irritation to David; but something sinister and unresolved lingers, for on his deathbed David arranges Shimei's death.[38] Once flattered as having wisdom "like the angel of God to discern good and evil" (2 Sam. 14:17), David proves incapable of deciding the issue of loyalty between Ziba and Mephibosheth, where one might expect some resolution.[39] He offers the good life in Jerusalem to Barzillai, but his offer is rejected, albeit graciously, and David must settle for Chimham. More important actions on David's part turn out to have distinctly negative consequences. Of long-lasting significance is his encouragement of competition between the northern and southern tribes, regarding who should be first to restore the king to the throne. In the wake of the resulting tribal animosity, Sheba calls the northern tribes to revolt (2 Sam. 19:11–12, 41–3 [Heb. 19:12–13, 42–4]; 20:1–2). To make matters worse, David's appointment of Amasa to replace Joab as commander of the army turns out to be a serious mistake when Amasa fails to rally Judah promptly against Sheba (2 Sam. 19:13 [Heb. 19:14]; 20:4–6).

If David was on the sidelines during the battle with Absalom's followers, he is even more removed from the events of Sheba's rebellion, where Joab and the wise woman of Abel resolve the crisis. Oddly, David's restoration to the throne of a united Israel and Judah and the actual reconciliation between the northern and southern tribes are not recounted, and therefore we can only wonder with what exuberance or perhaps resignation these events were greeted.

The account of David's final days brings an uneasy measure of resolution and reprieve. The chronological problem of 2 Samuel 21–4 has been much debated. There are indeed flashbacks here, and summaries of earlier periods of David's life – but since the events described in these chapters are narrated at this point in the story, we may view them both as a commentary on the preceding chapters and as a further stage in David's career.[40] Israel suffers. Significantly, we hear the accounts of a famine (2 Samuel 21), alleviated after David sends seven of Saul's "sons" to their deaths, and of pestilence (2 Samuel 24), for which David offers his house in expiation, only after we have witnessed David losing sons to violence and after his house has been nearly decimated. Also in 2 Samuel 21 we encounter a weary David (21:15), whom someone else must save from a Philistine giant (vv. 16–17). David has become a liability to his followers; they demand that he no more go out to battle with them (2 Sam. 21:17). And giant-slaying, for which David was once famous, is left to others. As if he sensed that David is now well on the way to becoming a non-person, the narrator begins to rewrite his story, ascribing David's famous victory against Goliath to one Elhanan (2 Sam. 21:19). If David is able to recite psalms of praise (2 Samuel 22 and 23), we cannot hear them without overtones of irony in view of the actual course of his fortunes: "Yhwh has recompensed me according to my righteousness, according to my purity in his eyes."

David lives to appoint his successor, though it is hard to resist the impression that David in 1 Kings 1–2 lacks any real power of decision. He is the object of manipulation, and as such, more pathetic than tragic. An unflattering picture of David emerges in these final chapters: he appears senile and impotent, easily duped but vindictive to the end. David dies and is buried in the city of David, but we hear nothing of public or private mourning at his death, such as one would expect for a great and beloved king. David himself had openly lamented the deaths of Saul, Jonathan, Abner, and Absalom,[41] but how deeply does anyone – even Bathsheba who earlier lamented Uriah's death – mourn the king's death? In contrast to Saul, Jonathan, Abner, and Absalom, who died by the sword, David dies quietly, but not without bequeathing violence to his son Solomon. Solomon's succession to the throne is marked by deceit, intrigue, and murder, as he moves determinedly to protect his interests just as his father had done in the Bathsheba affair.[42] Thus we find Solomon, in a kind of poetically just closure, "reliving the circumstances of his own birth," as David Gunn puts it[43] – a sign that tragedy within the Davidic house is far from over.

*   *   *

Central to David's tragedy has been his encounter with a God whose relentless judgment he cannot escape. It is not simply a question of morality, of sin and punishment, for tragedy is more than this. Tragic guilt involves both the transgression of a prohibition and the guiltiness of being that calls down upon itself excessive consequences.[44] The divine metamorphosis from David's protector to his prosecutor does not suddenly result from David's sins of adultery and murder. Already before David commits these wrongful deeds, there are signs that Yhwh no longer unqualifiedly champions David's cause. An early note of dissonance is sounded in 2 Samuel 6, as David reaches the height of his fortune. David's first attempt to bring the ark of Yhwh to Jerusalem miscarries when Yhwh kills Uzzah for touching the ark. Perhaps this failure is meant to warn David that he does not control Yhwh.[45] David's response is anger (v. 8), fear (v. 9), and unwillingness to take the ark into the city (v. 10). He tries again, after being reassured that the ark brings blessing, and though this time he succeeds in establishing the ark in Jerusalem, the ensuing domestic dispute with Michal foreshadows the discord that will later plague the royal house.

Throughout the account of David's sin (2 Samuel 11), Yhwh is conspicuously absent, just as Yhwh is absent at the moment of sin in the garden of Eden. In view of Yhwh's active participation in David's affairs during his rise to the throne, it is striking that Yhwh does not intervene, even if indirectly, to prevent David from sinning. In 1 Samuel 25, for example, when David is prepared to kill Nabal and his entire male household, Yhwh seems to have used Abigail to prevent David from shedding innocent blood. On this earlier occasion, it is Yhwh who kills the husband, and David gets the wife without incurring guilt.[46] But the situation is different in 2 Samuel 11, and David (necessarily?) yields to temptation. Is it coincidence that Bathsheba is bathing – on the roof – when David takes his afternoon stroll, or is David, like the first couple, being tested? Even in the matter of Bathsheba's pregnancy, like Michal's childlessness, divine involvement cannot be ruled out.

In 2 Samuel 11–12, as was also the case in the garden of Eden, Yhwh appears only after the sin, to mete out punishment. And, again, as in the garden story, the guilty do not die – though Yhwh threatened the first couple with death in the day they ate the forbidden fruit, and David has pronounced a sentence of death upon himself. In both cases, however, wrongdoing is severely punished. Yhwh sends a prophet to condemn David. We have only to recall that Yhwh always spoke to Saul indirectly, through the prophet Samuel, to see in Nathan's appearance before David a subtle suggestion that David will no longer enjoy easy access to Yhwh. In Yhwh's name, Nathan recites what Yhwh has done for David – and how much more he would still do.[47] But now David will experience Yhwh's other side.

The certainty of God David knew during his rise to the throne becomes, after his sin, only a possibility that does not determine the action. "Who knows whether Yhwh will be gracious to me that the child may live?" (2 Samuel 12:22), asks David, hoping to persuade Yhwh to spare the child condemned to death for his sin. But Yhwh is not gracious.[48] Again, "If I find favor in Yhwh's eyes, he will bring me back," David says when he flees Jerusalem before Absalom (15:25), and "perhaps Yhwh will look upon my affliction and Yhwh will repay me with good for this cursing of me today" (16:12). Indeed, David does return to Jerusalem and he is restored to the throne; but is it a "repaying with good" if the price of David's return is his son's death and the near split of the kingdom?

In 2 Samuel 15:31, upon learning that his counselor has joined Absalom's conspiracy, David prays, "O Yhwh, please, turn the counsel of Ahithophel into foolishness." Immediately thereafter he meets Hushai, whom he sends back to persuade Absalom to reject Ahithophel's advice. Hushai succeeds because "Yhwh had ordained to defeat the good counsel of Ahithophel" (2 Samuel 17:14). Has Yhwh answered David's prayer, as some interpreters claim,[49] or is the defeat of Ahithophel's counsel rather the working out of nemesis within the Davidic house – a nemesis that calls for another royal son to die by the sword? The reason given for Yhwh's intervention is to "bring evil upon Absalom" (17:14), not to help David or to bring about David's restoration to the throne Absalom has sought to usurp. Whatever the connection between David's prayer, the defeat of Ahithophel's counsel, and Absalom's death, it is not a simple one. David could not induce Yhwh to spare his first son with Bathsheba; it would be tragically ironic indeed if he now could influence Yhwh to defeat his son Absalom. Although David is implicated in Absalom's death (and in Tamar's rape, Amnon's murder, and Absalom's rebellion), he is not responsible for these disasters. He is, however, accountable for them; his children's ruin is his punishment. But, we may ask, is it not a savage God who has chosen *this particular way* to punish him? Like Jephthah, when he vowed to sacrifice the one who met him upon his victorious return from battle, David, in praying that Yhwh confound Ahithophel's counsel, may not have intended the death of his child, but that is, tragically, what happens.

Only once more in the narrative, after his kingship is reestablished following both Absalom's revolt and Sheba's, do we again find David consulting Yhwh (2 Samuel 21). Famine has ravaged the land for three years before David seeks divine guidance, a clear sign that

David's former intimacy with Yhwh has been fractured. Yhwh responds to David's inquiry, but not as in earlier days, when he so often told David what to do. Now the Gibeonites tell him what he must do, and, as we saw in Chapter 4, a combination of events that eludes rational explanation leads God to heed supplications for the land. Elements of this account are echoed in 2 Samuel 24, where it is David's sin, not Saul's, that brings affliction upon the kingdom. Here, as in 2 Samuel 12, David confesses to sin – not once, but twice ("I have sinned," vv. 10, 17); and as in 2 Samuel 12, Yhwh instructs David through a prophet. Significantly, however, David's sin is attributed directly to Yhwh: "Again the anger of Yhwh was kindled against Israel, and he incited David against them, saying, 'Go, number Israel and Judah'" (v. 1).

Why Yhwh is angry we are not told. Reviewing sequentially the narrative of David's career, we can observe a shift in God's dealings with him, from practically unqualified support during David's rise, to absence at the moment of sin, to this final act of causing David to sin. David is allowed to select his punishment, and he asks to fall into Yhwh's, rather than human, hands because Yhwh is merciful (24:14). Yhwh then sends a plague which destroys thousands. Finally Yhwh repents of the evil; David confesses sin a second time, asks that the punishment fall upon his house rather than his people, and erects an altar as Yhwh commands. As in 2 Samuel 21, cause and effect are difficult to untangle as events come to a resolution: "Yhwh heeded supplications for the land and the plague was averted from Israel" (2 Sam. 24:25). This comment at the end of 2 Samuel is followed in 1 Kings 1–2 by the account of David's final days, where Yhwh is spoken of, and Yhwh's blessing is invoked, but Yhwh does nothing to make Solomon king. Yhwh's virtual absence here contrasts markedly with his direct involvement in clearing the way for David's kingship.[50]

Whether or not David is duped into proclaiming Solomon king is not entirely clear.[51] Although Bathsheba and Nathan claim David had promised the throne to Solomon, we have only their word for it; the text does not record such an important act on David's part. Solomon is crowned while the king still lives. Besides the suggestion that David is sexually impotent with the young and beautiful Abishag, and oblivious to the political intrigue already set in motion by rival factions within his family, the picture of David as a king who is no longer king offers further testimony to his incapacity and decreasing significance. In essence, nothing is left for him to do but curse his enemies and die. Perhaps for this reason his death receives little attention; he has already yielded his place in the narrative to "King Solomon" (1 Kings 1: 34, 39, 43, 51, 53). First, however, while David is still king – in fact, the last time the narrative refers to him as "king" – he praises Yhwh for letting him see his heir on the throne (1 Kings 1:48). Whether we view him in his final days as tragically pathetic or pathetically tragic, his appointment of Solomon has a tragic consequence for yet another son, a consequence David does not seem to consider: Adonijah will have to die before Solomon can be sure of his position.

On his deathbed, David charges Solomon to keep Yhwh's commandments:

that Yhwh may establish his word which he spoke concerning me, "If your sons take heed to their way, to walk before me in faithfulness with all their heart and with all their being, there shall not fail you a man on the throne of Israel." (1 Kings 2:4)

In words placed in David's mouth, Yhwh takes back the unconditional, eternal covenant promised in 2 Samuel 7. For the Davidic house, there are no more certainties.[52]

In a psalm attributed to David "on the day Yhwh delivered him from the hand of all his enemies and from the hand of Saul," David says of Yhwh:

> With the loyal you show yourself loyal,
>   with the blameless hero, you show yourself blameless,
> with the pure you act in purity,
>   with the crooked you show yourself perverse.
> You deliver a humble people,
>   but your eyes are upon the haughty to bring them low.[53]
>
> (2 Sam. 22:26–8)

The words both fit and do not fit what we know about David's experience of Yhwh, and therefore are an appropriate commentary on a story not unacquainted with tragic ambiguity. Yhwh is remarkably loyal to David during his rise to the throne, even though at times David could be considered a scoundrel. In meting out punishment for the Bathsheba/Uriah affair, when David was indeed crooked, Yhwh was savage, and perhaps "perverse" is not off the mark. Above all, the recognition that "your eyes are upon the haughty to bring them low" expresses the tragic theme of *hubris* that attracts nemesis, a theme so pervasive in the whole David story.

*   *   *

We have seen ample reason to speak of a tragic dimension in the story of David. We find it in the reversal of the hero's fortunes that takes place as a result of his sins, in the suggestions of hostile transcendence that accompany David's guilt, and in the series of unmitigated disasters that beset the Davidic house. Yet the tragic vision present in the story is not fully realized. What prevents David from attaining truly tragic proportions, something like the tragic grandeur of his predecessor Saul? There is no simple answer to this question, which brings us ever back to our initial question: who is David, and who is the son of Jesse? It is not just that David's personality is complex, elusive, and impenetrable – though this is one reason David comes through as less than tragic. David often surprises us with his unexpected responses, whose real motivation can never quite be determined, as, for example, with Saul in the cave or with his infant son. Another reason, the root of the matter, is found in the king himself, who simply does not assume the role of tragic hero. Though he suffers, he is not dignified by suffering, as is Saul. Saul we found to be an extremely complex and volatile personality, a man whose passions and powerful, conflicting emotions hurt both himself and those around him. At key points in the narrative, we are allowed intimate access to his violent nature, his pathetic, paranoid vulnerability, and more – we are privy to the inner struggle of his tormented spirit. What we see is not all bad or blameworthy. Saul is a towering figure, not just head and shoulders above the people in stature but also in his intensity, and, especially, by virtue of his resistance – his refusal to bow to fate – though fate, in the end, crushes him.

David, by contrast, seems small. He displays none of Saul's heroic defiance, and little, if any, of his inner struggle. Although the story grants David little privacy – indeed, it reveals more intimate details of his personal life than we heard of Saul – David remains inaccessible, his motives and feelings all too often unknown. What, for example, prompts David to commit the sins of adultery and murder in the first place? boredom? a sense of limitless power? disregard for his subjects' rights? lust and then fear of discovery? Whatever it is that motivates David, it is no noble flaw. He does not, like Saul and Jephthah, do the wrong thing while trying to do the right thing. Saul, we recall, sins by imploring divine favor before battle, even though it means offering the sacrifice without waiting for Samuel; he errs again, when he spares the best of Amalekite spoil, avowedly to sacrifice to Yhwh at Gilgal. Similarly, Jephthah promises a sacrifice to Yhwh if Israel attains victory over Ammon, not anticipating that he will find himself in the position of having to sacrifice his daughter. Whatever we think of Saul's and Jephthah's "flaws," they face head-on the consequences of their actions with a heroic determination that gives them a certain grandeur. Their refusal to compromise (as Saul might have, for example, by abdicating, or Jephthah, by not sacrificing his daughter) is a quality tragic heroes tend to have in common. David, as we have seen, does wrong willfully, almost as a matter of course, seemingly impervious to God's laws and kingship's requirements. And David is a consummate compromiser; he adapts to circumstances. David is too much the pragmatist to be broken by fate when he can bend. This is why he ultimately falls short of becoming a genuine tragic hero.

If his flaw is not noble, neither does David deal nobly with its consequences. When disaster strikes one child after another in quick succession, David mourns, weeps, and goes through the motions of grief, but only with Absalom does he display such anguish as is born of tragic guilt. We must ask, therefore, what happens to David as the meaning of punishment by evil and the sword gradually becomes known to him in its fullness? David's failure to take any outwardly appreciable measures to avoid his fate suggests the absence of genuine inner struggle. At the same time, the virtual textual silence regarding any inner struggle gives the impression that he displays little outward resistance.

In the first place, the fact of punishment seems to take him by surprise (2 Samuel 12); at the least, he responds strangely. Like Oedipus with Teiresias, David at first is blind to his guilt and cannot recognize himself in the prophet's words that identify him as a murderer. Does he react so strongly to the rich man's crime because of his own guilty conscience, as Fokkelman suggests,[54] or can it be that he has no sense of guilt, that he has followed his own advice to Joab ("Do not let this thing be evil in your eyes," 2 Sam. 11:25) and simply put the matter of Bathsheba and Uriah out of mind? Nathan must point out the king's error: "You are the man" (2 Sam. 12:7).

Upon learning what his transgression will mean for his house, David confesses, "I have sinned against Yhwh" (v. 13), and has nothing more to say. There is, as yet, no tragic recognition, no protest against the enormity of this punishment, no cry that it is more than he can bear. David is no Oedipus, lamenting in his extremity, "If there is any ill worse than ill, that is the lot of Oedipus." And when Nathan adds that Yhwh will spare his life and take the life of his child instead, David cannot even rise to the grand tragic occasion, but makes no reply. Only later will he wish he could have died in another son's place.

David's minimal response to Nathan might be interpreted to mean that the shock has reduced him to speechlessness, but it recalls his reaction on an earlier occasion when David had occasioned tragedy, the massacre of the priests of Nob (1 Samuel 22). When Saul had the priests of Nob killed and the city razed, one man, Abiathar, escaped to tell David. David admits, "I knew on that day, when Doeg the Edomite was there, that he would surely tell Saul. I am to blame for all the deaths in your father's house" (1 Sam. 22:22). Faced with such an atrocity, however, he displays no outward signs of remorse or outrage. He offers Abiathar sanctuary since "he that seeks my life seeks your life" (1 Sam. 22:23) – a gesture that requires no sacrifice on David's part. David destroys houses – Ahimelech's, Saul's, his own – but how deeply does David feel a sense of tragic responsibility?

David's responses to the misfortunes that befall his children, one by one, offer a key to understanding the kind of tragic hero David is. When Yhwh strikes David's unnamed son so that he becomes ill, David fasts and weeps. But when the child dies, David gets up, washes and anoints himself, changes his clothes, goes off to worship Yhwh, and then returns to his house to eat. What kind of grief is this? David's servants, not unreasonably, had expected him to show more distress over the child's death than over his illness, even to the extent of doing himself harm (12:18). When they remark upon this unusual behavior, David explains, "Now he is dead; why should I fast? Can I bring him back again? I shall go to him, but he will not return to me" (2 Sam. 12:23).[55] The matter is closed; life goes on, David comforts Bathsheba and soon gets another son. Thus, as punishment begins, there is compensation, with the second son, Solomon, given a distinct advantage: "Yhwh loved him" (12:24). Circumstances encourage David in adapting to his fate and perhaps in finding it endurable. If there had been no second child, he would have had to live with the death of the first and might even have come to appreciate its tragic dimension. Since there is a second son, David can compromise his potential as tragic hero.

David is to be painfully humiliated where it hurts most: he cannot control his house. This is both his punishment and his tragic flaw. When David learns that his son Amnon has raped his daughter Tamar (2 Samuel 13), he is "very angry," but does nothing to punish the crime.[56] Does he not see the connection we perceive between Amnon's moral violence and his own, or does he refuse to see it?[57] And does he feel no responsibility or remorse for having fallen prey to Amnon's deception and having sent Tamar to her violent fate? The inadequacy of David's response is indicated by Absalom's equally silent, but ultimately effectual reaction, juxtaposed to it:

> When King David heard all these things, he was very angry. But Absalom did not speak to Amnon either good or bad, for Absalom hated Amnon because he had raped Tamar his sister. (2 Sam. 13:21-2)

By doing nothing about the rape David becomes complicit in it. It is left to Absalom, who nurses his hatred for two full years, to avenge Tamar; David appears to have accepted the plight of a forsaken daughter who takes refuge in her brother's (not her father's) house.[58]

David's reaction to Amnon's murder by Absalom receives greater narrative attention than his response to Tamar's disgrace. In fact, the scene in which he learns of the prince's assassination (2 Sam. 13:30-6) contains elements that will reappear in the account of Absalom's death, when David will relive more intensely the trauma of losing his son and heir: the news that comes in two installments and the bitter weeping. At first David is told that "Absalom has slain all the king's sons; not one of them is left." But Jonadab assures the king that he has less reason to despair than he thinks: "Let not my lord the king take it to heart, thinking that all the king's sons are dead, for Amnon alone is dead" (v. 33). This is itself a compromise which David will find bearable. With the passage of time, he can be "comforted about Amnon, for he was dead" (v. 39).

Although David responds more emotionally to Amnon's assassination than to Tamar's rape, once again he does nothing about the crime. His eventual response to Amnon's death is neither insignificant nor uncharacteristic. The reaction of another bereaved father provides a telling contrast. For Jacob, seeing Joseph is dead is reason for *not* being comforted (Gen. 37:35). But for David, who is notorious

for his reaction to the death of Bathsheba's child, there is every reason
to believe that he will soon enough get over it. Then there was
Solomon to distract his attention; now there is Absalom. According
to 2 Sam. 13:37, "David mourned for his son day after day." But
which son, Amnon or Absalom? Verse 39 speaks of David's
longing for *Absalom*, and the next verse (14:1) informs us, as if to
underscore the point, that "Joab the son of Zeruiah knew that the
king's mind was on Absalom."

Unlike his tragic predecessor Saul, David does not seek out his
destiny but rather lets events unfold as they will. David the pragmatist
we have seen all along, biding his time, waiting for the kingship to
become his, not seizing it from Saul – in fact, refusing to seize it
(1 Samuel 24, 26) – but always ready to take advantage of the
moment: accepting Goliath's challenge when Saul and his army are
afraid (1 Samuel 17); meeting Saul's outrageous terms in order to
become the king's son-in-law (1 Samuel 18); stepping in immediately
after Saul's death to become king of Judah (2 Sam. 2:1–4); ready to
negotiate with Abner for the northern tribes, but on his own terms
(2 Sam. 3:12–14). People close to him – Jonathan, Michal, Abiathar,
Abigail with her husband's lands and wealth – even enemies-
become-allies (from their point of view) like Achish and Abner are
stepping-stones, who in one way or another all prove useful to him
in his acquisition of power. After the divine judgment of 2 Samuel 12,
however, something happens to David. As his tragic fate begins to
unfold, David appears no longer prepared to seize the moment by
taking initiative himself; he tends rather to *react* to events set in
motion by others. Especially when it comes to dealing with his
children, his responses are regularly inadequate or inappropriate,
and ultimately destructive. It is left to Joab to bring about Absalom's
return to Jerusalem, and then to Absalom (after being denied an
audience with his father for two years) to seize the initiative and force
the king to see him – both important developments that will have
fateful consequences.

Joab takes matters into his own hands "in order to turn about the
state of things" (2 Sam. 14:20), sending a wise woman to David with
a story designed to make the king agree to Absalom's return. In
contrast to the way he was taken in by Nathan's parable, David
perceives that the woman's story applies to him: "Is the hand of Joab
with you in all this?" (v. 19). Has David grown wiser? He is,
narratively speaking, coming closer to his moment of tragic recog-

nition, which he will reach through Absalom. David yields to Joab's purpose ("See now, I will do this thing. Go, bring back the youth Absalom," v. 21), but he refuses to participate ("Let him dwell in his house; he is not to see my face," v. 24). His indecision and vacillation – allowing Absalom to return but refusing to see him – make this a particularly portentous compromise. Once again David displays his inability to act firmly when his children are involved.[59]

When David flees Jerusalem before Absalom, he again takes a course of least resistance, without any apparent plan of action (2 Sam. 15:20; 17:16). He plays into the hands of his tragic fate by leaving ten wives of secondary rank to keep his house (2 Sam. 15:16), thus allowing Nathan's prophecy to be fulfilled: "They pitched a tent for Absalom upon the roof, and Absalom went in to his father's wives in the sight of all Israel" (16:22). (When David returns to his house after Absalom's death, still the king, he deals with the matter by putting the ill-treated women away, displaying once again his ability to put an ugly situation behind him, 2 Sam. 20:3.) Another king, at another time, facing the battle in which he would die, eschewed any compromises and deliberately sought out the God who had rejected him, compelled by some inner force to hear again what he already knew (1 Samuel 28). In fleeing from Absalom, David faces a battle that, as far as he knows, could spell the end of his rule and even his death. Shimei, for one, claims that Yhwh has given David's kingdom to Absalom, and calls it divine vengeance for David's crimes against Saul's house (2 Sam. 16:8). David accepts Shimei's cursing as inspired by Yhwh, "Let him alone, let him curse, for Yhwh has bidden him" (16:11). He does not, however, take it as the final word: "It may be that Yhwh will look upon my affliction and that Yhwh will repay me with good for this cursing of me today" (v. 12).

Like Saul, David seeks out the God who has brought judgment upon him, but he does not rely on direct inquiry as he had in earlier days. Does he refrain from asking Yhwh what to do because he can no longer fully trust Yhwh? It is difficult to imagine that David has decided to leave matters in Yhwh's hands,[60] for if David defers to Yhwh's will, he also acts in his own interest. During his retreat from Jerusalem, he professes, "If I find favor in the eyes of Yhwh, he will bring me back" (15:25), and "let him do to me whatever is good in his eyes" (15:26). But, in the same breath, he sends Jonathan and Ahimaaz back to Jerusalem as spies. He prays to Yhwh to confound the counsel of Ahithophel, but at the same time sends Hushai back to

Jerusalem to defeat Ahithophel's counsel, saying, "If you return to the city... then *you* will defeat for me the counsel of Ahithophel" (15:34). Again we see clearly David the pragmatist, whose desire to provide for every contingency disqualifies him as a true tragic hero.

Only with his moving lament, "My son Absalom, my son, my son Absalom, if only I had died instead of you, Absalom, my son, my son," does David reach the point of tragic recognition, forced as he is to confront the tragic consequences of his actions. I said earlier that there is something suggestive of King Lear in David's lament, as well as in David's extremity as he flees from Absalom. There is also in the moment of tragic recognition something of a lesser tragic hero, Willy Loman, except that the recognition works in reverse. After his son Biff forces him to hear the truth about himself and his illusions, Willy, astonished at the notion his son nevertheless might love him, says, "Isn't that – isn't that remarkable? Biff – he likes me!"[61] David, in effect, says of Absalom, "I really loved him," as if he had not really known it before. For a time he assumes the role of tragic hero, but he cannot sustain it. Joab calls him back to reality by pointing out that this is no way for a king to behave. If, warns Joab, David does not "go out and speak kindly to your servants," the army will abandon him by morning. Having lost his son, David could lose the kingdom too – and, in spite of everything, he *does* want the kingdom.

The king does his duty; he takes his place at the gate for the people to see (2 Sam. 19:8 [Heb. 19:9]). When we next hear of him, he is at work consolidating his position, appealing to the elders of Judah and offering command of the army to Amasa, who had been Absalom's general (19:11–14 [12–15]). David never wrestles, like Saul, to wrench meaning out of his misfortunes, and though he never seems quite to recover from them, he manages with the help of Joab and others to continue with the business of kingship.[62] The tragic David yields to the pragmatic one. He will later yield to the pathetic one, but still pragmatic enough to give his successor instructions about running the kingdom after he is dead (1 Kings 1–2).

If David's complexity, elusiveness, and impenetrability make him a questionable tragic hero, his flexibility and lack of tragic dignity born of tragic responsibility are the deciding factors. Perhaps he belongs in a class of tragic figures like Willy Loman, Nora Helmer, Blanche Dubois, and J. B., for he does not measure up to an Agamemnon, Antigone, Lear, or Saul. In his willingness to bend, to accommodate himself to fate, he lacks the largeness of spirit that sets great tragic heroes apart from lesser mortals. He has, as we have seen, his moment of tragic grandeur, but it passes. The real tragedy in the story of David lies in the burden of divine judgment David must bear, and not in his manner of bearing it – a judgment of destruction upon his house, yet to come to an end.

The tragedy of the house of David has only just begun when David dies. The remainder of the Deuteronomistic History, from 1 Kings 3 to 2 Kings 25, chronicles the woeful events that afflict the Davidic house from the division of the kingdom after Solomon's death to the catastrophe of exile. David has begotten a line of kings that will end miserably, even as Saul's house ended miserably – a dynasty whose members, the "good" ones notwithstanding, stumble blindly on to compound the guilt of the house of David so thoroughly that even righteous King Josiah is unable to alter the terrible course of destiny.[63] As the Deuteronomistic History closes (2 Kings 25:27–30), some four centuries have elapsed since David's death, and the Davidic king, Jehoiachin, lives out his days in Babylonian captivity, where he "dined regularly at the king's table." Jehoiachin's rueful fate echoes hauntingly the fate of Mephibosheth, the last of the house of Saul, which David displaced.[64] He, too, was to end his days in virtual house arrest, a pensioner at the royal court. David's house has come to this; its dynastic hopes rest precariously on a Mephibosheth *redivivus*.[65]

Afterword

An den langen Tischen der Zeit
zechen die Krüge Gottes.
   ·   ·   ·

Sie sind die gewaltigsten Zecher:
sie führen das Leere zum Mund wie das Volle
und schäumen nicht über wie du oder ich.

[At the long tables of time
the goblets of God are guzzling.
   ·   ·   ·

They are the heftiest guzzlers:
they raise both the empty and full to their lips
and do not foam over as you or I do.]

Paul Celan

I began this book by saying it would deal with tragedy as we meet it in particular biblical texts and not as we abstract it in theory. I end it with an afterword which is not a conclusion. For to write a conclusion I would need to draw together arguments from previous chapters – perhaps to dispute with those who maintain there is no tragedy in the Bible and to show how my analysis proves that the stories of Saul, of Jephthah, of the members of Saul's house, and of David are tragic – and, finally, to tie my observations up into a neat interpretive package, thus sparing the reader the need to engage what I hope are substantive arguments about the Bible's tragic dimension in the preceding chapters. Because my interest lies in texts, not theory, I have avoided, insofar as possible, generic claims about the Bible's tragic vision in favor of detailed analysis of specific instances of biblical tragedy (using a working definition of tragedy broad enough to include the Greeks, Shakespeare, biblical literature, and modern works). It would be inconsistent with the hermeneutical assumptions that have guided this study for me to try to summarize

– because it cannot be summarily stated what makes these narratives tragic – or to rehash – because it would only try the reader's patience – meanings I have sought to probe and draw out of complex and subtle narratives in Chapters 2–5 of this book.

Tragedy, I have argued, poses questions about the elusive and necessary relationship of guilt, suffering, and evil that it can only resolve aesthetically, not thematically.[1] My aim has been to show that the tragic vision is by no means alien to the Bible, to investigate some places where it can be found, and thereby to illustrate the diversity that exists in the way the tragic vision finds expression and aesthetic resolution in biblical literature. Rather than attempt to prove on the basis of predetermined external criteria that the narratives of Saul, of Jephthah, of Saul's house, and of David can be read as tragedies (such proof being neither possible nor desirable), I have speculated about the nature of their tragic visions, focusing on recalcitrant materials in these texts that cannot be adequately accounted for or explained away or reduced to something else. Because the tragic is a vision of fundamental disorder and cosmic unintelligibility contained within the literary work that, as Timothy Reiss observes, it undermines from within,[2] critical interpretation will also find itself caught up in an unresolvable tension. Is it possible to interpret malevolent transcendence?[3]

By discussing these texts at all, I have participated in the attempt all interpretation makes to impose order on them and make intelligible their irrational dimension, though I have tried to suggest rather than to define wherein the tragic lies, to *point to* the tragic rather than to *name* it. To locate Saul's tragedy (and by extension that of his house) in divine hostility, Jephthah's in divine absence, and David's in divine judgment does not mean that the tragic in these narratives can be reduced to simple origins or find adequate explanation in mere descriptive categories. These narratives all raise questions about the nature of human guilt, responsibility, and accountability. They also, through their portrayal of divinity as ambiguous, ambivalent, or in some other impalpable way problematic, implicate the deity in human misfortune and suffering.

If tragedy is a threat to stability and order, as Plato argued in *The Republic*, perhaps reading the Bible in terms of its tragic dimension will be considered somewhat subversive. Clearly my readings call into question comfortable assessments of texts resistant to easy solutions, in particular, assessments that try to rationalize or minimize the possibility of cosmic indifference to human misfortune. Tragedy threatens order by virtue of its recognition of random and unpredictable disorder. The random, the chaotic, the unintelligible, the contingent, are dimensions of reality as we know it, dimensions that the Bible knows also and whose fissures it does not, I have sought to illustrate, try to smooth over. Indeed, the Bible's uncompromising portrayal of reality as embracing dissolution and despair as well as resolution and repair is the source of its extraordinary narrative range and power. Any less expansive, multifaceted, and honest representation of accumulated experience and wisdom would be inadequate and inauthentic. Nor does the tragic vision itself leave us without hope, for if it despairs of knowing the ways of the universe – "the secrets of God and the limit of the Almighty," as Zophar puts it (Job 11:7)[4] – at the same time it shows us the dignity and amplitude of human beings coming to terms with the possibilities and limits of mortality.

Tragedy does not exhaust the interpretive possibilities of the narratives examined here; it does, however, open up an array of deeper questions they raise about order and human limits, about the human condition and the larger scheme of things, questions subject to multiple interpretations. And interpret we shall, again and again, in an effort to comprehend the Bible's vision of the incomprehensible, or perhaps to inquire how it deals, or fails to deal, with questions that matter to us, its readers.

Notes

1. BIBLICAL NARRATIVE AND THE TRAGIC VISION

1 My subject is the Jewish Bible, and when the terms "Bible" and "biblical" appear in this study they refer to it. Considerable interest has been shown in the possibility of Christian tragedy and tragedy in the New Testament; see *inter alia*, Cox (1969), and the sources listed there; Stone (1984). For interesting observations on tragicomedy in the Gospel of Mark, see Via (1975).

2 E.g. Boling (1975), pp. 206–10; Trible (1984), pp. 93–116; Fuchs (1989); Webb (1987), p. 75; Polzin (1980), p. 179; Bal (1988a), pp. 44, 46; Burney (1970), p. 320; Hertzberg (1969), p. 218.

3 E.g. Whybray (1968), pp. 24–5, 36–7 *et passim*; Conroy (1978), pp. 49, 51, 100 *et passim*; Perdue (1984), p. 71; the most thorough treatment of David as tragic is Whedbee (1988).

4 See e.g. Gellrich (1988), pp. 8–22, 94–162; Booth (1983), pp. 82–90; Krieger (1960), pp. 3–5; Else (1957), p. 306 *et passim*; Mason (1985), pp. 3, 100 *et passim*.

5 Gellrich (1988), p. 10. See also pp. 114–16, 124–5, 142–4; similarly, Booth (1983), pp. 89–90.

6 For this distinction between Euripides, Sophocles, and Aeschylus in terms of their portrayal of the gods and their tragic heroes, see Knox, in Easterling and Knox (1989), pp. 72–87. My comments about the significant differences among the Greek tragedies is based primarily on Kitto (1986); the essays by Winnington-Ingram, Easterling, and Knox, in Easterling and Knox (1989); Lucas (1959); Lesky (1965). Also influential on my thinking have been two recent works employing structuralist and semiotic theory, Vernant and Vidal-Naquet (1988); and C. Segal (1986).

7 Aristotle, *Poetics* 1460b.

8 Abel (1967), p. 20. Abel's judgment offers an example of what happens when we give definitions priority over texts. Kitto (1986) classifies Euripides' *Alcestis*, *Iphigenia in Tauris*, *Ion*, and *Helen* as tragicomedies, a term he admits is "not altogether a satisfactory one" (p. 311), and he considers the *Electra* and the *Orestes* to be melodramatic.

9 Bayley (1981), p. 5. Farnham (1950), pp. 2–12, argues for significant

differences among Shakespeare's early, middle, and late tragedies; Frye (1967) groups them along different lines as tragedies of order, passion, and isolation.

10 Frye (1967), pp. 14–15, discusses the similarities of the history plays to tragedy. Whereas he reads Shakespeare's romances as the fulfillment of his comic vision in *A Natural Perspective* (1965), Frye also considers the possibility of reading them as the fulfillment of Shakespearean tragedy at the end of *Fools of Time* (1967). Bradley (1949), p. 3, speaks of *Richard II* and *Richard III, Julius Caesar, Antony and Cleopatra,* and *Coriolanus* as "tragic histories or historical tragedies." I mention Shakespeare because he and the Greek tragedians supply my chief models for the tragic. I know too little about Racine and Corneille, except that their tragedies are of the first order, or about Schiller and other representatives of the Germanic tradition for them to have shaped my understanding. For illuminating distinctions between the German *Trauerspiel* and tragedy, see Benjamin (1977), pp. 57–158. The discussions of modern works by Sewall (1980) and Krieger (1960) have also contributed considerably to my understanding of tragedy.

11 Frye (1966), p. 162.

12 Steiner (1980), p. 8.

13 Frye (1966), p. 209. Frye points out that the rise can have taken place before the action begins. Cf. Lesky (1965), pp. 8–9.

14 Mason (1985), p. 10. Mason's theoretical approach is both common-sensical and naive, assuming that we all "feel" the same way he does when we read tragedy, but his insistence that we begin with texts rather than definitions is laudable. On "degrees" of tragedy, see also Gassner (1981), p. 305.

15 I take the term from Sewall (1980), as does Humphreys (1985). Krieger (1960) distinguishes between tragedy as a literary form and tragic vision. The distinction may be useful but for my purposes is not practical. Texts that share a tragic vision are what I call tragic. I fully agree with Krieger, pp. xi–xii, that discrete literary works should not be treated as "mere manifestations" of a particular all-encompassing vision; rather their distinctive features and resistance to categorization provide the subject of inquiry.

16 Jaspers (1952), p. 45.

17 Reiss (1980), p. 11.

18 Reiss (1980), p. 11. This is Krieger's point in distinguishing between the tragic existent and the tragic visionary; see esp. Krieger (1971), pp. 36–52.

19 Krieger (1971), p. 4.

20 Reiss (1980), p. 17; similarly, Booth (1983), pp. 85–6; C. Segal (1986), pp. 46–7.

21 Krutch (1981), p. 228; cf. Burke (1968), pp. 199–201. For a balanced and nuanced presentation of arguments for and against modern tragedy, see Gassner (1981).

22 E.g. Sewall (1980); Krieger (1960); Oates (1972); Mahoney (1985); Cox (1969); B. Simon (1988); Bouchard (1989). Sewall, whose influence on my thinking will be evident to those familiar with his book, applies the concept of tragic vision profitably to a broad spectrum of literature, ranging from classics like *Oedipus Tyrannus*, the book of Job, *Doctor Faustus*, and *King Lear*, to modern works such as *The Scarlet Letter*, *Moby-Dick*, *The Brothers Karamazov*, *Absalom, Absalom!*, *The Trial*, and *Long Day's Journey into Night*.

23 Miller (1957), esp. pp. 7–8, 31–6. The citation is from p. 33. See also Friedrich Dürrenmatt's (1966) essays, "Theaterprobleme," pp. 92–131, and "Anmerkung zur Komödie," pp. 132–7, esp. his interesting remarks on presenting the tragic through comedy, pp. 122–4.

24 Steiner (1980), p. 4; similarly, Kierkegaard (1987), pp. 150–1. See also the discussion of Frye (1982), pp. 169–98.

25 Kurzweil (1970), p. 340.

26 Kurzweil (1970), p. 338.

27 Tsevat (1966).

28 Frye (1982), pp. 169–98.

29 Good (1990), pp. 25–6, 375–8.

30 Ricoeur (1967), pp. 211–31; cf. Goldmann (1981), pp. 138–9; Mason (1985), pp. 33–5. Frye (1982), p. 181, attributes the "malice within the divine nature" in the Saul story to "a kind of inspired blundering"; it is ironic that a literary critic would fall back on the type of explanation he frequently criticizes biblical scholars for making. "Inspired," definitely; "blundering," by no means.

31 See Gellrich (1988), pp. 260–4; Frye (1966), pp. 209–11.

32 Kierkegaard (1987), p. 144.

33 Frye (1966), p. 41.

34 Jaspers (1952), pp. 52–5; Ricoeur (1967), pp. 220–2.

35 Knox (1955), p. 22.

36 Jaspers (1952), p. 52.

37 See Girard (1977), pp. 40–4, 64–77 *et passim*. "Tragedy," he points out, "is the balancing of the scale, not of justice but of violence" (p. 45).

38 Lawrence (1920), p. 9, from the Preface to *Touch and Go: A Play in Three Acts* (italics his); also cited by Mason (1985), pp. 99–100; see also Frye (1966), p. 210.

39 The translation is Clines' (1989), p. 276.

40 Jaspers (1952), pp. 30–1.

41 Cox (1969), pp. 10–11.

42 See Mason (1985), pp. 136–62, who presents a case for such a position, claiming, for example, tragic status for pathetic tragic victims such as Cassandra in Euripides' *The Trojan Women*.

43 My understanding of Job has been most influenced by the insights of Tsevat (1966); Good (1973 and 1990); Landy (1984); and Clines (1989).

44 Tsevat (1966); Clines (1989), pp. xxxviii–xlvi.

45 Good (1973), pp. 475–6; (1990), pp. 194–9, argues persuasively that the adversary's words in Job 1:11 and 2:5 are a self-imprecation that forces God's hand.

46 For arguments that Job embodies a comic vision, see Whedbee (1977); Frye (1982), pp. 196–8.

47 Frye (1966), p. 209.

48 Robertson (1977), pp. 48–9.

49 Rimmon-Kenan (1983), p. 16; italics hers. Rimmon-Kenan follows Genette in distinguishing between *histoire, récit*, and *narration*; see Genette (1980), pp. 27–32.

50 I take this idea from Frye's description of the Iliad (1967), p. 15: "We may compare the Greek dramatic tragedies with the Iliad, which, though complete in itself, is part of an epic cycle that keeps on going. As complete in itself, it is a tragedy, the tragedy of Hector; as part of the epic cycle, its central figure is Achilles, who does not die in the Iliad, but leaves us with a powerful intimation of mortality." For the thesis that 1 Samuel – 1 Kings 2 is "a unified structure in which the lives of Samuel, Saul, and David are all intertwined in such a way that they follow the same basic pattern" and that "Saul emerges as the hero of the story," see Preston (1982). The citation is from p. 28.

51 Thus my analysis of Saul begins with his introduction in 1 Samuel 9 – actually with its preparation in 1 Samuel 8 – and ends with his death in 2 Samuel 1; analysis of David begins with his introduction in 1 Samuel 16 – anticipated in 1 Samuel 13 and 15 – and ends with his death in 1 Kings 2. On the Saul "story," cf. the remarks of Gunn (1980), p. 13.

52 As Fish (1980), p. 68 *et passim*, points out, texts are not independent of theories. Since in the excursuses I approach the texts with different questions, the result is, not surprisingly, readings that move in different directions.

53 Sewall (1980), p. 5.

54 Mason (1985), p. 10; see his discussion, pp. 10–18. See also the comments of Booth (1983), pp. 85–6.

2. SAUL: THE HOSTILITY OF GOD

1 Steiner (1980), p. xiii.

2 See Ricoeur (1967), pp. 211–31, and the discussion in Chapter 1 above.

3 Frye (1982), p. 181.

4 Von Rad (1962), p. 325.

5 See e.g. McCarthy (1965); Jobling (1978), pp. 4–25, (1986), pp. 44–87; Polzin (1989), pp. 80–125.

6 Humphreys (1978, 1980, 1982, and 1985).

7 Gunn (1980, 1981).

8 Humphreys (1985), p. 23.

9 Humphreys (1985), p. 27. The obvious problem with such reconstructions is the lack of evidence for their existence. There are problems with the reconstructed structure of the tragic stratum (e.g. there is nothing constructive from Saul's point of view in Humphreys' "second

constructive phase" in 1 Sam. 16:14–19:10; and this section has as much claim to the description "Saul's disintegration" as the "second destructive phase" [p. 25]). Moreover, Humphreys' argument is also circular: the material that does not fit the reconstructed structure is assigned to a later hand because it breaks the structure (see e.g. p. 44). See also the criticisms of Edelman (1990), p. 209.

10 Krieger (1971), pp. 4, 42, 47–51. My interest in describing the Samson saga as comic or classic is not to force it into a mold (comedy is no more definable than tragedy and is, in fact, usually defined in relation to tragedy) but to show it as offering an alternative vision to that of the Saul story. I use "comic vision" in much the same sense that Krieger uses "classic vision," although Krieger makes a point of distinguishing between "classic" and "comic." He acknowledges, however, that all the works he treats as classic "are in some sense, whether superficial or profound, comic as well" (1971, p. xi; see also pp. 221–52). My use of Krieger to inform my understanding of the comic vision bears a certain resemblance to his use of Kierkegaard to support his theory of tragedy (see 1960, pp. 7–21), and I owe more to his insights than my brief remarks indicate. The subtitles of Krieger's books illustrate the distinction he draws between the two visions: the tragic vision is "the confrontation of extremity"; the classic vision, "the retreat from extremity." He distinguishes these from the ethical vision, an "evasion of extremity," and the religious vision, the "transcendence of extremity." For an analysis of their interrelationships, see esp. 1971, pp. 3–80.

11 Langer (1953), p. 334.

12 Vickery (1981) offers a sustained but unconvincing argument for Samson as a tragic hero. Humphreys (1985), pp. 68–78, sees little evidence for claiming tragic status for Samson and considers Samson more pathetic than tragic. Crenshaw's discussion of tragic and comic dimensions (1978, pp. 121–37) abounds with sweeping generalizations and tenuous comparisons. He says, for example, "Samson's inner compulsion to bring about his own collapse resembles the career of Israel's first king who also fell into the hands of the Philistines" (p. 127), but he does not show *how* it resembles it nor does he explore the nature of this inner compulsion. Whereas he admits that "certain features of the Samson saga resemble comedy more than tragedy" (p. 127), Crenshaw never deals adequately with the relationship between comic and tragic elements, settling instead for labeling the saga "tragi–comedy" (p. 129). Particularly perplexing in Crenshaw's analysis are the attempts to make non-tragic events tragic (e.g. emphasizing the suffering of Samson's innocent victims; see n. 62 below), and confusing "comic" with "funny," to see humor in the tragic moments (e.g. "His punishment [the blind Samson grinds at the mill in the prison] was equally funny" [p. 128]).

13 See the interesting comparison by Booth (1983, pp. 61–78) between *Love's Labor's Lost* and *King Lear* as comedy and tragedy, where he labels *Love's Labor's Lost* as a "deviant comedy."

14 Frye (1966, p. 216) observes that, whereas a tragedy "may contain a comic action, it contains it only episodically as a subordinate contrast or under-plot."

15 Within the framework of Judges, one might identify it with the (apparent) time of stability under the "minor judges," Ibzan, Elon, and Abdon; on the minor judges as representing periods of peace, see Boling (1975), pp. 189, 215; Webb (1987), p. 176; or, taking the story independently, one may say, following Frye, that it simply assumes that matters were once better (1966, p. 171). As Gunn (1984), p. 121, points out, in the final form of the narrative, disharmony prevails and Israel blocks its own movement toward a harmonious society; see also Exum (1990).

16 The reprisal/counter-reprisal aspect of the Samson saga has been best analyzed by Gunkel (1913). Another comic feature is that Samson's great feats occur in a kind of vacuum; the conflict with the Philistines does not seem so serious, since only Samson engages in it.

17 Taking Judg. 16:30 as part of Samson's prayer; for fuller discussion, see Exum (1983), p. 34 and n.

18 See Greenberg (1983), p. 12.

19 To have Samson live, blinded, would be worse, as Milton recognized. Following Mendenhall (1973), pp. 76–7, I take *nqm* as vindication, not vengeance. Vindication is Yhwh's prerogative, with Samson acting as the legitimate agent.

20 1 Samuel 8 is the immediate backdrop, the crisis against which Saul's kingship begins. Polzin (1989), pp. 18–54, 112–15, discusses the larger literary context in 1 Samuel 1–3, and earlier in Judges 19–21.

21 Gunn (1980), p. 108.

22 On the symbolism of the robe, see the discussions of Gunn (1980), pp. 80, 95; Fokkelman (1986), pp. 608–9 *et passim*; and Polzin (1989), pp. 218–19.

23 Saul, from the outset, is not prepared to encounter Samuel (in 1 Samuel 9, his servant provides both the idea to consult the seer and the money to pay him, perhaps a divination fee; see Paul [1978]). At the beginning and end of his career, Saul makes a journey of inquiry (*darash*, 9:9; 28:7) that leads him to Samuel. He is urged on by a servant or servants who know where to seek the answers: "Behold, there is a man of God in this city," 9:6; "Behold, there is a woman-master of spirits at En-dor," 28:7. His servant's description of Samuel, "all that he says comes true" (9:6), is darkly ironic in its anticipation of all the troubles Samuel will prophesy for Saul.

24 Steiner (1980), pp. xiii–xiv.

25 Bergson (1980), p. 94.

26 Preston (1982), p. 36. For detailed comparison, see U. Simon (1988).

27 So Good (1965), p. 78. Polzin (1989), p. 271, n. 16, stresses the negative quality of the act.

28 So Humphreys (1980), pp. 79–80. The reading I present here supports this assessment.

29 The translation is Grene's (1954), pp. 68–9.
30 Perhaps lameness makes Mephibosheth an unsuitable claimant to the throne, though this is not what Ziba's speech in 2 Sam. 16:3 implies. David's loyalty to Jonathan and Mephibosheth is questionable (2 Samuel 9), and Mephibosheth's loyalty to David is questioned (2 Sam. 16:3–4). In his defense, Mephibosheth blames his lameness, and Ziba's deception, for his inability to follow David when David flees from Absalom (2 Sam. 19:24–30).
31 Frye (1966), p. 168.
32 For detailed discussion of the parallels between these two parts of the Samson saga, see Exum (1981), pp. 3–9.
33 On the nature of Saul's "sin," see the discussions of Gunn (1980), pp. 33–40; Donner (1983); Miscall (1986), pp. 84–8; Fokkelman (1986), pp. 32–44; Long (1989), pp. 88–93. Gunn's suggestion that Samuel's instructions are ambiguous with regard to their emphasis on time (Samuel intends that Saul should wait *until he comes*; Saul understands that he must wait *seven days*) is ingenious, and Gunn's reading heightens the tragic quality of Saul's choice. Nonetheless, I would stress other aspects of the story, *viz.* Saul's dilemma and the fact that he feels constrained to act (*wa'et'appaq*, "I forced myself," or as Polzin [1989], p. 129, suggests "got control of himself"); and in particular the fact that he does the wrong thing by trying to do the right thing. Saul does *wait*. If he were headstrong, he would have gone ahead earlier, either with the battle (was it necessary to implore divine favor?) or with the sacrifice, since his troops were already deserting him.
34 The particle *hinneh* draws attention to this fact; see Fokkelman (1986), p. 37. Cf. also Gunn (1980), p. 66. It would even seem Saul has not finished, for he called for the *'olah* and the *shelamim* but has offered only the *'olah*. We will meet a clearer example of such fatedness in the story of Jephthah, when his daughter appears (*hinneh*) as the fulfillment of the terms of his vow; see the discussion in the next chapter. Saul offers the burnt offering to win God's favor before battle, and Jephthah vows a burnt offering to win God's favor before battle.
35 There is general agreement that 1 Sam. 10:8 contains the instructions referred to by Saul and Samuel, in spite of problems (e.g. Saul and Samuel have already been to Gilgal together and sacrifices were offered [1 Sam. 11:14–15]; in 1 Samuel 10, Saul was but a youth, whereas in 1 Samuel 13 he has a grown son). For a possible solution, see Polzin (1989), p. 251, n. 6; see also Long (1989), pp. 43–66, 190–3.
  "What a difference," observes Peter Miscall (1986), p. 88, "if Samuel denounced Saul for sacrificing too soon and without him!" Samuel complicates the situation between Saul and Yhwh. Eslinger (1985), pp. 264–82, has shown that Yhwh and Samuel do not share the same view of kingship. Polzin (1989), pp. 126–31, discusses the ambiguous, rather negative, portrayal of Samuel in this chapter and throughout 1 Samuel, and, like Eslinger, offers a corrective to analyses that identify Samuel's point of view too readily with that of the deity. The issue of Saul's guilt

is not so easily resolved as Polzin's reading of 1 Samuel 13 would have it; in particular, I cannot accept his conclusion that Samuel's denunciation is "a trumped-up charge to keep Saul on the defensive and under his prophetic control" (p. 129). Fokkelman, too (1986, p. 34), notes that "the prophet is also a mortal and not perfect," but while keeping "open the possibility here that the narrator was alive to some imperfection in Samuel," by 1 Samuel 15 Fokkelman has decided that Saul is entirely in the wrong.

36 Good (1965), pp. 67, 69–70, thinks 1 Samuel 13 is Samuel's rejection of Saul whereas 1 Samuel 15 is Yhwh's. He takes Samuel's anger in 15:11 as a sign that Samuel resents having to reject Saul a second time. This is ingenious but not convincing. On 1 Samuel 13 as Samuel's attempt to manipulate Saul, see Polzin (1989), 129–31. Polzin also observes that Samuel's departure for Gibeah (of Saul) associates him with Saul.

37 Gunn (1980), p. 47. Gunn has analyzed the scene very well (see esp. pp. 41–56) and I follow here his argument that the scene revolves around different understandings of the compatibility of *zebah* and *herem*. I am not convinced, however, by Gunn's attempt to read v. 9 as saying that Saul and the people spared Agag and the best of the spoil respectively. Saul shares responsibility with – and for – the people, as he recognizes, v. 24. With regard to the sparing of Agag, I doubt we can second-guess Saul's intention. It is worth noting, however, that God has explicitly commanded Saul not to "spare/have compassion" (*hml*). Saul is rejected because he does "spare/have compassion," whereas, later, David's sins of adultery and murder are forgiven, though he deserved death "because he had no compassion (*hml*)," 2 Sam. 12:6. On the way to Gilgal Saul sets up a monument to himself; again I do not think this act helps us decide the issue of Saul's intentions. Fokkelman challenges Gunn's conclusions about *zebah* and *herem* (1986, p. 104, n. 28); Fokkelman apparently thinks *Leitwortstil* permits only one (correct) interpretation. Cf. also Long (1989), pp. 141–57, who considers Saul guilty and his self-defense weak.

38 Perhaps the addition of "and your words" in 1 Sam. 15:24 is a hint that Saul understood the "commandment of Yhwh" Samuel referred to in 13:13 as Samuel's own instructions.

39 Good (1965), p. 68; Gunn (1980), p. 74. On *yr'* as "respect" or "honor," see Gunn (1980), p. 53; Preston (1982), p. 45, n. 8. Fokkelman (1986), p. 104, n. 28, gives *yr'* a negative interpretation. Saul has previously shown his respect for the people by letting them ransom Jonathan from his oath (1 Samuel 14).

40 I see no reason to consider Saul's desire to worship Yhwh insincere, even if he is also concerned with appearances. For a positive assessment of Saul in 1 Samuel 15, see Gunn (1980), pp. 38–56, 70–5, who argues that here, as in 1 Samuel 13, Saul interprets the divine command one way; Samuel and Yhwh, another way. For a negative assessment, see Sternberg (1983), pp. 45–82; (1985), pp. 482–515; Fokkelman (1986),

pp. 95–108. On the possibility of divergent interpretations of 1 Samuel 15, see Miscall (1986), pp. 99–114. Polzin (1989), pp. 135, 145, 218 *et passim*, sees Saul's attention to ritual as increasingly leading him to sorcery and divination.

41 Saul does apparently see Samuel again, 1 Samuel 19. The statement in 15:35 that Saul did not see Samuel again signals forcefully the break with the old order represented by Samuel and prepares for the introduction of the new order symbolized by David in 1 Samuel 16. The narrator's claim that Yhwh repented contradicts Samuel's assertion that Yhwh does not repent (even though Yhwh has told Samuel he has repented). Thus we have reason to question Samuel. For a different interpretation, but in the context of Samuel's intentions, see Polzin (1989), pp. 143–7. Especially interesting are Polzin's remarks about the double meaning of *ns'* and *shub* in 1 Sam. 15:25–31, where Saul asks Samuel to "forgive/bear my sin" and "return/repent with me."

42 For fuller discussion of 1 Samuel 14, see Chapter 4 below.

43 For fuller discusion, see Exum (1983).

44 Langer (1953), p. 342.

45 Obedience (*sm' bqwl*) is repeatedly connected with the notions of kingship (divine versus human) and rejection (of Yhwh or of Saul). In 1 Samuel 8, Yhwh instructs Samuel to obey/listen to (*sm' bqwl*) the people and make them a king like the nations even though their request means the rejection (*m's*) of Yhwh as king (cf. also 12:1). 1 Samuel 12 announces divine forbearance if the people and their king obey Yhwh (vv. 14–15; note the pun on Saul's name, vv. 13, 17, 19). Saul, however, obeys the people rather than Yhwh and is therefore rejected (*m's*) as king (1 Samuel 15). As Gunn (1980), p. 74, observes, "It is appropriate that Saul, whose appointment as king came from 'obeying the people' should meet with rejection through 'obeying the people.'" The people are not rejected; only Saul. The themes come together a final time in 28:16–19.

46 Clearly it is difficult to generalize about such matters, since the same literary devices can serve both classic and tragic modes, but the comparison is useful insofar as it illuminates the texts under discussion. See also my remarks about differences between the Akedah and the sacrifice of Jephthah's daughter in Chapter 3 below.

47 See Humphreys (1980), pp. 83–5.

48 The final resolution to Saul's tragedy, including the fate of his house, is reached in 2 Samuel 21, where Saul's and Jonathan's bones are brought home to Benjamin for burial; see Chapter 4 below.

49 This scene corresponds to what Frye (1966), p. 179, calls "the point of ritual death" in comedy.

50 Though it is not stated explicitly in 16:21–30 that Yhwh granted Samson's prayer, there can be little doubt that Yhwh is the agent. I have suggested elsewhere (1983, p. 39, n. 21) that the absence of direct reference to the deity may be the narrator's way of distancing Yhwh from the spectacle of Samson's death. See also Exum (1990).

51 For further discussion, see Exum (1981), pp. 21–5.

52 Frye (1966), pp. 170, 208–9.

53 See Blenkinsopp (1963); Greenstein (1981), pp. 250–2.

54 I owe this insight to Robertson (1984), p. 102.

55 Greenstein (1981) notes a number of anomalies in the story besides this one, all of which he sees as part of the riddle the text poses for us: "With Samson, the expected is the unexpected" (p. 246). This unpredictability or toying with our expectations is another feature of the comic. Tragedy tends to develop along more clearly defined lines and is less likely to surprise (cf. Sypher [1980], p. 207).

56 Yhwh also says, v. 17, that Saul will "restrain" or "hold back" his people. The verb (*ya'tsor*) is usually translated "rule" or "govern" (so the Revised Standard Version, Jewish Publication Society Version, and Jerusalem Bible). Saul delivers Israel from the Philistines and rules Israel only for a time. He does not seem to restrain Yhwh's people, in fact his sin is listening to them (1 Samuel 15). Perhaps these predictions find fulfillment in David. Eslinger (1985), pp. 309–10, offers a different understanding of "restrain" in this context, taking it as divine sarcasm: Yhwh selects a *nagid*, not a *melek*, precisely to restrain Israel from becoming "like the nations"; similarly, Ackerman (1991), p. 12, but without attributing sarcasm to the deity.

57 Good (1965), p. 58.

58 See C. Segal (1981), pp. 44–6. Mason (1985), pp. 40–60, underscores the importance of social bonds for Greek tragedy; corporate responsibility holds true equally for the Bible.

59 On the root *sh'l* and its associations with Saul and Samuel through what he calls homiletical etymology, see Garsiel (1985), pp. 73–5. Cf. Zakovitch (1980), pp. 41–2.

60 See E. Segal (1972).

61 Wharton (1973), esp. pp. 53–4.

62 Crenshaw (1978), pp. 124–6, seeks to arouse sympathy for "innocent victims" – Samson's wife, the thirty Philistines at Ashkelon, the young boy upon whom the blinded Samson leans, and the Timnite's younger sister, "by far the most pitiful" (p. 125).

63 See Frye (1965), p. 79. I disagree with Zakovitch (1984), p. 111, that Samson learns from his mistakes.

64 Landy (1984), p. 140.

65 Babcock-Abrahams (1975), p. 153. The following discussion of the trickster is drawn essentially from Babcock-Abrahams' excellent analysis of trickster on a cross-cultural basis and the literature cited there. See also the essays by Steinberg and Camp in Exum and Bos (1988). "Trickster" is a scholarly construct; for some of the inherent problems see Bal (1988b). Babcock-Abrahams observes, "...it would perhaps be better to call both this type of tale and persona by the literary term 'picaresque' which combines with the notion of trickery and roguish behavior the idea of the uncertain or hostile attitude of an individual to

existing society and an involvement in narrative focussed on movement, within and beyond that society" (p. 159). On Samson as a trickster figure, see Niditch (1990).

66 Babcock-Abrahams (1975), p. 147.

67 Radin (1956), p. ix.

68 Girard (1977), pp. 12, 104–9, 270–2.

69 1 Sam. 22:6, 9–10; 23:7, 13, 19–20, 25; 24:1; 26:1; 27:4; note Saul's gratitude for the Ziphites' compassion (*hml*, 23:21; recall Saul's sparing Agag in 1 Samuel 15).

70 Confession of sin does not necessarily lead to forgiveness; e.g. Josh. 7:20, a case whose similarities to Saul's have been interestingly explored by Sternberg (1985), pp. 497–9, 509; (1983), pp. 63–4. See Chapter 3 below, on the people's confession of sin in Judg. 10:10, the uncertain divine response, and its relation to the story of Jephthah. Bailey (1990), pp. 115–16, argues that for the Deuteronomistic Historian, confession of sin alone is not enough for forgiveness; it must be accompanied by supplication/repentance. In the case of 2 Samuel 12, Bailey sees David's behavior in vv. 16–17 as supplication (rather than mourning) and places importance on David's worshipping (*wayyishtahu*) Yhwh in v. 20. Note that Saul asks for forgiveness and pleads with Samuel to return/repent (*shub*) with him, after which Saul worships (*wayyishtahu*) Yhwh. Polzin (1989), pp. 141–5, offers insightful observations about repentance and forgiveness in 1 Samuel 15, showing that there is nothing mechanical in the Deuteronomistic Historian's concept of forgiveness.

At several points Polzin touches on the problem of human guilt and hostile transcendence (e.g. pp. 125, 243–4, n. 17), but backs off from it, preferring to speak of divine and human freedom and of "mystery." It is not simply a case of one critic's "hostile transcendence" being another critic's "mysterious ways"; rather Polzin's reading strategy, by privileging the narrator's privileging of God, prevents him from analyzing Yhwh in the same way he analyzes other characters in the story. Similarly Fretheim (1985), who is concerned to defend God, especially against Gunn's critical comments about divine malevolence.

71 For Saul's similarities to the judge-deliverers and for similarities between this incident and Judges 19–21, see Polzin (1989), pp. 112–15; Garsiel (1985), pp. 80–1, 87–99.

72 As Polzin (1989), p. 180, notes, the two accounts of David's escaping Saul when Saul casts his spear at him foreshadow the two accounts of David's sparing Saul's life. In the latter account, Saul's spear reappears as a possible murder weapon, but David refuses to let Abishai kill the king.

73 Reading *'rk* as "your enemy"; cf. Symmachus, Aquila, Theodotion, Vulg., Targ. Some commentators follow LXX (cf. Syr.) in reading *r'k*, in which case Samuel's statement is not so radical, and merely reiterates what he has said before (15:28).

74 Ricoeur (1967), p. 218; cf. Frye (1982), p. 181.

75 Ricoeur (1967), pp. 220–1. Italics his.
76 In addition to the studies of Vickery (1981) and Crenshaw (1978) mentioned above, see also the remarks of Gunn (1984), pp. 121–2 and Landy (1984), pp. 140–3.
77 Landy (1984), p. 142.
78 Humphreys (1985), p. 69.
79 Booth (1983), p. 78. He adds that all of us are sometimes foolish.
80 Knowing and not knowing, telling and not telling are two of the key motifs in the Samson saga. The characters repeatedly fall short of comprehending the ways in which Yhwh is involved in events; they do not know because they are not told. The large number of questions that appear in the saga affords the listener more riddles than the famous one in Judg. 14:14. On the secrecy motif, see Eissfeldt (1925); Wharton (1973); on the Samson saga as riddle, see Greenstein (1981).
81 See Exum (1990).
82 Frye (1966), p. 224.

3. JEPHTHAH: THE ABSENCE OF GOD

1 See Green (1975); Heider (1985), esp. pp. 223–400; see also de Vaux (1964); Burney (1970), pp. 329–31.
2 See also Micah 6:6–7; Jer. 7:31; 19:5; Ezek. 16:20–1; 20:25–6; 23:37–9. Not surprisingly, scholarly opinion varies considerably on such a sensitive and controversial issue as human sacrifice; in particular the nature of the *molek* sacrifices is debated. For fuller discussion of the issues, see Green (1975), pp. 169–87; Heider (1985); J. Day (1989).
3 Webb (1987), pp. 46–8; cf. Polzin (1980), p. 177.
4 Gunn (1980), p. 125.
5 Zakovitch (1981), pp. 40, 45, proposes that *zonah*, usually translated "harlot," refers to a divorced woman.
6 Trible (1984), pp. 97, 100, 104; cf. Bal (1988a), p. 44.
7 A similar ambiguity occurs in the story of Gideon. The spirit clothes him; he sounds the trumpet and calls out the troops (Judg. 6:34–5). He next asks for a sign, "If you will deliver Israel by my hand" (6:36; cf. Jephthah's "If you will indeed give the Ammonites into my hand," 11:30). Is he no longer under the influence of the spirit when he asks for a sign or does the spirit not obviate the need for a sign?
8 Marcus (1986a), pp. 13–18, lists the evidence for both positions. It seems to me, on the basis of 1 Sam. 18:6 and Exod. 15:20, that Jephthah may well have expected a woman.
9 I owe this reference to Sewall (1980), p. 7. In this analysis, I have tried to avoid implicating the deity too strongly, since the very ambiguity of the divine silence seems to me crucial to the story. It is not the case here, as in the story of Saul, that God is openly antagonistic. On the other hand, if we compare extra-biblical parallels where a father vows what turns out to be his own child, a chief feature is that the supernatural

figure to whom the vow is made has something different in mind from the father; e.g., the frequently cited parallels of Idomeneus, Maeander, and Agamemnon in Euripides' *Iphigenia in Tauris*, and many interesting examples and variations from Grimm's fairy tales ("Hans mein Igel," "Der König vom goldenen Berg," "Das singende springende Löweneckerchen," "Das Mädchen ohne Hände"). The rabbis did not shrink from implicating the deity, and offered the interpretation that God punished Jephthah for his carelessly worded vow by causing his daughter to appear as its fulfillment (*Bereshit Rabbah* 60:3; *Wayyiqra Rabbah* 37:4).

10 The case of the daughters of Zelophehad (Numbers 27) indicates that women could preserve the family name and ensure that the ancestral inheritance remain within the family.

11 The phrase is Krieger's (1960).

12 See below, Excursus 1 and note 22. See also my remarks in Chapter 1 above about there being no way out without denying oneself, where tragic heroes are concerned.

13 There is no mention of Jephthah's wife or the possibility of other offspring.

14 An analysis of the narrative based on the sacrificial theory of René Girard would prove particularly illuminating. The hero returns from battle contaminated by violence. A cleansing rite is necessary, but something goes amiss. Violence is unleashed first in the hero's own family (his daughter) and then on another Israelite tribe (Ephraim). The pattern of escalating violence continues within the cyclical pattern of Judges, culminating in full-scale internecine war and mass rape and murder in Judges 20–1. The connection between women and sacrifice also calls for exploration; see Girard (1977), pp. 119–42 *et passim*; Jay (1985).

15 Cf. the rabbinic explanation that Jephthah died through his limbs dropping off in various cities, where they were then buried; thus Jephthah was buried in many places (*Bereshit Rabbah* 60:3; *Wayyiqra Rabbah* 37:4).

16 Rösel (1980).

17 See Marcus (1986a), pp. 18–21; Parker (1979). The correspondence between condition and promise is not always present in the extra-biblical parallels; see Parker (1989), pp. 70–87.

18 See esp. Krutch (1981).

19 Ricoeur (1967), p. 220.

20 The ending which has Iphigenia spared is generally regarded as spurious. In Euripides' *Iphigenia in Tauris*, Artemis substitutes a hind for the sacrifice and transports Iphigenia to Tauris. In Aeschylus' *Agamemnon*, Clytemnestra avenges Iphigenia's sacrifice, as an unwilling victim at Aulis, by her father. On versions of the Iphigenia myth, see Henrichs (1981), pp. 198–208.

21 As Thiselton (1974) shows, pp. 293–6, the power of such utterances is not magical but lies rather in their nature as what J. L. Austin called

performative utterances. The blessing, for example, has power insofar as it constitutes the *act* of blessing. Such utterances also have power in that they usually invoke the deity. My approach to words here is inspired by Hartman's chapter (1981), pp. 118–57, "Words and Wounds."

22 The present story clearly assumes this, whereas Lev. 27:1–8 stipulates monetary payment by which a person vowed to God could be released. In the midrashic literature, one finds various attempts to explain Jephthah's ignorance of the law; see Marcus (1986a), pp. 46–7.

23 See Landy (1986); Jobling (1986), pp. 124–32.

24 Jobling (1986), p. 128.

25 Jobling (1986), pp. 128–31; the citation is from p. 129. Webb (1987), p. 55, similarly observes, "These are not the words of a man who is desperate for peace." Webb, pp. 54–60, also draws attention to the ambivalent and uneasy nature of Jephthah's suit.

26 On this translation, see Bal (1988a), p. 49, and the discussion in Excursus 2 below.

27 Hartman (1981), p. 150.

28 For fuller discussion, see Exum (1989). Fuchs (1989) also discusses how the narrative subordinates the daughter to its androcentric interests, specifically in order to make Jephthah a more sympathetic character.

29 This is not to say that we are to condone Jephthah's sacrifice of his daughter, but only that human sacrifice was practiced. As we have seen, no outright condemnation of Jephthah's sacrifice appears in the text.

30 See Girard (1977).

31 The situation of the sacrificial victim is more complex than can be considered here. Married women are not good candidates for sacrifice because a married woman has ties to both her parents' and her husband's families, either of which might consider her sacrifice an act of murder, and thus take vengeance; see Girard (1977), pp. 12–13. On the opposition between sacrificial purity and the pollution of childbirth, see Jay (1985), pp. 283–309. Girard argues that anyone who does not have a champion makes an appropriate sacrifice.

32 Deborah is an important exception who proves the rule.

33 This is crucial according to Girard (1977), p. 13 *et passim*.

34 *Pace* Meyers (1988), pp. 24–6, I am unwilling to forgo the use of the term "patriarchal" to describe the male gender bias of narrative, a usage widespread in feminist literature. Meyers holds that this usage reflects a misunderstanding of patriarchy as a social system. I understand patriarchy not just as a social system, but as an ideology behind it. To the extent that texts produced by patriarchal culture are androcentric, they may also be termed patriarchal. Meyers is correct that I apply contemporary feminist standards to feminist readings of the text; such an approach is necessary if the study of women in ancient literature is to become anything other than the study of men's views of women.

35 Marcus (1986a), p. 34; see also Trible (1984), p. 106.

36 Cf. Lerner's remarks on the complicity of women in patriarchy (1986), pp. 5–6, 233–5.

37 Thus a reading such as Trible's (1984), pp. 93–109, that makes Jephthah all-bad, irredeemably guilty, and wholly responsible for the crime of murder, and his daughter helpless and totally innocent, simply reinforces the victim–victimizer dichotomy. Bal (1988a), in contrast, completely reinterprets the daughter's death and the meaning of the women's remembrance; see pp. 45–68, 96–113, 119–22, 161–8 *et passim*.

38 Soggin (1981), p. 217; Gray (1986), p. 319; P. Day (1989), p. 58; see also the older commentaries of Burney (1970), pp. 332–4; Moore (1985), pp. 304–5.

39 Bal (1988a), pp. 46–68, P. Day (1989). Day sees the story as aetiological, and is concerned with identifying the ritual rather than with its meaning for Jephthah's daughter as a character in the story. Bal uses narrative theory to offer a sustained analysis of the meaning of the daughter's sacrifice and the women's ritual.

40 Tsevat (1975); Wenham (1972); Keukens (1982); Bal (1988a), pp. 46–8; P. Day (1989), p. 59. The frequent references to Anat as *btlt 'nt* in the Ugaritic texts indicate that the word refers to a woman who has not borne children, not to a woman who has not had sexual intercourse.

41 Bal (1988a), pp. 48–9; P. Day (1989), p. 60.

42 Bal (1988a), p. 49. Bal's emphasis on speech–act complements nicely my comments above on the power of words. Bal deconstructs the male concept of virginity via a detour into Freudian theory. Her resultant (re)reading of the story, a counter-reading, challenges the more traditional interpretations found within biblical scholarship, and illustrates one way to reinscribe a female perspective.

43 Bal (1988a), p. 51, takes this phrase as related to the *value* of the girl as a possible wife, not, as I want to read it here, a reference to her unfulfilled life. In either case, the emphasis is androcentric. In the present text, the *women's* ritual commemorates the *death of a virgin*, whereas one might imagine that a woman's ritual would celebrate fertility. Is this an androcentric inversion of female expression? Such androcentric appropriation of female experience can be seen, for example, in Genesis 2–3. In this classic illustration of womb envy, the creative power of women is assumed by the prototypical Man who, just as Zeus gives birth to Athena from his head, symbolically gives birth to woman with the help of the creator god (no creator goddess is involved).

44 I thank my colleague Ellen M. Ross for suggesting this idea. As my discussion above indicates, if Jephthah's daughter were married, her husband, not her father, would have power over her. If she had borne children, she would not be sacrificially pure.

45 Lerner (1986) traces male control of female sexuality from its locus within the patriarchal family to regulation by the state. On woman's sexuality "not so much as part of her feminine being but, rather, as an exclusive form of male experience," see Aschkenasy (1986), esp. pp. 123–4. Within the Bible, the Song of Songs is the great exception.

46 Kristeva (1986), p. 26; on patriarchy's division of eroticism and procreativity, see Lerner (1986), esp. pp. 141–60.

47 The Israelite women engage in ritual whereas the men are busy fighting, in the war with Ammon (10:17–11:33) and among themselves (12:1–6).
48 Lerner (1986), p. 242.

4. THE FATE OF THE HOUSE OF SAUL

1 See B. Simon (1988).
2 Kierkegaard (1987), p. 150.
3 I am speaking here of poetics, not historicity, for the degree of historicity of David and Michal's relationship may be questioned. Jobling (1978), p. 20, raises the question whether Jonathan is a literary construct, and Edelman (1990), p. 218, observes that the covenant between David and Jonathan is a literary fiction. "What rightful heir," she asks, "would give up his throne to another because of mere friendship?"
4 Berlin (1983), pp. 24–5.
5 Jobling (1978), pp. 4–25. This is not to exclude political implications of the term; see Thompson (1974).
6 An important early study of male bonding that elicited a good deal of critical response is Tiger (1984 [1st ed., 1969]). For a recent feminist analysis, see Sedgwick (1985). A classic example of male bonding in the ancient Near East is that of Gilgamesh and Enkidu in the Gilgamesh Epic. Damrosch (1987), pp. 204–6, offers perceptive observations on the "friendship-as-marriage" motif in David's relationship with Jonathan.
7 See the structural analysis of Jobling (1978), pp. 4–25.
8 We might also take David's concern with a reward in 1 Sam. 17:26, "What shall be done for the man who kills this Philistine?," as a sign of his political ambitions.
9 This is not to suggest that a woman in Michal's position might not have political motives; the point is that the text presents her only motive as love.
10 On the importance of Michal to David's claim to Saul's kingdom, see Flanagan (1983), pp. 51–4.
11 Earlier he demanded his wife from Abner, the power behind Ishbosheth's throne. As Clines (1972), p. 271, observes, from Abner David demands something from *Saul*'s house as a sign of Abner's loyalty. From Ishbosheth he demands what is legally his. No man stands in David's way. He can have the wife of another (Michal), the wife of a fool (Abigail), and the wife of a loyal soldier (Bathsheba). Only Yhwh cuts him short.
12 Jobling (1978), pp. 4–25.
13 Jobling (1978), pp. 4–25; Leach (1966).
14 Jobling (1978), p. 7.
15 Leach (1966), p. 90.
16 Jobling (1978), p. 20, calls him an "extreme case of character emptied into plot." In my view, the portrayal of Jonathan as supporting David but loyal to Saul is a narrative necessity not only to enable Jonathan to mediate the kingship but also to portray him with dignity. If Jonathan,

like Saul, resisted David, he would seem obdurate and foolish, whereas Saul's complexity allows him to be sympathetic in his opposition to David. If, on the other hand, Jonathan went over fully to David's side (e.g. joining David's band of outlaws rather than staying behind with his father), we would think him a traitor.

17 Cf. Miscall (1986), p. 90.

18 I follow Hertzberg (1964), pp. 115–16, in understanding the people's sin as neglect of cultic regulations; see also Blenkinsopp (1964), p. 424. On the people as the real "sinners" in this account, see Polzin (1989), pp. 136–9.

19 *Contra* Fokkelman (1986), pp. 71–2, I do not think Saul knows for certain the guilt is in Jonathan. Nor am I convinced by Fokkelman's argument, pp. 64, 71–80, that Saul considers his son his rival for the throne and wants to kill him out of jealousy.

20 Reading *li* with a number of ancient witnesses.

21 Hertzberg (1964), p. 111.

22 Polzin (1989), p. 136, reads Jonathan's statement in v. 30 as contrary to fact, and thus agreeing with the narrator's assessment. It is not clear to me, however, how this reading squares with Jonathan's criticism of Saul in v. 29.

23 Edelman (1986), pp. 235–9; (1990), pp. 210–11. Edelman's negative assessment of Jonathan lends support to my reading. Among Jonathan's shortcomings, she notes his failure to repent and accept his guilt when he learns he has inadvertently broken the ban. Instead, she points out, he challenges the appropriateness of the ban, claiming that it diminished the scale of the victory. She sees the narrator's statement that the defeat extended from Michmash to Aijalon as contradicting Jonathan's assessment. See also Smith (1899), pp. 114, 120.

24 For readings that stress the positive portrayal of Jonathan and its function as showing Saul in a more negative light, see, *inter alios*, Polzin (1989), pp. 133–9; Fokkelman (1986), pp. 48–80; Long (1989), pp. 107–29.

25 The text does not pursue the matter.

26 I take the "he" in 1 Sam. 18:3, "he loved him as himself," to refer to Jonathan, as in v. 1.

27 The argument is rhetorically nice: Jonathan frames reference to David's deeds with protestations of his innocence.

28 The text says that Jonathan made David swear by his love for him, but that is not the same thing as saying David loved Jonathan.

29 Jobling (1978), p. 14.

30 We are not told why David wept so profusely. Is he disconsolate at parting from Jonathan, or distraught over having to flee the royal court?

31 See the discussion of Miscall (1983), pp. 105–26.

32 Cf. Miscall (1986), p. 142.

33 I prefer to follow the Hebrew here; instead of becoming a snare to David, Michal's love becomes a snare to Saul.

34 Recall that he had no parting words for Jonathan; see above.

35 Reading the verb tense as past perfect.
36 See Clines (1972), pp. 269–72.
37 Alter (1981), p. 122, observes that the emphasis on the bride price suggests that David wants Michal back for political and not personal reasons. So also, Aschkenasy (1986), p. 142.
38 Between the two lists of David's children, David moves ever closer to the throne at the expense of Saul's house – Michal is brought to David; Abner is killed; Ishbosheth is murdered – until he is finally anointed king of Israel.
39 Usually understood as "jumping" or "whirling," but perhaps some activity with his hands such as clapping or snapping his fingers, as an accompaniment to his dance; cf. Avishur (1976); Ahlström (1978); Fokkelman (1990), pp. 379–80; McCarter (1984), p. 171.
40 Alter (1981), pp. 123–5.
41 Berlin (1983), pp. 72–3. I fail to see how "leaping and whirling" is necessarily more exaggerated than "whirling with all his might," but I agree that David's perspective, "dancing," or simply "sporting" (*wesiḥaqti*), is an attempt on David's part to put his behavior in a more positive light.
42 Carlson (1964), pp. 92–6, and Rosenberg (1986), pp. 117–18, also draw attention to the ideological function of this encounter.
43 Alter (1981), p. 124; Aschkenasy (1986), pp. 140–5; Fokkelman (1990), p. 204; Clines (1991).
44 See Exum (1988).
45 Alter (1981), p. 123.
46 For a discussion of gender ideology as it affects the presentation of Michal as a nagging wife, see Exum (1989).
47 In effect, Michal will be like David's ten wives of secondary rank, whom he shuts up and who remain under house arrest "until the day of their death [the same phrase as 6:23], living as if in widowhood" (2 Sam. 20:3). Carlson (1964), p. 96, sees in David's words reference to the humiliation David suffers as a result of his sin with Bathsheba and his later misfortunes.
48 Rimmon-Kenan (1983), p. 17, cites E. M. Forster's famous definition of plot ("'The king died and then the queen died' is a story. 'The king died and then the queen died of grief' is a plot.") and counters it by pointing out that "there is nothing to prevent a causally-minded reader from supplementing Forster's first example with the causal link that would make it into an implicit plot."
49 Some commentators, e.g. Gressman (1910), p. 139; Carlson (1964), p. 93; Hertzberg (1964), p. 281; Ackroyd (1977), p. 71, see Michal's childlessness as divine punishment either for her disrespectful attitude to the ark, or her lack of proper religious enthusiasm, or her royal arrogance.
50 I have heard Fuchs use this term in papers read at meetings of the Society of Biblical Literature. To my knowledge, Clines (1991) is the only other critic to raise the possibility of Michal's refusing David.

51 Fokkelman (1986), p. 270, undercuts the danger when he suggests Michal averts it by "making it into a game."

52 King (1988), pp. 100, 146–8; Coogan (unpublished paper).

53 See the articles in Exum and Bos (1988); see also Aschkenasy (1986), pp. 161–79; Marcus (1986b).

54 Proverbs 31 offers a good example. The woman has considerable power over the household, while her husband "sits among the elders of the land" (v. 23). The distinction between power and authority is helpful; authority is legitimate power, power recognized by society. See Rosaldo (1974), pp. 21–2; Lamphere (1974), p. 9; see also Hackett (1985), pp. 17–22; Meyers (1988), pp. 40–4.

55 Fokkelman (1986), p. 269.

56 The phrase "Hauptfrauen der freien Israeliten" is Crüsemann's (1980), p. 226, who thinks the remark refers only to lower-class women. Cf. McCarter (1984), p. 187, who believes Michal refers to "all the young women of Israel, whether slave or free."

57 As Mieke Bal has pointed out to me, this is itself a gender issue because it makes gender solidarity impossible. Lerner (1986), ch. 6, argues that using class to divide women is one of the strategies of patriarchal ideology: "The division of women into 'respectable women,' who are protected by their men, and 'disreputable women,' who are out in the street unprotected by men and free to sell their services, has been the basic class division for women. It has marked off the limited privileges of upper-class women against the economic and sexual oppression of lower-class women and has divided women one from the other. Historically, it has impeded cross-class alliances among women and obstructed the formation of feminist consciousness" (p. 139).

58 Ps.-Jerome (*Patrologia Lat.* 23.1329–402) and Josephus (*Ant.* VII.4.3) resolve the problem ingeniously by proposing that after her sister's death, Michal raised Merab's children. In *Bereshit Rabbah* 82:7 we find the attempt to avoid the implication that David ceased to honor Michal's marital rights by understanding the phrase "she had no child to the day of her death" to mean she died in childbirth.

59 Fokkelman (1986), pp. 267–8.

60 Apart from Nathan, who acts as God's agent, the only other person to criticize David's behavior to his face is Joab, and he, too, comes to an unhappy end: immediately afterwards David demotes him, and on his deathbed orders Solomon to execute him.

61 Cf. the important role of the queen mother in Kings.

62 For a suggestive analysis of the gender-determined nature of women's deaths in Greek tragedy, see Loraux (1987).

63 Freedman (1972), pp. 117, 123; Cross and Freedman (1975), pp. 47, 50.

64 Holladay (1970), p. 183; cf. Shea (1986), p. 19: "You were wonderful, (in) your love to me, / more than the love of women." On the difficulties of the LXX witnesses, see McCarter (1984), p. 72.

65 Though adding that Saul's head was hung in Dagon's temple, the Chronicler does not relate the exposure of Saul's and his son's bodies; cf.

1 Chr. 10:8–12 with 1 Sam. 31:8–13. Chronicles also omits the bloody events of 2 Samuel 2–4 and 21, along with other material unfavorable to David.

66 The longer form of his name, Abiner, appears in 1 Sam. 14:50. On the likelihood that Abner was Saul's cousin, not his uncle (1 Chr. 8:33), see McCarter (1980b), p. 256. On Saul's genealogy and genealogical fluidity, see Flanagan (1981), pp. 59–61; (1983), pp. 39–41, 45–7.

67 See Hertzberg (1964), p. 250, who posits Ishbosheth's youth or infirmity as reason for his "evident absence" in the battle against the Philistines.

68 The reigns of Ishbosheth and David do not correspond. Either there is a mistake or deliberate suppression of the length of Ishbosheth's reign, or perhaps David ruled in Judah while Saul was still king; see Freedman (1975), p. 16; Levenson (1982), pp. 241–2; VanderKam (1980), p. 528. Or Ishbosheth's reign was preceded by an interregnum during which Abner was consolidating Saul's territory after the defeat at Gilboa; so Soggin (1975), pp. 35–40; McCarter (1984), p. 89. For a social–scientific reconstruction that sees Saul and David as chiefs during the period of transition to the monarchy, see Flanagan (1981); on the succession, see Flanagan (1983).

69 See Soggin (1975), pp. 31–2, n. 1, and the references listed there; Flanagan (1981), p. 59; (1983), p. 47; but cf. McCarter (1980b), p. 254.

70 McCarter (1984), p. 105, translates David's words in 2 Sam. 3:33 as a statement, reading *ho*, "alas," in place of the interrogative particle. In light of all the questions surrounding Abner in this brief scope of material, I prefer the usual translation, taking it as an echoing question.

71 McCarter (1984), p. 109, reads *hlwk* at the end of v. 24 as *hlw'*, and reads it with the following verse as a question, following some LXX manuscripts: "Don't you know the treachery of Abiner son of Ner?" (p. 106). But see Alter (1981), pp. 101–2, on the forcefulness of *wayyelek halok*. 4QSam^a follows it with another question, "For was it to dupe you that he came?" See Ulrich (1978), p. 131; cf. McCarter, who disputes this interpretation.

72 Polzin (1989), p. 175. Polzin points out that David refuses to respond as Saul desires. On the Oedipal rivalry between Saul and David, see Bach (1989), pp. 53–6.

73 Polzin (1989), pp. 173–4, raises this question about Saul, but points out that it does not provide a suitable explanation for Saul's inquiry after David's identity, since Saul asks the same question of David when Abner brings David before him. Abner is in a different position.

74 Edelman, personal communication. See (1991), chapter 12, for fuller discussion.

75 In the parallel 1 Samuel 24, Saul asks David the same question. There David addresses Saul as "my father." In 1 Samuel 26, he calls himself Saul's "servant," an echo of his (non)answer to Saul in 1 Sam. 17:58, "I am the son of your servant Jesse the Bethlehemite."

76 Miscall (1986), p. 160.

77 Sternberg (1985), pp. 240–1.

78 So Hertzberg (1964), p. 251; McKane (1963), pp. 185–6; see also the older commentaries cited by Eissfeldt (1966a), pp. 139–40.

79 Yadin (1948), pp. 110–16; Eissfeldt (1966a and 1966b [which reports on Yadin's article]); followed by de Vaux (1958), p. 125; (1971), pp. 130–1; Fensham (1970); Grønbaek (1971), p. 229; Blenkinsopp (1972), p. 86; Soggin (1975), pp. 43–4, and n. 21; McCarter (1984), p. 95.

80 Hertzberg (1964), p. 252.

81 Ackroyd (1977), p. 38; so the New English Bible and the Jewish Publication Society Version.

82 Camp (1981), p. 23, offers some speculations, but I fail to find anything rhetorically superior in Abner's speech to Joab. Both speeches appeal to kinship bonds ("Joab your brother," 2 Sam. 2:22; "to return from pursuing their brothers," v. 26) though in different circumstances.

83 Emendation of *lule* for *lu* yields, "If you had only spoken up, the men would already have given up the pursuit of their brothers this morning," an even stronger indictment of Abner.

84 By raising such questions, I do not mean to suggest that we should psychoanalyze the characters. My interest lies not in possible answers but rather in the great number of questions the text raises precisely by avoiding them.

85 McCarter (1984), p. 107. Cf. Hertzberg's emendation (1964), p. 255, which yields a meaning similar to the one I suggest here.

86 Clines (1972), p. 271; (1991).

87 Gunn (1978), p. 72, following Veijola (1975), p. 61, observes that Israel's dismay over Abner's death (2 Sam. 4:1) does not suggest that Israel was eager to transfer allegiance to David. It is also possible that they are dismayed at Abner's death in David's territory, with its implications of Davidic involvement, if, in fact, Abner represented them in negotiations with David.

88 Hertzberg (1964), p. 260: "We must, however, assume that Abner was destined for the command of the Israelite army, and some envy on this account may have been a contributory factor in Joab's rash decision." See also Eissfeldt (1966a), p. 136; McCarter (1984), p. 122; VanderKam (1980), pp. 531–2; Soggin (1975), p. 46; Ackroyd (1977), p. 46. This was also Joab's motive according to Josephus, *Ant.* VII.1.5.

89 Abishai wanted to kill Saul while Saul and Abner slept (1 Samuel 26). Not to be left out of the picture, he is associated with Joab in the murder of Abner.

90 See, *inter alios*, Weiser (1966); McCarter (1980a); Lemche (1978); Whitelam (1984); Cryer (1985); VanderKam (1980); Hertzberg (1964), p. 261; Grønbaek (1971), pp. 243, 270; Whitelam (1979), pp. 105–12.

91 It may be that *beshalom* indicates the conclusion of a treaty between David and Abner; see Whitelam (1979), pp. 106–7.

92 On his deathbed, however, David will call for Joab's death for the

murders of Abner and Amasa (1 Kings 2:5). In the meantime, Joab has served David for many years; see Whybray (1968), pp. 40–3.

93 Polzin (1989), pp. 206–7, 211–13; Gunn (1980), pp. 96–100.

94 On David's ambivalent relationship to these aggressive brothers, see Gunn (1978), pp. 39–40; Rosenberg (1986), pp. 164–71.

95 His return of Michal to David is predicated upon Abner's cooperation.

96 See n. 68 above.

97 See McCarter (1984), pp. 106–7, 124–7; and esp. the discussion, p. 125.

98 For perceptive remarks about the relation of narration and dialogue in the Bible, see Alter (1981), pp. 63–87; Berlin (1983), pp. 64–72.

99 Similarities between 2 Sam. 21:1–14 and the Anat–Baal–Mot myth have been noted by Cazelles (1955), pp. 168–70; Blenkinsopp (1972), p. 93.

100 Malamat (1955), pp. 10–11; Soggin (1975), pp. 47–8. On the treaty background, see also Fensham (1964); Polzin (1969), pp. 233–40; Blenkinsopp (1972), pp. 91–3. For a different view, see Whitelam (1979), pp. 116–17.

101 Fensham (1964); Polzin (1969); Green (1975), pp. 164–7; Cazelles (1955), pp. 167–8.

102 Cf. Deut. 21:22–3; Josh. 8:29; 10:26–7.

103 Buber (1933), pp. 113–14.

104 Blenkinsopp (1972), p. 92; Cazelles (1955), p. 170.

105 The translation of 2 Sam. 21:4 suggested by Edelman (1986), p. 116, for which she acknowledges D. Pardee (n. 124), is equally plausible: "We have no man (in authority) who can order the death penalty in Israel."

106 Kapelrud (1955) rightly emphasizes the connection between kingship and fertility as the background of this story but wrongly associates the events it describes with a fertility rite. On the ritual background, see also Cazelles (1955), who concludes that the "Canaanite aspect has been weakened by the author" (p. 174).

107 Perhaps there is a hint here of Cain's sevenfold and Lamech's seventy-sevenfold vengeance (Gen. 4:24).

108 Buber (1933), pp. 113–14; cf. the analysis of Fokkelman (1990), pp. 289–91, who seeks to resolve the ambiguity. I find Fokkelman's assumptions about David, e.g. that he "had of course been aware for a long time of what Rizpah was doing," and that he "had perhaps been appalled and deeply impressed by Rizpah's dedication," to be totally unfounded in the text, which states simply that David was told what Rizpah had done and straightway had the bones buried (2 Sam. 21:11–12).

109 It is ironic that, at this point, David offers his house, since his house has already suffered considerably for his sins; see the discussion in Chapter 5. The punishment he chooses here does not befall them; in fact, Yhwh has apparently already decided to stop the messenger of death when David offers himself and his house.

110 On 2 Samuel 21 and 24 as parallel accounts of cultic acts at rival cultic sites, see Blenkinsopp (1972), p. 94; Cazelles (1955), pp. 174–5.

111 Brueggemann (1988), p. 392, underplays the issue of divine responsibility: "To be sure, 'Yhwh incited,' but David proposed the census and David must answer for his policy."

5. DAVID: THE JUDGMENT OF GOD

1 See Gunn (1989); Miscall (1989); Ackerman (1990); Perdue (1984). Whybray (1968), p. 36, concludes that "it is the very richness and variety of his literary creation which raises the figure of David to a stature comparable with the great tragic heroes of literature."

2 See Miscall (1983), pp. 57–83; (1986), pp. 120–5; perhaps David more than any other biblical character lends himself to Miscall's indeterminate readings.

3 Fokkelman (1981), p. 86.

4 I am speaking here of the larger movement of the plot; clearly it is not a case of simple straight up-and-downness. There are ambivalences in the relationship between Saul and David on both sides; for example, David has to kill, as it were, a symbolic father.

5 Commentators on the books of Samuel commonly distinguish, on source-critical grounds, between the History of David's Rise in 1 Samuel 16–2 Samuel 5 and the so-called Court History of David or Succession Narrative in 2 Samuel 9–20 and 1 Kings 1–2 (with possible beginnings in 2 Samuel 2–7). On the History of David's Rise, see McCarter (1980a); (1980b), pp. 27–30; Weiser (1966); Grønbaek (1971); Rendtorff (1971). The hypothesis of a Succession Narrative goes back to Rost (1926); see also von Rad (1966); Whybray (1968); Ridout (1971); Gunn (1978). Undoubtedly the material has a complicated pre-history that contributes to its complexity; my concern, however, is not the development of the tradition but rather the tragic dimension of the text as it now stands, including 2 Samuel 21–4, chapters frequently and misleadingly labelled "appendices" and often ignored in assessments of David's reign.

6 Gunn (1978), pp. 94–6, draws attention to the way David does nothing to acquire the kingdom as part of a larger theme of "giving and grasping."

7 McCarter (1980b), p. 30, recognizes in the repeated refrain, "Yhwh was with him" (1 Sam. 16:18; 17:37; 18:14; 18:28; 2 Sam. 5:10), the theological leitmotiv of the story of David's rise, noting its appearance at its beginning and end.

8 The two introductions to David in 1 Samuel 16 and 17 contain contradictory information. For readings that take seriously the literary function of the double introduction, see Gros Louis (1977), pp. 20–3; Alter (1981), pp. 147–53; Polzin (1989), pp. 161–75.

9 The issue of his good presence may well depend on where the reader's sympathies lie; for Saul, at any rate, David initially brings relief, but soon becomes a source of apprehension.

10 Ahimelech's inquiry of God on David's behalf is not mentioned in 1 Sam.

21:1–9 [Heb. 2–10], but Doeg and Saul both refer to it (22:10, 13), and Ahimelech, far from denying it, indicates it is not the first time he has inquired for David. The incident with Ahimelech is problematic, for David deceives Ahimelech regarding his mission, and his lie brings destruction upon the city of priests. Though David admits he knew Doeg would tell Saul of his presence at Nob, he can hardly have anticipated the extent of Saul's vengeance. Would Abiathar have joined David's band if he considered David responsible for Nob's destruction, or does he have no other choice, being now also a renegade?

11 Saul is still king, with an army and a following, whereas David's followers are, by and large, renegades. Since David knows he is also Yhwh's anointed and the kingdom will one day be his, he can afford to spare Saul now, setting a precedent for protecting the anointed king. On the key political issues in these chapters, see Rosenberg (1986), pp. 133–9.

12 We are not always told by what means David inquires of God; in 1 Sam. 23:9–12 and 30:7–8 it is through Abiathar and the ephod, and similar means may be supposed in the other cases. There is, as Alter (1981), p. 69, points out, no reason to take this as actual dialogue.

13 David raids other peoples and tells Achish he raided the southern territory of Judah, the Jerahmeelites, and the Kenites (1 Sam. 27:8–11).

14 On the different modes of legitimizing David's kingship in 2 Samuel 5–8, see Whedbee (1988).

15 Cf. Rosenberg (1986), pp. 126–7, 130, who points out certain advantages of sedentary kingship.

16 Fokkelman (1981), pp. 50–1, argues for retaining the Kethiv, "messengers," but the point about David's remaining in Jerusalem while Joab and the army engage in battle is still the same. Rosenberg (1986), p. 126, nicely exploits both readings.

17 Saul embodies the divinely disapproved institution, monarchy, and pays the price of that *hubris*, whereas David's monarchy for Yhwh is acceptable. David's *hubris* is thus not *that* he is king but how: his *hubris* is in violating the limits of kingship, obedience to God, which implies justice to the king's subjects.

18 Suggestions of force may be played down but are not edited out: "he took her." Note, too, that after David "takes" her (v. 4), Bathsheba is referred to as "the woman" and "the wife of Uriah," but not by name, until 12:24. For further discussion, see Bal (1987), pp. 10–36.

19 Obviously some time has passed between v. 4 and v. 5, but we do not know exactly how much. There is no indication that David sees (wants?) Bathsheba again between the first encounter and his sending for her again (11:27) to make her his wife.

20 I am not impressed by Sternberg's detailed investigation (1985), pp. 201–13, of the question, "Does Uriah know?" Bal (1987), pp. 17–20, 26–8, in a critique of Sternberg, shows how irrelevant the question is.

21 In assuming the matter can be summarily dismissed, David again violates Bathsheba and Uriah; cf. Rosenberg (1986), p. 172.

22 Dividing v. 10 with Fokkelman (1981), pp. 83–6, who makes a convincing case against the Masoretic division. The secret crimes of the paterfamilias – which are not so secret after all, since we read about them in detail – will become matters of public punishment for his house. Having his wives raped "before all Israel and before the sun" is meant to disgrace David, or as the wise Ahithophel puts it, to make Absalom "odious to your father" (2 Sam. 16:21) and strengthen Absalom's support. No thought is given to the disgrace experienced by the ten women. David later puts them away "in a house under guard" (2 Sam. 20:3), so that they suffer for what they represent.

23 On the threat to the house as a central element of tragedy, see B. Simon (1988), esp. pp. 1–26.

24 Note that like Bathsheba, Tamar is beautiful (13:1), and, like Bathsheba, she is objectified (2 Sam. 13:17 may be translated literally, "Send [a key word of 2 Samuel 11] this outside away from me").

25 The Septuagint reads "sevenfold," a reading accepted by McCarter (1984), pp. 292–9, among others. Exod. 22:1 [Heb. 21:37] calls for fourfold compensation for the theft of a sheep; Ackerman (1990), pp. 49–50, suggests that David's sons are depicted as sacrificial lambs as part of the divine judgment against David. Already the Talmud (*Yoma* 22b) drew a connection between fourfold compensation and the death of four of David's children: the unnamed son, Tamar, Amnon, and Absalom.

26 The ceremonial nature of the kiss is suggested by 2 Sam. 15:5, where Absalom combines rhetoric with ceremonial kissing to win adherents for his cause. Whybray (1968), p. 28, perceptively points to an ominous note in the silence surrounding the reconciliation.

27 The last time Absalom made a request, he also dissembled to hide a sinister plan (2 Sam. 13:24–9). David should have reason to be suspicious.

28 On the narrator's control of sympathy, see Conroy (1978), pp. 111–12.

29 Fokkelman (1981), p. 179, notes, "The foreigners are more faithful to David than are his own people."

30 *Contra* Fokkelman (1981), pp. 188–90.

31 Following the Jewish Publication Society's translation for the obscure Hebrew; the Septuagint reads, "as a bride comes home to her husband. You seek the life of only one man..."

32 *Contra* Fokkelman (1981), pp. 177–8.

33 Conroy (1978), p. 97. Fokkelman (1981), p. 177, sees David's response as "very efficient action," and observes that once again David flees into the wilderness when his life is threatened. But the circumstances are quite different: then Saul was king, now David is.

34 As Conroy (1978), pp. 96–7, observes, the climax in the plot and the emotional climax come at different points in the story. On the handling of suspense in 2 Sam. 18:19–32, see, esp., the discussions of Conroy (1978), pp. 46–7, 51–2, 67–75; Fokkelman (1981), pp. 250–62; Gunn (1978), pp. 45–6.

35 David's unusual reaction is the kind of madness that tragedy brings;

compare, for example, Lear, for whom madness is the only alternative. But for David this condition is temporary. David's troubles have afflicted the entire country. The sword has ravaged David's house, as Yhwh said, but in the battle "the forest devoured more people... than the sword" (18:8).

36 Michal, who rebukes David for his behavior before the ark, pays dearly for her outspokenness; see above, Chapter 4. Nathan rebukes David (2 Samuel 12), but Nathan speaks for Yhwh, and that is a different matter from a subject criticizing the king's behavior.

37 Conroy (1978), p. 100, draws attention to references to death and discord throughout the account of David's return. Fokkelman (1981), p. 311, sees a different pattern in these encounters, from negative to positive.

38 Note the echoes of earlier events. David, like Saul in 1 Sam. 11:13, refuses to put anyone to death on his day of success. Like David, when confronted by Nathan with his sin, Shimei confesses, "I have sinned"; and like Nathan/Yhwh, David says, "You shall not die." Shimei will later meet death when he leaves Jerusalem, just as David experienced his greatest tragedy and longed to die when he fled Jerusalem. On the significance of Shimei, see further, Ackerman (1990), p. 54.

39 Solomon will have greater success with his decision "divide the child" (1 Kings 3:25) than David achieves with the verdict "divide the land" (2 Sam. 19:29). For although Mephibosheth, like the real mother, offers all to the other claimant, King David makes no further ruling.

40 For recent attempts to understand 2 Samuel 21–4 in their present context, see Childs (1979), pp. 273–5; Whedbee (1988), pp. 162–4; Brueggemann (1988); Fokkelman (1990), pp. 271–363. Cf. the earlier, insightful observations of Carlson (1964), pp. 194–259.

41 He also laments Amnon's death, though no words of David are recorded, and he mourns, in effect, his first-born son before the child dies.

42 Gunn (1978), p. 82.

43 Gunn (1978), p. 82.

44 See Ricoeur (1967), pp. 214–26, and the discussion in Chapter 1 above.

45 There is an interesting pattern in the way Yhwh first opposes, but then agrees to, human designs. Yhwh is opposed to kingship and the first king fails, but the second king, the one Yhwh chooses after his own heart, succeeds. Here the first attempt to bring the ark to Jerusalem fails, but the second succeeds with Yhwh's blessing. In 2 Samuel 7 David proposes to build a temple for Yhwh, but Yhwh refuses, conceding, however, that David's son Solomon may build it.

46 On 1 Samuel 25 as foreshadowing 2 Samuel 11, see Levenson (1982), pp. 237–8.

47 On the themes of giving and taking in this oracle, see Fokkelman (1981), pp. 84–6.

48 Gunn (1978), pp. 98, 110, perceptively notes the ambivalent portrayal of Yhwh as a character in the story; *contra* Fokkelman (1981), p. 92, n. 5.

49 Von Rad (1966), p. 200; Fokkelman (1981), p. 191; Gunn (1978), pp. 108–9. Inordinate theological significance has often been ascribed to David's conditional statements in 2 Sam. 15:25–6 and 16:10–12 and his prayer in 15:31. They are interpreted, e.g., as his submission to Yhwh's will, signs of trust or faith which God rewards by restoring the kingdom to David. See esp. von Rad (1966); Brueggemann (1972); (1974); (1985), pp. 51–5. Whereas Fokkelman speaks of a "fundamental and distinctive election of submission to God's will" (p. 186), he also claims that "David's return is entirely the work of God and at the same time entirely the work of David himself" (p. 187; see also pp. 190–1, 193, 201, 205, 301–2). Conroy (1978), p. 98, sees David's return as Yhwh's doing, and a sign of abiding divine favor, but adds that the hero is not restored to his "happy initial condition or even to something better." Gunn (1978), pp. 94–108; (1989), pp. 138–40, places heavy emphasis on David's recognition that the kingdom is a gift. Only Gunn (1978), pp. 98, 108–10, allows for divine ambivalence.

In my opinion, the real issue here is not whether or not David will retain the kingship (though it is an issue for David), and certainly not his faith, but the king's humiliation (prophesied in 2 Samuel 12). He must be brought to this point; it is his nemesis. What Nathan prophesied has come to pass, and when the king is at his lowest point, Absalom's death compounds the agony. As Fokkelman (1981), p. 302, notes, after David's restoration there is no expression of gratitude or recognition of God's help on David's part.

50 See Gros Louis (1977), pp. 18–20.

51 For numerous examples of David as deceiver and as one who is in his turn deceived, particularly after the Bathsheba/Uriah incident, see Marcus (1986b). Marcus makes a strong case that David is being deceived here.

52 The conditional nature of the Davidic covenant in 1 Kings 2 may be the result of Deuteronomistic editing, as most commentators believe, but its placement here is remarkable. It occurs at the perfect point to undermine tragically the confidence of David's house expressed in 2 Samuel 22 and 23.

53 The translation of the last line is problematic, but the idea that Yhwh humbles the proud is clear enough. Cf. similar ideas in the Song of Hannah (1 Samuel 1). See also Polzin (1989), pp. 30–6, for comparison of 1 Samuel 1 and 2 Samuel 22, which he sees as a poetic *inclusio*.

54 Fokkelman (1981), pp. 76–7.

55 Perdue (1984), pp. 76–7, points to the difficulty of assessing David's response. "Are these the words of a grief-striken father," he asks (p. 77), "or of a callous ruler realizing he had failed to negate Nathan's prophecy predicting trouble from the king's own house, a prediction whose initial sign was the death of the child?"

56 The Septuagint adds "and he would not harm Amnon, for he loved him, since he was his first-born." Cf. the similar remark about Adonijah in 1 Kings 1:6.

57 Ackerman (1990), pp. 45–6.
58 Hertzberg (1964), p. 324, assumes Tamar lived in Absalom's house before the rape, but as McCarter (1984), p. 326, observes, that cannot be determined.
59 This is David's major problem according to Whybray (1968), pp. 37–9. On the tensions between his public and private life as a source of David's difficulties, see Gros Louis (1977); Ridout (1971), pp. 141–61; Gunn (1978), pp. 88–94. A compelling political reading of David's private affairs is given by Rosenberg (1986), pp. 113–99.
60 See note 49 above.
61 The scene occurs near the end of Act Two of *Death of a Salesman*.
62 Whybray (1968), pp. 24, 40–3, speaks of Joab's tragedy, and evaluates Joab positively. A more sober assessment of Joab is given by Rosenberg (1986), pp. 164–71.
63 The last years of the kingdom are tragically violent. Josiah's son Jehoahaz is put in chains by Neco and dies in Egyptian captivity, and not many years later, his grandson experiences a similar fate. Jehoiachin is taken into exile to Babylonia, where he is imprisoned, and though later set free, he remains in exile "all the days of his life" (2 Kings 25:29, 30). Zedekiah, the last king of David's line to sit on the throne in Jerusalem, meets a deeply tragic end: his sons are killed before his eyes, his eyes are put out, and he is carried to Babylon as a prisoner (2 Kings 25:7).
64 Polzin (1989), pp. 213–15, perceptively observes that the long, drawn-out decline of Saul is but part of a larger pattern that is repeated in the account of the Davidic house, and of that of monarchy in general, in both Israel and Judah.
65 The tragic account ends but the Davidic hopes continue. One might view the Deuteronomistic History as the tragedy of the nation, with the non-tragic David and the non-tragic "history" to be found in the Latter Prophets and Writings. On what he refers to as the Primary and Secondary Histories in the Bible as pessimistic and optimistic histories, see Clines (1990), pp. 85–105. On the different pictures of David in the Deuteronomistic History and Chronicles–Ezra–Nehemiah, see Gunn (1989), pp. 144–8; Miscall (1989). As Clines, Gunn, and Miscall point out, the interesting question is not historical; i.e. whether one source is more historically reliable, but, rather, literary. As Miscall puts it, "the two works unsettle one another but they do not cancel each other out" (p. 157). On David in the Psalms, see Petersen (1986), pp. 139–41; Mays (1986), pp. 151–5.

AFTERWORD

1 Krieger (1960), p. 3; (1971), pp. 4–8, 36–9; (1981), pp. 42–3; cf. Ricoeur (1967), pp. 211–13, 225–6.
2 Reiss (1980), p. 17; Krieger (1981), p. 43; see also my comments on this point in Chapter 1.
3 Bouchard (1989), p. 14, raises the question and engages it as a theological

task, pp. 10–48 *et passim*. See also Ricoeur (1967), pp. 211–31. On p. 226, Ricoeur notes, "Explicit formulation of the tragic theology would mean self-destruction for the religious consciousness."

4 Translating somewhat freely. Clines (1989), p. 253, renders Job 11:7, "Can you uncover the mystery of God? / Can you attain to the perfection of Shaddai's knowledge?"; Good (1990), p. 79, "Can you discover Eloah's farthest edge, / or discover as far as Shaddai's boundary?"

Bibliography

Abel, Lionel   1967   "Introductory Remarks." In Abel 1967: 15–30.

Abel, Lionel, ed.   1967   *Moderns on Tragedy: An Anthology of Modern and Relevant Opinions on the Substance and Meaning of Tragedy.* Greenwich, CT: Fawcett.

Ackerman, James S.   1990   "Knowing Good and Evil: A Literary Analysis of the Court History in 2 Samuel 9–20 and 1 Kings 1–2." *Journal of Biblical Literature* 109:41–60.

1991   "Who Can Stand before YHWH, This Holy God? A Reading of 1 Samuel 1–15." *Prooftexts* 11:1–24.

Ackroyd, P. R.   1977   *The Second Book of Samuel.* Cambridge Bible Commentary. London: Cambridge.

Ahlström, G. W.   1978   "*krkr* and *tpd.*" *Vetus Testamentum* 28:100–1.

Alter, Robert   1981   *The Art of Biblical Narrative.* New York: Basic Books.

Aschkenasy, Nehama   1986   *Eve's Journey: Feminine Images in Hebraic Literary Tradition.* Philadelphia: University of Pennsylvania Press.

Avishur, Y.   1976   "*KRKR* in Biblical Hebrew and Ugaritic." *Vetus Testamentum* 26:256–61.

Babcock-Abrahams, Barbara   1975   "'A Tolerated Margin of Mess': The Trickster and His Tales Reconsidered." *Journal of the Folklore Institute* 11:147–86.

Bach, Alice   1989   "The Pleasure of Her Text." *Union Seminary Quarterly Review* 43:41–58. [= *The Pleasure of Her Text: Feminist Readings of Biblical and Historical Texts,* ed. A. Bach, pp. 25–44. Philadelphia: Trinity Press International, 1990.]

Bailey, Randall C.   1990   *David in Love and War: The Pursuit of Power in 2 Samuel 10–12.* JSOT Supplement Series, 75. Sheffield: JSOT Press.

Bal, Mieke   1987   *Lethal Love: Feminist Literary Readings of Biblical Love Stories.* Bloomington: Indiana University Press.

1988a   *Death & Dissymmetry: The Politics of Coherence in the Book of Judges.* University of Chicago Press.

1988b   "Tricky Thematics." In Exum and Bos 1988:133–55.

Barthélemy, Dominique, ed.   1982   *Critique textuelle de l'Ancien Testament.* Orbis Biblicus et Orientalis 50/1. Fribourg, Suisse: Éditions Universitaires. Göttingen: Vandenhoeck & Ruprecht.

Bayley, John   1981   *Shakespeare and Tragedy.* London: Routledge & Kegan Paul.

Benjamin, Walter   1977   *The Origin of German Tragic Drama*, tr. John Osborne. London: NLB.

Bergson, Henri   1980   "Laughter." In *Comedy*, ed. Wylie Sypher, pp. 59–190. Baltimore: Johns Hopkins University Press.

Berlin, Adele   1983   *Poetics and Interpretation of Biblical Narrative.* Sheffield: Almond Press.

Blenkinsopp, Joseph   1963   "Structure and Style in Judges 13–16." *Journal of Biblical Literature* 82:65–76.

   1964   "Jonathan's Sacrilege. I Sm 14, 1–46: A Study in Literary History." *Catholic Biblical Quarterly* 26: 423–49.

   1972   *Gibeon and Israel: The Role of Gibeon and the Gibeonites in the Political and Religious History of Early Israel.* Cambridge University Press.

Boling, Robert G.   1975   *Judges.* Anchor Bible, 6A. New York: Double-day.

Booth, Stephen   1983   *King Lear, Macbeth, Indefinition, and Tragedy.* New Haven: Yale University Press.

Bouchard, Larry D.   1989   *Tragic Method and Tragic Theology: Evil in Contemporary Drama and Religious Thought.* University Park: Penn-sylvania State University Press.

Bradley, A. C.   1949   *Shakespearean Tragedy.* London: Macmillan.

Brooks, Cleanth   1955   *Tragic Themes in Western Literature.* New Haven: Yale University Press.

Brueggemann, Walter   1972   "On Trust and Freedom: A Study of Faith in the Succession Narrative." *Interpretation* 26:3–19.

   1974   "On Coping with Curse: A Study of 2 Sam. 16:5–14." *Catholic Biblical Quarterly* 36:175–92.

   1985   *David's Truth in Israel's Imagination and Memory.* Philadelphia: Fortress Press.

   1988   "2 Samuel 21–24: An Appendix of Deconstruction?" *Catholic Biblical Quarterly* 50:383–97.

Buber, Martin   1933   "Weisheit und Tat der Frauen." In *Kampf um Israel: Reden und Schriften (1921–1932)*, pp. 107–14. Berlin: Schocken.

Burke, Kenneth   1968   *Counter-Statement.* Berkeley: University of California Press.

Burney, C. F.   1970   *The Book of Judges.* New York: KTAV. Originally published 1903.

Camp, Claudia V.   1981   "The Wise Women of 2 Samuel: A Role Model for Women in Early Israel." *Catholic Biblical Quarterly* 43:14–29.

   1988   "Wise and Strange: An Interpretation of the Female Imagery in Proverbs in Light of Trickster Mythology." In Exum and Bos 1988:14–36.

Carlson, R. A.   1964   *David, the Chosen King*, tr. E. J. Sharpe and S. Rudman. Uppsala: Almqvist & Wiksell.

Cazelles, H.   1955   "David's Monarchy and the Gibeonite Claim (II Sam. xxi, 1–14)." *Palestine Exploration Quarterly* 87:165–75.

Childs, Brevard   1979   *Introduction to the Old Testament as Scripture.* Phila-delphia: Fortress Press.

Clines, David J. A. 1972 "X, X *ben* Y, *ben* Y: Personal Names in Hebrew Narrative Style." *Vetus Testamentum* 22:266–87.

  1989 *Job 1–20*. Word Biblical Commentary, 17. Dallas, TX: Word Books.

  1990 *What Does Eve Do to Help? and Other Readerly Questions to the Old Testament*. Journal for the Study of the Old Testament Supplement Series, 94. Sheffield: JSOT Press.

  1991 "The Story of Michal, Wife of David, in Its Sequential Unfolding." In *Telling Queen Michal's Story, An Experiment in Comparative Interpretation*, ed. D. J. A. Clines and T. C. Eskenazi, pp. 129–40. Journal for the Study of the Old Testament Supplement Series, 119. Sheffield: JSOT Press.

Conroy, Charles 1978 *Absalom Absalom! Narrative and Language in 2 Sam. 13–20*. Rome: Biblical Institute Press.

Coogan, Michael David "The Woman at the Window: An Artistic and Literary Motif." Unpublished paper.

Corrigan, Robert W., ed. 1981a *Comedy: Meaning and Form*. 2d ed. New York: Harper and Row.

  1981b *Tragedy: Vision and Form*. 2d ed. New York: Harper and Row.

Cox, Roger L. 1969 *Between Earth and Heaven: Shakespeare, Dostoevsky, and the Meaning of Christian Tragedy*. New York: Holt, Rinehart and Winston.

Crenshaw, James L. 1978 *Samson: A Secret Betrayed, a Vow Ignored*. Atlanta: John Knox.

Cross, Frank Moore, Jr., and Freedman, David Noel 1975 *Studies in Ancient Yahwistic Poetry*. SBL Dissertation Series, 21. Missoula, MT: Scholars Press.

Crüsemann, Frank 1980 "Zwei alttestamentliche Witze: I Sam 21:11–15 und II Sam 6:16. 20–23 als Beispiele einer biblischen Gattung." *Zeitschrift für die alttestamentliche Wissenschaft* 92:215–27.

Cryer, F. H. 1985 "David's Rise to Power and the Death of Abner: An Analysis of 1 Samuel xxvi 14–16 and Its Redaction-Critical Implications." *Vetus Testamentum* 35:385–94.

Damrosch, David 1987 *The Narrative Covenant: Transformations of Genre in the Growth of Biblical Literature*. San Francisco: Harper and Row.

Day, John 1989 *Molech: A God of Human Sacrifice in the Old Testament*. University of Cambridge Oriental Publications, 41. Cambridge University Press.

Day, Peggy L. 1989 "From the Child is Born the Woman: The Story of Jephthah's Daughter." In *Gender and Difference in Ancient Israel*, ed. P. L. Day, pp. 58–74. Minneapolis: Fortress Press.

Detienne, Marcel, and Vernant, Jean-Pierre, *et al.* 1989 *The Cuisine of Sacrifice among the Greeks*, tr. Paula Wissing. University of Chicago Press.

Donner, Herbert 1983 *Die Verwerfung des Königs Saul*. Wiesbaden: Franz Steiner.

Driver, S. R. 1890 *Notes on the Hebrew Text of the Books of Samuel*. Oxford: Clarendon Press.

Dürrenmatt, Friedrich 1966 *Theater-Schriften und Reden*. Zürich: Arche.

Easterling, P. E., and Knox, B. M. W., eds. 1989 *The Cambridge History of Classical Literature*, vol. I, part 2. *Greek Drama*. Cambridge University Press.

Edelman, Diana 1986 "The Rise of the Israelite State under Saul." Unpublished Ph. D. dissertation, University of Chicago.

1990 "The Deuteronomist's Story of King Saul: Narrative Art or Editorial Product?" In *Pentateuchal and Deuteronomistic Studies: Papers Read at the XIIIth IOSOT Congress*, ed. C. Brekelmans & J. Lust, pp. 207–20. Leuven University Press.

1991 *King Saul in the Historiography of Judah*. Journal for the Study of the Old Testament Supplement Series, 121. Sheffield: JSOT Press.

Eissfeldt, Otto 1925 *Die Quellen des Richterbuches*. Leipzig: J. C. Hinrichs.

1966a "Ein gescheiterter Versuch der Wiedervereinigung Israels (2 Sam 2, 12–3, 1)." In *Kleine Schriften* III, pp. 132–46. Tübingen: J. C. B. Mohr. [= *La Nouvelle Clio* 3 (1951), pp. 110–27.]

1966b "Noch einmal: Ein gescheiterter Versuch der Wiedervereinigung Israels." In *Kleine Schriften* III, pp. 147–50. Tübingen: J. C. B. Mohr. [= *La Nouvelle Clio* 4 (1952), pp. 55–9.]

Else, Gerald 1957 *Aristotle's Poetics: The Argument*. Cambridge: Harvard University Press.

Eslinger, Lyle M. 1985 *Kingship of God in Crisis: A Close Reading of 1 Samuel 1–12*. Bible and Literature Series, 10. Sheffield: Almond Press.

Exum, J. Cheryl 1981 "Aspects of Symmetry and Balance in the Samson Saga." *Journal for the Study of the Old Testament* 19:3–29. Errata in *JSOT* 20:90.

1983 "The Theological Dimension of the Samson Saga." *Vetus Testamentum* 33:30–45.

1988 Review of Peter Miscall, *1 Samuel: A Literary Reading*. Hebrew Studies 29:177–80.

1989 "Murder They Wrote: Ideology and the Manipulation of Female Presence in Biblical Narrative." *Union Seminary Quarterly Review* 43:19–39. [= *The Pleasure of Her Text: Feminist Readings of Biblical and Historical Texts*, ed. A. Bach, pp. 45–67. Philadelphia: Trinity Press International, 1990.]

1990 "The Centre Cannot Hold: Thematic and Textual Instabilities in Judges." *Catholic Biblical Quarterly* 52:410–31.

Exum, J. Cheryl, ed. 1984 *Tragedy and Comedy in the Bible*. Semeia 32. Decatur, GA: Scholars Press.

1989 *Signs and Wonders: Biblical Texts in Literary Focus*. Decatur, GA: Scholars Press.

Exum, J. Cheryl, and Bos, Johanna W. H., eds. 1988 *Reasoning with the Foxes: Female Wit in a World of Male Power*. Semeia 42. Atlanta: Scholars Press.

Farnham, Willard 1950 *Shakespeare's Tragic Frontier*. New York: Barnes & Noble.

Fensham, F. C.   1964   "The Treaty between Israel and the Gibeonites."
Biblical Archaeologist 27:96–100.
  1970   "The Battle between the Men of Joab and Abner as a Possible
  Ordeal by Battle?" *Vetus Testamentum* 20:356–7.
Fish, Stanley   1980   *Is There a Text in This Class? The Authority of
Interpretive Communities.* Cambridge: Harvard University Press.
Fisher, Loren R.   1971   "Two Projects at Claremont." *Ugarit-Forschungen*
  3:25–32.
Flanagan, James W.   1981   "Chiefs in Israel." *Journal for the Study of the
Old Testament* 20:47–73.
  1983   "Succession and Genealogy in the Davidic Dynasty." In *The Quest
  for the Kingdom of God*, ed. H. B. Huffmon, F. A. Spina, and A. R. W.
  Green, pp. 35–55. Winona Lake: Eisenbrauns.
Fokkelman, J. P.   1981   *Narrative Art and Poetry in the Books of Samuel*, vol.
  I. *King David*. Assen: van Gorcum.
  1986   *Narrative Art and Poetry in the Books of Samuel*, vol. II. *The Crossing
  Fates.* Assen: van Gorcum.
  1990   *Narrative Art and Poetry in the Books of Samuel*, vol. III. *Throne and
  City.* Assen: van Gorcum.
Freedman, David Noel   1972   "The Refrain in David's Lament over Saul
  and Jonathan." In *Ex Orbe Religionum*, ed. C. J. Bleeker, S. G. F.
  Brandon, and M. Simon, pp. 115–26. Studies in the History of
  Religions, 21. Leiden: Brill.
  1975   "Early Israelite History in the Light of Early Israelite Poetry." In
  *Unity and Diversity: Essays in the History, Literature, and Religion of the
  Ancient Near East*, ed. Hans Goedicke and J. J. M. Roberts, pp. 3–35.
  Baltimore: Johns Hopkins University Press.
Fretheim, Terence E.   1985   "Divine Foreknowledge, Divine Constancy,
  and the Rejection of Saul's Kingship." *Catholic Biblical Quarterly* 47:
  595–602.
Frye, Northrop   1965   *A Natural Perspective: The Development of Shake-
spearean Comedy and Romance.* New York: Harcourt, Brace & World.
  1966   *Anatomy of Criticism.* New York: Atheneum.
  1967   *Fools of Time: Studies in Shakespearean Tragedy.* University of
  Toronto Press.
  1982   *The Great Code: The Bible and Literature.* New York: Harcourt Brace
  Jovanovich.
Fuchs, Esther   1989   "Marginalization, Ambiguity, Silencing: The Story
  of Jephthah's Daughter." *Journal of Feminist Studies in Religion* 5:35–45.
Garsiel, Moshe   1985   *The First Book of Samuel: A Literary Study of
Comparative Structures, Analogies and Parallels.* Ramat-Gan: Revivim.
Gassner, John   1981   "The Possibilities and Perils of Modern Tragedy."
  In Corrigan 1981b:297–306. Reprinted from *Tulane Drama Review* 1
  (1957), pp. 3–14.
Gellrich, Michelle   1988   *Tragedy and Theory: The Problem of Conflict since
Aristotle.* Princeton University Press.

Genette, Gérard   1980   *Narrative Discourse: An Essay in Method*, tr. Jane E. Lewin. Ithaca: Cornell University Press.

Girard, René   1977   *Violence and the Sacred*, tr. Patrick Gregory. Baltimore: Johns Hopkins University Press.

Goldmann, Lucien   1981   "The Concept of Tragedy and the 'Science' of Literature." In Corrigan 1981b: 136–9. Reprinted from *Racine* (Rivers Press, 1972).

Good, Edwin M.   1965   *Irony in the Old Testament*. Philadelphia: Westminster.

  1973   "Job and the Literary Task: A Response." *Soundings* 56: 470–84.

  1990   *In Turns of Tempest: A Reading of Job with a Translation*. Stanford University Press.

Gray, John   1986   *Joshua, Judges, Ruth*. The New Century Bible Commentary. Grand Rapids: Eerdmans.

Green, Alberto R. W.   1975   *The Role of Human Sacrifice in the Ancient Near East*. ASOR Dissertation Series, 1. Missoula, MT: Scholars Press.

Greenberg, Moshe   1983   *Biblical Prose Prayer*. Berkeley: University of California Press.

Greenstein, Edward L.   1981   "The Riddle of Samson." *Prooftexts* 1: 237–60.

Grene, David, tr.   1954   *Sophocles, Oedipus the King*. The Complete Greek Tragedies, ed. by David Grene and Richmond Lattimore. University of Chicago Press.

Gressmann, Hugo   1910   *Die älteste Geschichtsschreibung und Prophetie Israels*. Die Schriften des Alten Testaments, II/1. Göttingen: Vandenhoeck & Ruprecht.

Grønbaek, Jakob H.   1971   *Die Geschichte vom Aufstieg Davids (1. Sam. 15–2. Sam. 5): Tradition und Komposition*. Copenhagen: Munksgaard.

Gros Louis, Kenneth R. R.   1977   "The Difficulty of Ruling Well: King David of Israel." In *Literary Critical Studies of Biblical Texts*, ed. Robert W. Funk. *Semeia* 8: 15–33.

Gunkel, Hermann   1913   "Simson." In *Reden und Aufsätze*, pp. 38–64. Göttingen: Vandenhoeck & Ruprecht.

Gunn, David M.   1978   *The Story of King David: Genre and Interpretation*. Journal for the Study of the Old Testament Supplement Series, 6. Sheffield: JSOT Press.

  1980   *The Fate of King Saul: An Interpretation of a Biblical Story*. Journal for the Study of the Old Testament Supplement Series, 14. Sheffield: JSOT Press.

  1981   "A Man Given Over to Trouble: The Story of King Saul." In *Images of Man and God: Old Testament Short Stories in Literary Focus*, ed. Burke O. Long, pp. 89–112. Sheffield: Almond Press.

  1984   "The Anatomy of Divine Comedy: On Reading the Bible as Comedy and Tragedy." In Exum 1984: 115–29.

  1989   "In Security: The David of Biblical Narrative." In Exum 1989: 133–51.

Hackett, Jo Ann   1985   "In the Days of Jael: Reclaiming the History of Women in Ancient Israel." In *Immaculate and Powerful: The Female in Sacred Image and Social Reality*, ed. C. W. Atkinson, C. H. Buchanan, and M. R. Miles, pp. 15–38. Boston: Beacon Press.

Hartman, Geoffrey H.   1981   *Saving the Text: Literature/Derrida/Philosophy*. Baltimore: Johns Hopkins University Press.

Heider, George C.   1985   *The Cult of Molek: A Reassessment*. Journal for the Study of the Old Testament Supplement Series, 43. Sheffield: JSOT Press.

Henrichs, Albert   1981   "Human Sacrifice in Greek Religion: Three Case Studies." *Le sacrifice dans l'antiquité. Entretiens sur l'antiquité classique* 27:195–242.

Hertzberg, H. W.   1964   *I & II Samuel*, tr. J. S. Bowden. The Old Testament Library. Philadelphia: Westminster.

   1969   *Die Bücher Josua, Richter, Ruth*. Das Alte Testament Deutsch, 9. Göttingen: Vandenhoeck & Ruprecht.

Holladay, William L.   1970   "Form and Word-Play in David's Lament over Saul and Jonathan." *Vetus Testamentum* 20:153–89.

Humphreys, W. Lee   1978   "The Tragedy of King Saul: A Study of the Structure of 1 Samuel 9–31." *Journal for the Study of the Old Testament* 6:18–27.

   1980   "The Rise and Fall of King Saul: A Study of an Ancient Narrative Stratum in 1 Samuel." *Journal for the Study of the Old Testament* 18:74–90.

   1982   "From Tragic Hero to Villain: A Study of the Figure of Saul and the Development of 1 Samuel." *Journal for the Study of the Old Testament* 22:95–117.

   1985   *The Tragic Vision and the Hebrew Tradition*. Philadelphia: Fortress.

Jaspers, Karl   1952   *Tragedy Is Not Enough*, tr. H. A. T. Reiche, H. T. Moore, and K. W. Deutsch. Boston: Beacon Press.

Jay, Nancy   1985   "Sacrifice as Remedy for Having Been Born of Woman." In *Immaculate and Powerful: The Female in Sacred Image and Social Reality*, ed. C. W. Atkinson, C. H. Buchanan, and M. R. Miles, pp. 283–309. Boston: Beacon Press.

Jobling, David   1978   *The Sense of Biblical Narrative: Structural Analyses in the Hebrew Bible*, vol. I. Journal for the Study of the Old Testament Supplement Series, 7. Sheffield: JSOT Press.

   1986   *The Sense of Biblical Narrative: Structural Analyses in the Hebrew Bible*, vol. II. Journal for the Study of the Old Testament Supplement Series, 39. Sheffield: JSOT Press.

Kapelrud, A. S.   1955   "King and Fertility: A Discussion of II Sam 21:1–14." In *Interpretationes ad Vetus Testamentum pertinentes Sigmondo Mowinckel = Norsk teologisk tidsskrift* 56:113–22. [= *God and His Friends in the Old Testament*, pp. 41–50. Oslo: Universitetsforlaget, 1979.]

Keukens, Karlheinz H.   1982   "Richter 11, 37f.: Rite de passage und Übersetzungsprobleme." *Biblische Notizen* 19:41–2.

Kierkegaard, Søren   1987   *Either/Or*, Part I, ed. and tr. with Introduction and Notes by H. V. Hong and E. H. Hong. Princeton University Press.

King, Philip J. 1988 *Amos, Hosea, Micah – An Archaeological Commentary.* Philadelphia: Westminster.

Kitto, H. D. F. 1986 *Greek Tragedy: A Literary Study.* London: Methuen. Reprint of 3d ed., 1961.

Knox, Bernard 1955 "Sophocles' Oedipus." In Brooks 1955:7–29.

Krieger, Murray 1960 *The Tragic Vision: The Confrontation of Extremity,* vol. I of *Visions of Extremity in Modern Literature.* Baltimore: Johns Hopkins University Press.

   1971 *The Classic Vision: The Retreat from Extremity,* vol. II of *Visions of Extremity in Modern Literature.* Baltimore: Johns Hopkins University Press.

   1981 "The Tragic Vision Twenty Years After." In Corrigan 1981b:42–6.

Kristeva, Julia 1986 *About Chinese Women,* tr. A. Barrows. New York: Marion Boyars.

Krutch, Joseph Wood 1981 "The Tragic Fallacy." In Corrigan 1981b: 227–37. Reprinted from *The Modern Temper.* New York: Harcourt, Brace and World, 1957.

Kurzweil, Baruch 1970 "Job and the Possibility of Biblical Tragedy." In *Arguments and Doctrines,* ed. Arthur A. Cohen, pp. 323–44. Philadelphia: Jewish Publication Society.

Lamphere, Louise 1974 "Strategies, Cooperation, and Conflict among Women in Domestic Groups." In *Woman, Culture, and Society,* ed. M. Z. Rosaldo and L. Lamphere, pp. 97–112. Stanford University Press.

Landy, Francis 1984 "Are We in the Place of Averroes? Response to the Articles of Exum and Whedbee, Buss, Gottwald, and Good." In Exum 1984:131–48.

   1986 "Gilead and the Fatal Word." In *Proceedings of the Ninth World Congress of Jewish Studies,* pp. 39–44. Jerusalem: World Union of Jewish Studies.

Langer, Susanne 1953 *Feeling and Form.* New York: Scribner's.

Lawrence, D. H. 1920 *Touch and Go, A Play in Three Acts.* New York: Thomas Seltzer.

Leach, Edmund 1966 "The Legitimacy of Solomon: Some Structural Aspects of Old Testament History." *Archives Européennes de Sociologie/ European Journal of Sociology* 7:58–101.

Lemche, N. P. 1978 "David's Rise." *Journal for the Study of the Old Testament* 10:2–25.

Lerner, Gerda 1986 *The Creation of Patriarchy.* New York: Oxford University Press.

Lesky, Albin 1965 *Greek Tragedy,* tr. H. A. Frankfort. London: Ernest Benn.

Levenson, Jon D. 1982 "I Samuel 25 as Literature and as History." In *Literary Interpretations of Biblical Narratives,* vol. II, ed. K. R. R. Gros Louis with J. S. Ackerman, pp. 220–42. Nashville: Abingdon.

Long, V. Philips 1989 *The Reign and Rejection of King Saul: A Case for*

Literary and Theological Coherence. SBL Dissertation Series, 118. Atlanta: Scholars Press.

Loraux, Nicole   1987   *Tragic Ways of Killing a Woman*, tr. Anthony Forster. Cambridge: Harvard University Press.

Lucas, D. W.   1959   *The Greek Tragic Poets*. London: Cohen & West.

McCarter, P. Kyle, Jr.   1980a   "The Apology of David." *Journal of Biblical Literature* 99:489–504.

    1980b   *I Samuel*. Anchor Bible, 8. New York: Doubleday.

    1984   *II Samuel*. Anchor Bible, 9. New York: Doubleday.

McCarthy, Dennis J.   1965   "II Samuel 7 and the Structure of the Deuteronomic History." *Journal of Biblical Literature* 84:131–8.

McKane, W.   1963   *I and II Samuel: The Way to the Throne*. London: SCM.

Mahoney, John L.   1985   *The Persistence of Tragedy: Episodes in the History of Drama*. Boston: Trustees of the Public Library.

Malamat, Abraham   1955   "Doctrines of Causality in Hittite and Biblical Historiography: A Parallel." *Vetus Testamentum* 5:1–12.

Marcus, David   1986a   *Jephthah and His Vow*. Lubbock, Texas: Texas Tech Press.

    1986b   "David the Deceiver and David the Dupe." *Prooftexts* 6:163–71.

Mason, H. A.   1985   *The Tragic Plane*. Oxford: Clarendon Press.

Mays, James Luther   1986   "The David of the Psalms." *Interpretation* 40:143–55.

Mazar, B.   1963   "David's Reign in Hebron and the Conquest of Jerusalem." In *In the Time of Harvest. Essays in Honor of Abba Hillel Silver*, ed. D. J. Silver, pp. 235–44. New York: Macmillan.

Mendenhall, George   1973   *The Tenth Generation: The Origins of the Biblical Tradition*. Baltimore: Johns Hopkins University Press.

Meyers, Carol   1988   *Discovering Eve: Ancient Israelite Women in Context*. New York: Oxford University Press.

Miller, Arthur   1949   *Death of a Salesman*. New York: Penguin.

    1957   *Arthur Miller's Collected Plays with an Introduction*. New York: Viking Press.

Miscall, Peter D.   1983   *The Workings of Old Testament Narrative*. Semeia Studies. Philadelphia: Fortress Press; Chico: Scholars Press.

    1986   *I Samuel: A Literary Reading*. Bloomington: Indiana University Press.

    1989   "For David's Sake: A Response to David M. Gunn." In Exum 1989:153–63.

Moore, George F.   1985   *A Critical and Exegetical Commentary on Judges*. The International Critical Commentary. Edinburgh: T. & T. Clark. Originally published 1895.

Niditch, Susan   1990   "Samson as Culture Hero, Trickster, and Bandit: The Empowerment of the Weak." *Catholic Biblical Quarterly* 52:608–24.

Oates, Joyce Carol   1972   *The Edge of Impossibility: Tragic Forms in Literature*. New York: Vanguard Press.

Oz, Amos   1982   *'l h'dmh hr'h hz't* in *'rtswt htn*. Tel Aviv: Am Oved

Publishers Ltd. ET = "Upon This Evil Earth." In *Where the Jackals Howl and Other Stories*, tr. Nicholas de Lange. Toronto: Bantam Books, 1982.

Parker, Simon B.   1979   "The Vow in Ugaritic and Israelite Literature." *Ugarit-Forschungen* 11:693–700.

   1989   *The Pre-Biblical Narrative Tradition*. SBL Sources for Biblical Study, 24. Atlanta: Scholars Press.

Paul, Shalom M.   1978   "1 Samuel 9, 7: An Interview Fee." *Biblica* 59:542–4.

Perdue, Leo G.   1984   "'Is There Anyone Left of the House of Saul...?': Ambiguity and the Characterization of David in the Succession Narrative." *Journal for the Study of the Old Testament* 30:67–84.

Petersen, David L.   1986   "Portraits of David: Canonical and Otherwise." *Interpretation* 40:130–42.

Polzin, Robert   1969   "*hwqy*' and Covenantal Institutions in Early Israel." *Harvard Theological Review* 62:227–40.

   1980   *Moses and the Deuteronomist. A Literary Study of the Deuteronomic History*, Part 1. New York: Seabury.

   1989   *Samuel and the Deuteronomist. A Literary Study of the Deuteronomic History*, Part 2. San Francisco: Harper and Row.

Preston, Thomas R.   1982   "The Heroism of Saul: Patterns of Meaning in the Narrative of the Early Kingship." *Journal for the Study of the Old Testament* 24:27–46.

von Rad, Gerhard   1962   *Old Testament Theology*, vol. I, tr. D. M. G. Stalker. New York: Harper and Row.

   1966   "The Beginnings of Historical Writing in Ancient Israel." In *The Problem of the Hexateuch and Other Essays*, pp. 166–204. New York: McGraw-Hill.

Radin, Paul   1956   *The Trickster: A Study in American Indian Mythology*. New York: Philosophical Library.

Reiss, Timothy J.   1980   *Tragedy and Truth*. New Haven: Yale University Press.

Rendtorff, Rolf   1971   "Beobachtungen zur altisraelitischen Geschichtsschreibung anhand der Geschichte vom Aufstieg Davids." In *Probleme biblischer Theologie*, ed. H. W. Wolff, pp. 428–39. Munich: Kaiser.

Ricoeur, Paul   1967   *The Symbolism of Evil*, tr. E. Buchanan. Boston: Beacon Press.

Ridout, George P.   1971   "Prose Compositional Techniques in the Succession Narrative (2 Sam. 7, 9–20; 1 Kings 1–2)." Unpublished Ph. D. dissertation, Graduate Theological Union.

Rimmon-Kenan, Shlomith   1983   *Narrative Fiction: Contemporary Poetics*. London: Methuen.

Robertson, David   1977   *The Old Testament and the Literary Critic*. Philadelphia: Fortress.

   1984   "Tragedy, Comedy, and the Bible – A Response." In Exum 1984:99–106.

Rosaldo, Michelle Zimbalist 1974 "Woman, Culture, and Society: A Theoretical Overview." In *Woman, Culture, and Society*, ed. M. Z. Rosaldo and L. Lamphere, pp. 97–112. Stanford University Press.

Rösel, Hartmut N. 1980 "Jephtah und das Problem der Richter." *Biblica* 61:251–5.

Rosenberg, Joel 1986 *King and Kin: Political Allegory in the Hebrew Bible.* Bloomington: Indiana University Press.

Rosenzweig, Franz 1976 *Der Stern der Erlösung. Gesammelte Schriften* II. The Hague: Martinus Nijhoff.

Rost, Leonhard 1926 *Die Überlieferung von der Thronnachfolge Davids.* Beiträge zur Wissenschaft vom Alten und Neuen Testament III/6 = 42. Stuttgart: W. Kohlhammer.

Scheler, Max 1981 "On the Tragic," tr. Bernard Stambler. In Corrigan 1981b:17–29. Also in Abel 1967:249–67. Reprinted from *Cross Currents* 4 (1954), pp. 178–91.

Sedgwick, Eve Kosofsky 1985 *Between Men: English Literature and Male Homosocial Desire.* New York: Columbia University Press.

Segal, Charles 1981 *Tragedy and Civilization: An Interpretation of Sophocles.* Cambridge: Harvard University Press.

1986 *Interpreting Greek Tragedy: Myth, Poetry, Text.* Ithaca: Cornell University Press.

Segal, Erich 1972 "Marlowe's *Schadenfreude*: Barabas as Comic Hero." In *Veins of Humor*, ed. Harry Levin, pp. 69–71. Harvard English Studies, 3. Cambridge: Harvard University Press.

Segal, Erich, ed. 1983 *Greek Tragedy: Modern Essays in Criticism.* New York: Harper and Row.

Sewall, Richard B. 1980 *The Vision of Tragedy.* New Haven: Yale University Press.

Shea, William H. 1986 "Chiasmus and the Structure of David's Lament." *Journal of Biblical Literature* 105:13–25.

Simon, Bennett 1988 *Tragic Drama and the Family: Psychoanalytic Studies from Aeschylus to Beckett.* New Haven: Yale University Press.

Simon, Uriel 1988 "A Balanced Story: The Stern Prophet and the Kind Witch." *Prooftexts* 8:159–71.

Smith, Henry Preserved 1899 *Samuel.* The International Critical Commentary. Edinburgh: T. & T. Clark.

Soggin, J. Alberto 1975 "The Reign of 'Esba'al, Son of Saul." In *Old Testament and Oriental Studies*, pp. 31–49. Biblica et Orientalia, 29. Rome: Biblical Institute Press.

1981 *Judges.* tr. J. S. Bowden. The Old Testament Library. Philadelphia: Westminster.

Steinberg, Naomi 1988 "Israelite Tricksters: Their Analogues and Cross-cultural Study." In Exum 1988:1–13.

Steiner, George 1980 *The Death of Tragedy.* New York: Oxford University Press.

Sternberg, Meir 1983 "The Bible's Art of Persuasion: Ideology, Rhetoric, and Poetics in Saul's Fall." *Hebrew Union College Annual* 54:45–82.

1985   *The Poetics of Biblical Narrative: Ideological Literature and the Drama of Reading*. Bloomington: Indiana University Press.

Stone, Jerry H.   1984   "The Gospel of Mark and Oedipus the King: Two Tragic Visions." *Soundings* 67:55–69.

Sypher, Wylie   1980   "The Meanings of Comedy." In *Comedy*, ed. W. Sypher, pp. 191–260. Baltimore: Johns Hopkins University Press.

Thiselton, Anthony C.   1974   "The Supposed Power of Words in the Biblical Writings." *Journal of Theological Studies* 25:283–99.

Thompson, J. A.   1974   "The Significance of the Verb *Love* in the David–Jonathan Narratives in 1 Samuel." *Vetus Testamentum* 24:334–8.

Tiger, Lionel   1984   *Men in Groups*. New York: Marion Boyers.

Trible, Phyllis   1984   *Texts of Terror: Literary–Feminist Readings of Biblical Narratives*. Philadelphia: Fortress Press.

Tsevat, Matitiahu   1966   "The Meaning of the Book of Job." *Hebrew Union College Annual* 37:73–106.

1975   *"bethulah; bethulim."* In *Theological Dictionary of the Old Testament*, ed. G. J. Botterweck and H. Ringgren, tr. J. T. Willis, pp. 340–3. Grand Rapids: Eerdmans.

Ulrich, Eugene Charles, Jr.   1978   *The Qumran Text of Samuel and Josephus*. Harvard Semitic Monographs, 19. Missoula, MT: Scholars Press.

Unamuno, Miguel de   1972   *The Tragic Sense of Life in Men and Nations*, tr. Anthony Kerrigan. Princeton University Press.

VanderKam, James C.   1980   "Davidic Complicity in the Deaths of Abner and Eshbaal: A Historical and Redactional Study." *Journal of Biblical Literature* 99:521–39.

de Vaux, Roland   1958   Review of H. W. Hertzberg, *Die Samuelbücher. Revue biblique* 65:124–5.

1964   *Studies in Old Testament Sacrifice*. Cardiff: University of Wales Press.

1971   *The Bible and the Ancient Near East*, tr. D. McHugh. Garden City, NY: Doubleday.

Veijola, Timo   1975   *Die ewige Dynastie. David und die Entstehung seiner Dynastie nach der deuteronomistischen Darstellung*. Helsinki: Suomalainen Tiedeakatemia.

Vernant, Jean-Pierre, and Vidal-Naquet, Pierre   1988   *Myth and Tragedy in Ancient Greece*, tr. Janet Lloyd. New York: Zone Books.

Via, Dan O., Jr.   1975   *Kerygma and Comedy in the New Testament: A Structuralist Approach to Hermeneutic*. Philadelphia: Fortress.

Vickery, John   1981   "In Strange Ways: The Story of Samson." In *Images of Man and God*, ed. Burke O. Long, pp. 58–73. Sheffield: Almond Press.

Webb, Barry G.   1987   *The Book of the Judges: An Integrated Reading*. Journal for the Study of the Old Testament Supplement Series, 46. Sheffield: JSOT Press.

Weiser, Artur   1966   "Die Legitimation des Königs David: Zur Eigenart und Entstehung der sogen. Geschichte von Davids Aufstieg." *Vetus Testamentum* 16:325–54.

Wenham, G. J.   1972   "*Betulah* 'A Girl of Marriageable Age.'" *Vetus Testamentum* 22:326–48.

Wharton, James A.   1973   "The Secret of Yahweh: Story and Affirmation in Judges 13–16." *Interpretation* 27:48–65.

Whedbee, J. William   1977   "The Comedy of Job." *Semeia* 7:1–39.

   1988   "On Divine and Human Bonds: The Tragedy of the House of David." In *Canon, Theology, and Old Testament Interpretation: Essays in Honor of Brevard S. Childs*, ed. G. M. Tucker, D. L. Petersen, and R. R. Wilson, pp. 147–65. Philadelphia: Fortress.

Whitelam, Keith W.   1979   *The Just King: Monarchical Judicial Authority in Ancient Israel.* Journal for the Study of the Old Testament Supplement Series, 12. Sheffield: JSOT Press.

   1984   "The Defence of David." *Journal for the Study of the Old Testament* 29:61–87.

Whybray, R. N.   1968   *The Succession Narrative: A Study of II Sam. 9–20 and I Kings 1 and 2.* Studies in Biblical Theology, Second Series, 9. Naperville, IL: Alec R. Allenson.

Yadin, Yigael [Sukenik]   1948   "Let the Young Men, I Pray Thee, Arise and Play before Us." *Journal of the Palestine Oriental Society* 21:110–16.

Zakovitch, Yair   1980   "A Study of Precise and Partial Derivations in Biblical Etymology." *Journal for the Study of the Old Testament* 15:31–50.

   1981   "The Woman's Rights in the Biblical Law of Divorce." *The Jewish Law Annual* 4:28–46.

   1984   " ∪ and ∩ in the Bible." In Exum 1984:107–14.

Index of authors

Index of proper names

Abdon, 53, 158
Abiathar, 123, 131, 133, 144, 146, 176
Abinadab, 26, 81, 96
Abishai, 41, 99, 101, 105, 125, 131, 163, 173
Abner, 14, 26, 70, 72, 81, 85, 92, 94–109, 125, 137, 146, 168, 170, 172–4
Abraham, 15, 45, 52, 60, 65
Absalom, 121, 129–37, 139, 143, 145–8, 159, 177, 179–80
Absalom, Absalom!, 155
Adonijah, 129–30, 141, 179
Aeschylus, 3, 7, 10, 17, 58, 153
  Agamemnon, 165
  Eumenides, 3, 7, 13
  Oresteia, 3, 7, 11, 13
Agamemnon, 57, 148, 165. *See also* Aeschylus: *Agamemnon*
Ahimaaz, 131, 133–4, 147
Ahithophel, 132, 139, 147–8, 177
Amalek, Amalekites, 24, 28, 32–3, 39, 108, 115, 124–5, 143
Amasa, 129, 136, 148, 174
Ammon, Ammonites, 16, 22, 35, 46–57, 59, 61–5, 126–7, 133, 143, 164, 168
Amnon, 129–30, 134, 139, 145, 177–9
Antigone, 10, 111, 148. *See also under* Sophocles
Aristotle, 2–3, 6, 153
  Poetics, 2
Armoni, 114
Asahel, 98, 101–2, 105, 107–8
Austen, Jane, 4

Bathsheba, 91, 121, 127–30, 137–41, 143–6, 168, 170, 176–7, 179
Brothers Karamazov, 155

Chaucer, 4, 122
  Monk's Tale, 4

David, 1, 12, 14–15, 16–44 *passim*, 70–119

passim, 120–49, 150–1, 153, 156, 160–3, 168–80
Deborah, 46, 47, 166
Deuteronomistic History, 9, 14–15, 149, 163, 180
Doctor Faustus, 155

Ehud, 46–7
Electra, 3. *See also under* Euripides; Aeschylus
Elon, 158
En-dor, medium at, 22–3, 25, 32, 53, 117, 134, 158
Euripides, 3, 153
  Alcestis, 153
  Bacchae, 3
  Electra, 153
  Helen, 153
  Heraclidae, 90
  Ion, 153
  Iphigenia in Aulis, 60
  Iphigenia in Tauris, 153, 165
  Medea, 3
  Orestes, 153
  Trojan Women, The, 155

Gibeon, Gibeonites, 26, 70, 82, 91, 94–5, 100, 105, 108–18, 140
Gideon, 40, 46–7, 57, 164

Hamlet. *See under* Shakespeare
Hushai, 131–3, 139, 147

Ibsen, 6
  Ghosts, 6
Ibzan, 53, 158
Iliad, 156
Iphigenia, 58, 165. *See also under* Euripides
Ishbaal, 125
Ishbosheth, 14, 26, 70, 72–3, 81, 85, 92, 94–109, 168, 170, 172

198

Index of citations

I SAMUEL

I KINGS

2 KINGS